From Conflict to Peace in a Changing World

Social Reconstruction in Times of Transition

Edited by Deborah Eade

An Oxfam Working Paper

First published by Oxfam GB in 1998. Reprinted in 1998, 1999 (twice)
This edition transferred to print-on-demand in 2007

© Oxfam GB 1998

ISBN 0 85598 395 7

A catalogue record for this publication is available from the British Library.

Available from:
Bournemouth English Book Centre, PO Box 1496, Parkstone, Dorset, BH12 3YD, UK
tel: +44 (0)1202 712933; fax: +44 (0)1202 712930; email: oxfam@bebc.co.uk

USA: Stylus Publishing LLC, PO Box 605, Herndon, VA 20172-0605, USA
tel: +1 (0)703 661 1581; fax: +1 (0)703 661 1547; email: styluspub@aol.com

For details of local agents and representatives in other countries, consult our website: www.oxfam.org.uk/publications
or contact Oxfam Publishing, Oxfam House, John Smith Drive, Cowley, Oxford, OX4 2JY, UK
tel +44 (0) 1865 472255; fax (0) 1865 472393; email: publish@oxfam.org.uk

Our website contains a fully searchable database of all our titles, and facilities for secure on-line ordering.

Published by Oxfam GB, Oxfam House, John Smith Drive, Cowley, Oxford, OX4 2JY, UK

Oxfam GB is a registered charity, no.202918, and is a member of Oxfam International.

Contents

Preface

Deborah Eade

Since its very inception in 1943, Oxfam GB has sought to respond to the impact of war and armed conflict on civilians and on the fabric of their societies. Today, conflict-related work continues to account for some two-thirds of Oxfam's annual grants expenditure, from the large-scale emergency relief programmes associated in recent years with Eastern Europe or the Great Lakes region of Africa, to the low-key work in areas which may at last be emerging from conflict, such as Central America, the Middle East, or Southern Africa.[1]

Not surprisingly, then, armed conflict has been a major and recurrent theme in Oxfam's publishing programme, whether the books and other materials are aimed primarily at international policy-makers, at development and relief practitioners, at the academic community, or at the general public. But, as **Jenny Pearce** points out in her contribution to this Working Paper, the danger today is that as 'the peace industry' gears into action, NGOs are drawn into concentrating on the definition of their own role and the expression of their own opinions, rather than giving voice to those whose lives are more directly affected. She argues that, instead of highlighting how people and societies themselves define and respond to crisis, NGOs and other aid agencies often imply (and sometimes perhaps believe) that these survivor-victims are passively waiting for outsiders to rescue them:

> The external agencies concerned with peace seem increasingly to focus the debate on *their* interventions (for instance, what *they* can do to articulate relief and development, what *they* can do to prevent conflict and build peace), and much less on the dynamic of *local* capacities and how these can shape the future prospects for peace-building.

This Working Paper reproduces articles and essays which first appeared in the quarterly journal, *Development in Practice*. The first part features papers by scholars, agency representatives, practitioners, and policy-makers on the ethical and legal dimensions of humanitarian endeavour. The second part comprises a collection of original essays which were commissioned from some of the highly experienced practitioners in the field of development and conflict who attended the June 1996 Symposium entitled *Building Bridges in Southern Africa: Conflict, Reconstruction and Reconciliation in Times of Change*, which was co-sponsored by the Johannesburg-based Centre for the Study of Violence and Reconciliation (CSVR) and Oxfam's South Africa Office. The two sections are complementary, each addressing conflict-related themes from a range of perspectives, and together painting an informative picture of the moral and practical complexities of crisis and intervention.

Hugo Slim opens the Working Paper by exploring the concepts of neutrality, impartiality, and solidarity; and the necessary links between human rights and international humanitarian law. Similar explorations are made by **David Bryer** and **Edmund Cairns** in their account of how Oxfam perceives these issues and shapes its own interventions in conflict. However, **Andy Storey** shows that much of the international humanitarian response to the 1994 crisis in Rwanda fell dismally short of could possibly be regarded as minimum standards of professionalism. Indeed, the main lesson to emerge from the 1996 evaluation was that humanitarian interventions cannot substitute for political action.[2] Here, **Juan Somavía** — architect of the 1995 World Summit for Social Development, and Chile's Permanent Ambassador to the United Nations — considers how today's expanded definitions of peace and security have, along with changes in the dynamics of war and insecurity, outstripped the capacity of traditional diplomatic methods and international instruments. He reviews the moral, political, and practical options available to the international community, and suggests ways in which the UN Security Council might enhance its ability to stem the abuse of power by governments and other actors. Within Europe, **Michel Chossudovsky** illustrates how IMF-sponsored economic structural adjustment policies served to exacerbate latent social tensions in the Former Yugoslavia — problems which, he argues, have been further intensified through the provisions of the Dayton Peace Accords. There are major lessons here for anyone who is concerned about the relationship between conflict and development. Drawing on the experience of Guatemala, a country with an atrocious history of State-sponsored political violence, **Elizabeth Lira** shows that, for peace to become a reality, the formal processes for recording human-rights violations must also be accompanied by society's willingness to recognise and assimilate its past. For the majority of the victims, such recognition requires material, as well as attitudinal, change. The question of how external agencies and NGOs might best engage in 'mental health' issues is taken up in a debate between **Derek Summerfield,** of the Medical Foundation for the Care of Victims of Torture, and **Alastair Ager**, Professor of Applied Psychology at the University of Edinburgh.

The Symposium drew together 30 individuals and organisations working in the areas of violence, conflict, and peace-building from across the Southern African region — the first time that NGOs had collectively addressed what it actually means to rebuild the social fabric. Participants were themselves working at many different levels, and discussions ranged from the very specific experiences of working with communities torn apart by war and violence, to the region-wide problems of weapons proliferation, the spread of HIV/AIDS, the manipulation of ethnic identities, and relations between civil society and the State. Healing strategies were also compared — from work with former child-soldiers in Mozambique to the Truth and Reconciliation Commission in South Africa, and the efforts of NGOs and the Church in Namibia to address internalised oppression, re-integrate exiles, and face the issues raised by survivors of detention camps during the war of liberation.

An invaluable dimension was the participation of speakers from Latin America: these helped to set the parameters for reflection and analysis, and ensured that the importance of changes in the international political and economic sphere was kept in view. Questions arising from the detailed presentation on El Salvador found many echoes in Southern Africa:

- Does reconstruction bring structural change?
- Does peace bring justice, and does justice bring peace?
- What is the role of collective memory in healing and reconciliation?
- How can we recognise and work with the many different levels of transition?
- What is the role of NGOs?
- With rising levels of violent crime in so many 'post-conflict' societies, can we even speak of peace at all?

And what are the gender-related dimensions of war, and of recovery and reconstruction? Negotiated peace settlements have seldom addressed women's specific economic and psychological needs, or built effectively on their social and political capacities. What happens, for example, to the women abducted by militias, and forced into sexual slavery? In Mozambique and Angola, as elsewhere, women's specific needs have been neglected in the demobilisation process. If they leave (or are abandoned by) their abductors, they lack any means of survival. Yet if they stay, they are not recognised as dependants in the demobilisation agreements. Women are in many ways excluded from access to land and training, and from the right (and opportunity) to take a full part alongside men in the process of shaping the political and economic reconstruction of their societies.

The papers arising from the Symposium thus focus on the daily challenges posed by working for a 'culture of peace'. A keynote paper by **Jenny Pearce** compares the 'post-conflict' developments in El Salvador, Nicaragua, and Peru. She places the accent on local involvement in shaping society, finding that formal peace processes may exclude rather than foster grassroots and popular participation — an issue developed in greater detail by **Martha Thompson**. A recurrent theme is that, although societies and communities must draw on their own self-healing potential, uninformed or badly timed external assistance can easily thwart these often very fragile and multi-layered processes: something highlighted by both **Anne Mackintosh** and **Graeme Simpson**. This may also affect how societies acknowledge their past: for while decisions about truth commissions, tribunals, and similar formal processes are taken at the highest political level (often with international support), it is among ordinary people and in mundane events that denial and recrimination must give way to recognition, reconciliation, and forgiveness. **Wiseman Chijere Chirwa** looks at how public symbols can help to establish a collective memory, while **Noel Muchenga Chicuecue**, **Viriato Castelo-Branco**, **Glenda Caine**, and **Francisco Tunga Alberto** focus on ways in which to help people consign *destructive* memories to the past.

The articles and essays collected here help to give concrete expression to the various conditions under which local and international agencies are working, and in which societies and individuals must somehow recover shared meanings and purpose. These contributions can only touch on some of the topics that need to be addressed. They do, nevertheless, give some insight into the ethical and practical issues involved in dealing with conflict and re-building societies that have been ravaged by war and violence.[3] Work on mediation and conflict-resolution cannot be approached in a social and economic vacuum. Conflict is a part of and influences to different degrees every sector of human activity: in societies in transition, conflict necessarily affects every kind of development intervention.

Deborah Eade
Editor, *Development in Practice*

Notes

1 See Linda Agerbak (1990): 'Breaking the cycle of violence: doing development in situations of conflict', *Development in Practice*, Vol 1 No 3; reprinted in Deborah Eade (ed) (1996).
2 David Millwood (ed) (1996).
3 For further reading, please see the Annotated Bibliography at the end of this Working Paper.

Relief agencies and moral standing in war: principles of humanity, neutrality, impartiality and solidarity[1]

Hugo Slim

In Dante's 'Inferno' there is a special place of torment reserved for those who have been neutral in this life. Their sin is so particular that they do not even merit a space in hell. Instead, they are confined to the outer part, or vestibule, of hell and separated from the rest of the damned by the river Acheron. The precise sin of this group of people is that of moral indecision and vacillation. Throughout their lives they never made a stand for something they believed. True to form, Dante inflicts upon them a torment which neatly fits their crime. They are destined to rush forever behind a banner which 'whirls with aimless speed as though it would never take a stand', while at the same time they are chased and stung by swarms of hornets.[2]

Many relief workers probably feel that they have already experienced the particular anguish of Dante's punishment. On frequent occasions, the international humanitarian system might be accurately described by Dante's image: a great crowd of international agencies rushing frantically behind the whirling banner of concern brandished by the international community, which seldom takes a definitive moral stand and plants its banner firmly in the ground. Indeed, the urgent and relentless flapping of UN and NGO flags from thousands of fast-moving white vehicles around the world today seems uncannily reminiscent of Dante's vision of the vestibule of hell. And even if relief workers and peace-keepers have not yet experienced such hell, there are those today who might be tempted to think that such a fate should certainly await them when the day of reckoning arrives. The organisation African Rights, in particular, has severely criticised the 'neutralism' of humanitarianism and what it considers to be the absurdity of current relief-agency claims to humanitarian neutrality in political emergencies and war (African Rights, 1994:24-8). Yet in classical humanitarianism, neutrality is prized as one of the four essential operational principles alongside humanity, impartiality, and independence.

So why has neutrality become a dirty word? Is it really a sin? Or do Dante and African Rights understand the word differently from conventional humanitarian practitioners? Is neutrality inevitably unprincipled, or is it in fact the operational means to highly principled ends? Is true humanitarian neutrality really impossible, when any humanitarian action inevitably plays to the advantage of one side or another? A passionate debate now rages about the moral positioning of humanitarian agencies and peace-keeping forces. And as most relief agencies and UN forces alike abandon the idea of neutrality, they are clinging with renewed vigour to the other traditional humanitarian principles of humanity and impartiality, or going beyond traditional humanitarian principles by justifying their position in terms of solidarity, or by giving more refined interpretations of impartiality.

The debate surrounding humanitarian neutrality and its fellow humanitarian principles is a debate about the moral stance or position of third parties in other people's wars. Where should an NGO, international agency, or UN force stand in a violent dispute between various groups? The issue of positioning concerns relief organisations not only at a corporate level, but also at an individual level. In order to operate in the midst of war, a relief agency needs to make its organisational position in that conflict known to the combatants. But at a personal level, it is also essential for staff morale that each individual has a strong sense of his or her individual position in relation to the prevailing violence. Playing a third-party role in a context of violence and injustice is personally taxing, and is one of the greatest challenges facing relief workers and UN soldiers in today's emergencies. The ability to do so with a sense of moral conviction and international legality is crucial to the morale of relief and development workers and also to the non-combatant civilians they seek to help.

The purpose of this paper is to explore the moral implications of the operations of relief agencies, acting as third parties in war-time. The paper begins by identifying the essential problem of moral stance and organisational positioning as one of locating humanitarian values within a context of organised inhumanity. The main part of the paper then examines current usage of the terms *humanity, neutrality, impartiality*, and *solidarity* as they are used to define humanitarian positions. The paper then briefly considers the psychological implications for relief workers of operating as non-combatant third parties in war, emphasising the importance of clear positioning to counter what I have termed 'by-stander anxiety'. Finally, the paper recognises that a range of different positions is both inevitable and desirable in a given conflict; but it concludes by emphasising the responsibility of any third-party organisation (military or civilian) to be transparent in its position and to preserve rather than distort traditional humanitarian principles and language. It ends by recommending concerted support for international humanitarian law (IHL) and its possible reform as the best way to focus the current debate about the place of humanitarianism in war.

Standing for humanitarian values

Relief agencies have problems with their identity and position in today's wars, because they are trying to do something which is intrinsically difficult: they invariably find themselves trying to represent the values of humanity and peace within societies which are currently dominated by the values of inhumanity and violence. More often than not, therefore, they are swimming against the current of that society, or certainly of its leadership. They are representatives of values which are often seen as a threat by leaders and peoples committed to violence and war. If humanitarian values are given too much consideration in situations of war or political violence, political and military leaders fear that they might undermine their followers' will to fight, or provide succour to their enemy.

Nevertheless, it is part of the paradox of human nature that humanitarian values can be present in war and since time immemorial have usually co-existed with violence to some degree.[3] Where there is organised violence, there is often mercy too. But the intricacies of the Geneva Conventions which were put together after World War II show how even the most united and victorious military and political leaders prefer humanitarian values to be rigidly controlled to prevent them from becoming an excessive threat to the war effort.

The task of representing humane values to various combatant parties will always place a humanitarian third party in a difficult position. In most cases, the values represented by the humanitarian will be greeted with distinct ambivalence. On the one hand, they may be recognised and even strangely cherished in some quarters of the warring parties and their societies: many humanitarians can recount a story about a gentle warrior whose cooperation was critical to saving many lives. On the other hand, they will also be treated with the utmost suspicion by crucial sections of any warring party, and perceived as a threat to the violence they are embarked upon. More cynically, but equally routinely, humanitarianism will be seized upon as something which can be abused to bolster the adversaries' own war efforts. The organisation and its individuals who dare to represent the values of humanity in war will thus usually meet a mixed response, with their values being seen simultaneously by different groups as ones to cherish, to attack, or to abuse.

While it has always been difficult to represent and position humanitarian values in war, the proliferation of relief and development agencies working in today's wars now seems to make that positioning even more difficult. One of the main reasons why humanitarian principles have been so difficult to clarify and affirm in the last five years must be that there are now so many different organisations trying to assert themselves as 'humanitarian'. The proliferation of NGOs in particular (which has been an inevitable consequence of Western donor policy in recent years) has led to wide differences in the ethical maturity and political sophistication of various organisations which are all competing to work in the same emergency. Anyone surveying the swarm of NGOs delivering primarily governmental humanitarian assistance in many of today's emergencies would be unwise to accept them all as equally principled and professional. With so many different organisations trying to establish a humanitarian position within today's wars, and with all of them using the same tired humanitarian language to do so, it is hardly surprising that the humanitarian scene has become overcrowded, its messages garbled and its stance somewhat undignified.

So what concepts *are* relief agencies using today to distinguish their third-party, humanitarian position in war? Many of the more mature have done some hard thinking about the principles of their position and the nature of their stance in today's conflicts. But despite their commitment to such thinking, attempts at a real breakthrough in the development of an over-arching principle for their position have achieved very little. To a large degree this is because different agencies have different views on where they stand. As a result, the new NGO codes and principles still lack the kind of clarity, brevity, and irresistible persuasiveness which might impress militiamen at checkpoints or convince a beleaguered government enduring the attacks of a rebel army.[4] The established humanitarian principles and conventional language which relief agencies have traditionally used to formulate their humanitarian stance are sounding distinctly hollow, confused, and even hypocritical in the mouths of today's multitude of international civilian and military organisations which operate with a humanitarian mandate. More precise understanding and usage of these terms might make for clearer positions. In the meantime, it is perhaps small wonder that the precise meaning of words like 'impartiality' has evaporated in recent years in a world where, in the same emergency, a Red Cross nurse can use the term to describe her medical programme and a UN commander can use the same word to describe air strikes.

Humanity, neutrality, and impartiality

Relief agencies traditionally assert their humanitarian position with the three key terms of *humanity, neutrality,* and *impartiality.* These three guiding principles (which also herald the opening of UN General Assembly Resolution 46/182 (1991), which attempted to define humanitarian assistance in the 'new world order' after the Cold War) are of course lifted straight from the top three of the Red Cross and

Crescent Movement's seven guiding principles as formalised in 1965.[5] Indeed, most humanitarian language which emerges from the mouths of NGOs and UN forces is in fact little more than the rebounding and frequently distorted echo of the language and principles of the Red Cross and Red Crescent Movement — an echo which, as we have seen, sounds particularly incongruous when it issues from the mouths of stridently political NGOs or heavily armed UN soldiers. Nevertheless, these three ideals are currently being actively reaffirmed in various forms in an effort to make them work again for today's civil wars, and for the new range of international third-party organisations which seek to find a role within these wars. The confusion seems to arise because different agencies are using the same language to describe different positions or no positions.

Humanity and its heresies

The first principle, that of humanity, apparently remains the least controversial, and is the principle most easily asserted by relief agencies, international politicians, and UN forces alike. However, much of the agreement on the principle of humanity seems to cluster around a somewhat heretical understanding of this principle. There are perhaps two particular heresies in play: first, a reductionist one which commodifies humanitarianism and relates it solely to material help; and secondly, an aggrandising one which tends towards making humanitarianism non-negotiable in war. The former is a heresy of substance (*what*), and the latter a heresy of approach (*how*).

The core of the Red Cross and Red Crescent definition of humanity is the desire '*to prevent and alleviate human suffering wherever it may be found ... to protect life and health and to ensure respect for the human being*'. Here is enshrined the classical definition of humanity. Although brief, it embodies a sense of humanity in all its fullness, showing the humanitarian quest to be much more than a purely physical pursuit aimed only at saving life. Rather, the actual meaning of humanity transcends mere physical existence to embrace 'respect for the human being'. This phrase is essential, because it extends the purview of humanitarianism to rights (such as religious freedom and fair trial) which are well beyond the simple right to life, and are clearly spelled out in the Geneva Conventions. As Pictet points out, the humanitarian ideal of the Red Cross and Red Crescent Movement actually extends to a person's 'life, liberty and happiness — in other words everything which constitutes his [sic] existence'(Pictet, 1979:26).

The first heresy which is so evident in current usage of the principle of humanity caricatures humanitarianism as an essentially materialistic concern for physical welfare, manifested in the provision of a range of commodities such as food, water, shelter, and medicine. This commodification of humanitarianism and its subsequent reduction to a package of 'humanitarian assistance' is a serious heresy which undermines wider humanitarian values. To interpret humanitarianism as an essentially minimalist endeavour relating to simple human survival is a misreading of its first principle. The Geneva Conventions are full of civil and political rights, as well as rights relating to simple physical survival. Restricting humanitarian concerns to relief commodities precludes many other vital aspects of the Geneva Conventions which relate to Pictet's notions of liberty and happiness. Without recognising humanitarianism's concern for all types of rights, humanitarian reductionists actually minimise the rights of those they seek to help. Recognition of this heresy may well be liberating and serve to free people from a conundrum which is more imagined than real. NGOs in particular seem to have convinced themselves that a humanitarian position and a human-rights position are somehow at odds with each other. This is obviously not the case: a truly humanitarian position on the plight of civilian populations in war, as articulated in the IV Geneva Convention, is firmly position in the full spectrum of human rights. Tragically, much time and ink may have been wasted in recent years, trying to find a way of reconciling human rights and humanitarianism, when in fact they were never divided in the first place.

The second heresy is exemplified in some new language. Instead of the simple principle of humanity, most relief agencies have now adopted the more cumbersome (and perhaps sinister) term 'the humanitarian imperative'.[6] This is presumably in the hope that by giving the principle of humanity an imperative gloss and making it unreservedly a moral absolute, the phrase will present humanitarianism as a non-negotiable, almost genetic and biological force, so always over-riding the position of the warring factions. In addition, the humanitarian imperative usually seems to relate solely to 'humanitarian assistance' — the minimum package of relief *commodities* which donor governments are prepared to allow as emergency aid and which typifies the first heresy.

Very much in the Gallic humanitarian tradition, this second heresy gives humanitarianism a non-negotiable aspect.[7] This is at odds with the spirit of classical humanitarianism, which has always recognised that it must negotiate its place in violence, assuming the right of human beings to wage war, but seeking to limit the effects of that war with the consent of the warring parties. The Geneva Conventions recognise that warring parties have rights as well as obligations in agreeing how humanitarianism should be realised in war.[8] By implying that the rights are all on the side of the relief agencies and the victims of war, current interpretations of 'the humanitarian imperative' may optimistically (and even illegally) imply the automatic presence of relief agencies in war and undermine the very serious negotiation which needs to take place between warring leaders and humanitarians to ensure that humanitarian action is fair.

Perhaps the worst aspect of the non-negotiable heresy is that it is so unrealistic. In reality, unless assistance is delivered by force, humanitarianism will always be negotiable. While it is highly likely that altruism in its most universal form is innate to human nature and even an important aspect in the survival and evolution of all species,[9] there is also no doubt that it is usually in fierce competition with human traits which tend towards inhumanity, like fear, oppression, self-determination, enmity, hatred, aggression and violence. There is, therefore, something rather simplistic and imperious about the new phrase 'the humanitarian imperative'. It displays some humanitarians' exaggerated sense of their own importance within a people's vision of their own conflict, suggesting that the new wave of humanitarian ideologues have failed to grasp that conflicting societies are usually deadly serious about their *right* to wage war. In contrast, less grandiose humanitarians who have experience of representing humanitarian values in war realise that they are usually pleading for a minority position, and one which has to be nurtured when it cannot be imposed.

Finally, it is also worth noting what might be an inconsistency rather than a heresy in the current use of the principle of humanity and its new imperative. Many relief agencies, like the politicians whom they frequently criticise, tend to be extremely selective about the various humanitarian 'imperatives' around the world. In an Orwellian fashion, it seems that all crises that threaten the lives of civilians are imperative, but some are more imperative than others. The more imperative emergencies are of course usually determined by the *Realpolitik* imperatives of relief agencies' donor governments, and by the financial or promotional imperatives of competing relief agencies. Thus behind the rhetoric there is an element of bluster and even hypocrisy when relief agencies talk about 'the humanitarian imperative'. Dropping the new term and reverting to the more extensive and more dignified original principle of *humanity* might be wise.

The temptation to abandon neutrality

Of the three classical principles which seek to underpin a humanitarian position, *neutrality* is the one from which most agencies and all military peacekeeping doctrine are in retreat. As suggested above, there is now a majority view that neutrality is either undesirable, because it is equated with being unprincipled, or is simply unachievable in practice, because relief aid is so frequently manipulated. However, the recent pariah status of neutrality in the humanitarian's lexicon seems to stem from a widespread misunderstanding of the term. As Denise Plattner has pointed out, although it is much talked about, there is no definition of neutral humanitarian assistance, and her 11 criteria go far to determine the parameters of what such a definition might encompass (Plattner, 1996).

In its strict sense, humanitarian neutrality is not the neutralism of Dante and African Rights. Truly neutral relief workers and peacemakers are not indifferent, unprincipled, and vacillating creatures destined for the vestibule of hell. On the contrary, they have a determined commitment to particular ideals. They have already taken a stand, and for them neutrality is ultimately the operational means to achieve their humanitarian ideals within an environment which is essentially hostile to those ideals. For the ICRC and for other relief agencies

which choose such a position, neutrality is thus a pragmatic operational posture. Far from being unprincipled or amoral, it allows them to implement their ideals, within the limits prescribed by international humanitarian law.

The Red Cross and Red Crescent definition of neutrality is enshrined in its third fundamental principle:

In order to continue to enjoy the confidence of all, the Movement may not take sides in hostilities or engage at any time in controversies of a political, racial, religious or ideological nature.

Within this principle, Pictet has emphasised the important distinction between military neutrality and ideological neutrality (Pictet, 1979: 54–9). Being neutral means taking no part in military operations and no part in ideological battles. Drawing on the work of scholars who have defined the constituent parts of State neutrality, and on Pictet's commentary on ICRC neutrality, Plattner agrees that the three key ingredients to a neutral position are *abstention, prevention*, and *impartiality*. For an organisation, as for a State, 'abstention' means no involvement in military or ideological activity. 'Prevention' obliges the organisation to ensure that neither party is able to use the organisation to its advantage. 'Impartiality' requires the organisation to apply equal terms to the warring parties in its dealings with them (Plattner, 1996:164). As such, Plattner concludes that 'neutrality may therefore be understood as a duty to abstain from any act which, in a conflict situation, might be interpreted as furthering the interests of one party to the conflict or jeopardising those of the other'(ibid., p. 165).

While perhaps approving this definition in theory, seasoned relief workers and peacekeepers will of course seize quickly on the word 'interpreted'. As they know only too well, in the extremely contested arena of war and political emergencies, the devil is in the interpretation of actions and events. Perception is everything and varies from faction to faction in conditions where one group's legitimate relief is seen by another group as an obvious contribution to the war effort of the enemy. African Rights is thus correct in condemning the 'tendency to believe that neutrality need only be asserted to be proved' (African Rights, 1994: 24). In reality it has to be proved by rigorous adherence to the principles of abstention, prevention, and impartiality, and by constant negotiation, thorough appraisal of the conditions of the respective parties, and continual recourse to the precepts of the Geneva Conventions.

Apart from the Red Cross and Red Crescent Movement, which still rigorously uphold it, few other agencies still draw on the concept of neutrality to stake out their position in war. One determined exception is UNICEF and its Operation Lifeline in South Sudan (OLS), which has worked hard to draw up and disseminate a set of humanitarian principles. In doing so, they have firmly embraced the principle of neutrality:

The guiding principle of Operation Lifeline is that of humanitarian neutrality — an independent status for humanitarian work beyond political or military considerations. (Levine, 1995)

The many NGOs which have rejected the notion of neutrality have done so for two main reasons. First, as Plattner points out, they feel that it often imposes an unacceptable silence upon them in the face of grievous violations of human rights (Plattner, 1996: 169–70). What Pictet has described as the inevitable 'reserve' required of the neutral (Pictet, 1979:53) is considered to be too high a price to pay for NGOs who mandate themselves as advocates of human rights and social justice. Secondly, abiding by neutrality's commitment to prevention and abstention seems increasingly unfeasible in the light of what we now know about the manipulation of relief supplies, and the fact that combatants and civilians are intrinsically mixed in today's civil wars. For example, in the same article in which UNICEF argues for neutrality, the apparent paradox of its position is made clear. Within a matter of a few column inches, it also eloquently makes the case for why such neutrality is not so simple and is perceived by many as impossible to achieve in today's wars:

The military are not a distinct group, separated from the civilian population, but are fathers, brothers, sons frequently returning to their homes. Clearly, in such circumstances, women and children who have received aid from OLS agencies are not going to refuse to feed their own family members. (Levine, 1995)

Despite these problems, UNICEF is one of the very few agencies which is trying to observe and apply the principle of neutrality in its work. But while neutrality may be right for some organisations, it is certainly not right for all of them. Some are bound to find it offensive to the mandates they give themselves. Also, as African

Rights points out, the majority of organisations will find that they simply do not have the means — in terms of diplomatic and political contacts, finances or professional competence — to negotiate and secure a rigorous position of neutrality in their relief work (African Rights, 1994:24). Nevertheless, these factors do not mean that neutrality in itself is not possible, nor that it is an unprincipled means of operating. In the right hands and in pursuit of the right ideals recognised in international humanitarian law, neutrality is an extremely valuable principle. Relief agencies need to decide if they are going to abide by it or not. If they are, they should ensure that they acquire the appropriate skills. If they are not, they should not discredit the principle simply on the grounds that it is at odds with their own mandate and capabilities.

Embracing impartiality

Because of their difficulties with neutrality, most NGOs have abandoned the concept and embraced its close relation, *impartiality*. In common with most other NGOs, ACORD (a European NGO consortium with extensive and considered experience of working in political emergencies and war in Africa) has determinedly reasserted the principle of impartiality over that of neutrality as the guiding ethic of its operations in war:

Whereas neutrality dictated that ACORD could take no position of any kind in a conflict, impartiality means upholding accepted human values irrespective of the allegiance of those involved.[10]

While ACORD rejects neutrality, it affirms the notion of impartiality. But it has misunderstood the principle of neutrality. For, as we have seen, neutrality may stop an organisation from taking sides (militarily or ideologically) and protect it from public criticism, but it does not prevent an organisation from having a principled position, based on firm ideals. The classical definition of impartiality, taken from the Red Cross and Red Crescent principles, is that an organisation

makes no discrimination as to nationality, race, religious beliefs, class or political opinions. It endeavours to relieve the suffering of individuals, being guided solely by their needs, and to give priority to the most urgent cases of distress.

As Pictet (1979:37–43) and others have pointed out, the principle of impartiality is therefore built on the twin pillars of non-discrimination of person and proportionality of need. In other words, the similarity of all people but the differences in their needs should at all times determine the judgements of the impartial humanitarian, in the light of the objective precepts of humanitarian law.

The attraction of impartiality over neutrality for most NGOs and UN forces is that the concept permits the impartial person to be judgemental — albeit not gratuitously so, but in line with agreed values. Pictet caricatures the difference between neutrality and impartiality thus: 'the neutral man [sic] refuses to make a judgement, whereas the one who is impartial judges a situation in accordance with pre-established rules' (1979: 53) . NGO policy has pounced on the objectivity of impartiality and its potential for being judgemental. For advocacy-driven NGOs and robust peace-keepers alike, impartiality seems to offer the most scope for justifying a strategy of speaking out or shooting out, while also maintaining humanitarian values.

The Medecins Sans Frontieres movement (MSF) has sought to emphasise that impartiality need not be passive or condone human-rights violations, by adhering to a more refined expression of the principle: the notion of 'active impartiality'.[11] The active dimension of MSF's impartiality refers to the fact that they will speak out and condemn any party in a conflict which they see as breaching human rights or humanitarian law. The development of this harder interpretation of impartiality is, therefore, determinedly not neutral and abstentionist. Public criticism will be made against people or groups on the basis of what they do, but not on the basis of who they are. Impartiality in this context relates to the various factions or parties involved, but rejects the idea of abstention in the face of human-rights abuses. The idea of active impartiality might therefore be summed up as impartiality to persons, but partiality to their actions.

Leaning towards solidarity

A fourth concept is gaining increasing currency within debates about humanitarian positioning: it is that of 'solidarity'. This represents the stance of those who wish to abandon both neutrality and impartiality. African Rights and others have suggested that, in many political emergencies and wars, the notion of solidarity might be the most appropriate guiding principle around which relief agencies could align their operational position. In its paper *Humanitarianism Unbound*, African Rights states that 'It is arguable that solidarity is the most important principle of all', adding that 'what solidarity operations have in common is a political goal shared with the people' (African Rights, 1994: 26, 27). The writer defines 'genuine solidarity in relief work' as including four main components:

1) Human rights objectivity and the pursuit of justice. This means a commitment to pursuing an agenda based on a set of rights. 2) Consultation with and accountability to the people with whom solidarity is expressed. 3) Shared risk and suffering with the people. 4) Concrete action in support of the people and their cause. This may include providing relief and/or political or human rights lobby and advocacy. (African Rights, 1994:27)

The idea of solidarity obviously involves taking sides. Such a concept may be anathema to many people who give to and work for NGOs, and it is certainly in opposition to classical humanitarian principles. But in both Christian moral theology and development work based on social justice, there is an important tradition of taking sides. Albert Nolan, a Dominican veteran of the South African liberation struggle, is a leading advocate of this position:

In some conflicts one side is right and the other side is wrong ... In such cases a policy of seeking consensus and not taking sides would be quite wrong. Christians are not supposed to try and reconcile good and evil, justice and injustice; we are supposed to do away with evil, injustice and sin.[11]

Such a solidarity-based approach is obviously easier when the sides are clearly drawn, when right and wrong are as distinct as night and day, and when the wronged can be easily distinguished from the wrong. But such clarity is not always the case in today's internal wars, and the principle of solidarity can seldom be applied with confidence in many conflicts. Solidarity is a principle which was right for those who backed long-established (and often non-violent) resistance movements like the civil-rights movement in the USA or the liberation movements in South Africa and Eastern Europe. It is also one which should always be actively applied in genocide as in Rwanda. But in wars like those in Somalia, Liberia, and Sierra Leone, the 'good' sides are not so clearly identifiable. At a practical level, the application of solidarity faces problems too. The tenuous nature of the chain of command in today's wars can compromise the principle of taking sides. Political and military leaders (whether intentionally or not) often have little control over those who carry out atrocities in their name, meaning that solidarity can all too easily become solidarity with excessive and uncoordinated violence.

In an attempt to avoid these pitfalls, a certain element of humanitarian discourse has adapted the notion of solidarity and claimed solidarity not with those who are 'right', but with those who are somehow regarded as 'innocent'. In this analysis (which might be called 'innocence-based solidarity'), the lowest common denominator of innocence is usually drawn along lines of sex and age. So women, children, and the elderly are perceived as 'the innocent' and as 'vulnerable groups' who merit the solidarity of relief agencies. But, as the above quotation from UNICEF makes clear, such a position is often simplistic and ill-informed. This kind of innocence-based solidarity is thus equally precarious as a general principle of humanitarian action. And Levine's lament about current humanitarian action is apt when considering the conflict between classical humanitarianism and its detractors: 'we have not worked out what it means to be neutral in a conflict yet in solidarity with all its victims'.[12] On the one hand, ICRC would claim that this is something they have worked out years ago, while Duffield and African Rights would probably claim that such a position is both undesirable and impossible.

Moral stance and personal morale

Beyond the desire to clarify humanitarian principles, there is another reason why a clear sense of the moral positioning of third-party organisations in war is so important: its effect on staff morale. Being a third party to the wanton cruelty and violence in so many of today's civil wars is personally testing for individual relief workers. Even with the clearest sense of purpose, an individual can feel all the recriminations of being a by-stander in the face of appalling atrocities. Experiencing the violence and destruction around them in places like Rwanda, Bosnia, and Liberia, it is usual for most relief workers to experience a gamut of

emotions which range from pity and compassion through powerlessness, frustration, and fear, to anger and outright hostility to all concerned. It is common for several of these emotions to be experienced simultaneously in an individual. It seems equally common for individuals to swing from one end of the spectrum to another at different intervals. At the hostile end of the spectrum, it becomes possible to categorise a whole people as somehow deranged and sub-human.

Humanitarians seldom do anything obvious to stop the causes of the violence around them. Their impact is usually only palliative; at best they become some small beacon of alternative humane values in the midst of inhumanity. Because of this frequent inability to stop the violence around them, many humanitarians and peace-keepers have to deal with what might be termed 'by-stander anxiety'.[13] It is this anxiety which perhaps underlies the concerns of NGOs in particular to be dissatisfied with classical humanitarianism and move towards notions of active impartiality and solidarity. Although not necessarily the case, public silence is feared as the hallmark of the by-stander, and so advocacy becomes all-important to NGOs.[14]

In such a context, it becomes extremely important for relief workers to know where their particular organisation stands and what position it is taking as a third party. Their own personal contribution must make sense as a moral and active one within the violence around them, and such activity must be clearly explained in terms of whichever principle — neutrality, impartiality, or solidarity — their organisation has chosen to pursue. In this way, the individual can interpret his or her role within the violence beyond that of a by-stander, consciously countering the invidious feelings of by-stander anxiety with a definite vision and understanding of his or her position.

Behind the words

To sum up, the semantic manoeuvring around humanitarian principles which currently preoccupies humanitarian policy-makers is symptomatic of the confusion which arises when so many different types of third-party organisation seek to clarify their moral position in political emergencies and war today. Not surprisingly, however, the variety of shifting positions and their mutating vocabulary create confusion, and the humanitarian community still seeks a decisive moral banner under which to go about its business. The result is that the notions of humanity, neutrality, and impartiality, which traditionally underpinned classical humanitarianism, are being stretched or abandoned and so risk being undermined in a process in which they come to mean different things to different people.

Yet behind the word-play there is a definite determination to preserve the old values of humanitarianism, while applying them within the byzantine politics (local and international) of today's emergencies. Most of the different attempts to reframe humanitarian principles seem to have three main ideals in common: a commitment to the principle of humanity — albeit it in a minimal form; a desire to speak out (or shoot out) in the face of human-rights abuses; and a guarantee of third-party immunity for humanitarian agencies. The current word-play of most relief agencies shows them attempting to combine these three ideals into a single position. Relief agencies are eager to assure themselves and others that they subscribe to a morality beyond the sanctity of human life alone. However, as has been argued, such an anxiety is based on an unnecessarily minimalist interpretation of the principle of humanity. In reality, the principle of humanity as respect for the whole human person and as developed in the Geneva Conventions easily embraces the wider moral concerns of NGOs. Instead of agonising over new mission statements and giving added nuance to old principles, many relief agencies should perhaps spend more time reading the Geneva Conventions (particularly the IV Convention) and adopt them as the best possible bulwark of their position in war. It is to their shame that the number of NGOs and their staff who are familiar with the Geneva Conventions, and who refer to them in their work, is pitifully few.

With so many agencies (civilian and military) now operating in and around humanitarian programmes, a range of positions from classical neutrality to solidarity is to be expected and desired in any given emergency. But every agency is responsible for making its position clear for the sake of the credibility of the important principles involved, as well as for morale of the suffering community in question and the individual relief workers working with them. The challenge is to clarify humanitarian terms and the principles to which they refer, so preserving their legitimacy and effectiveness in

war. The best way to do this is to work together with the laws and principles we have already — most notably the IV Geneva Convention — and so to concentrate our efforts on thinking how to improve what we have. Gathering round the banner of international humanitarian law in this way should bring a double boon: first it will provide a united front and common forum for action and thinking on humanity in war; and secondly, by taking so principled and obvious a stand, we might just avoid the vestibule of hell.

References

African Rights (1994) *Humanitarianism Unbound*, London: African Rights.

Levine, I. (1995) *Sudan: In Pursuit of Humanitarian Neutrality: Aid Under Fire*, Issues in Focus Series, No. 1, Geneva: UNDHA.

Pictet, J. (1979) *The Fundamental Principles of the Red Cross: A Commentary*, Geneva: Henri Dunant Institute.

Plattner, D. (1996) 'ICRC neutrality and neutrality in humanitarian assistance', *International Review of the Red Cross* No. 311.

Notes

1 This is a shortened version of a paper which also explored the moral stance of UN Peacekeeping Forces and which will be published as a chapter in *Aspects of Peacekeeping*, edited by Stuart Gordon (London: Frank Cass, forthcoming 1998).

2 Dante, *The Divine Comedy*, 'The Inferno', Canto 3, lines 53–4, Penguin Classics 1984, translated by Mark Musa.

3 See Jean Guillermand, 'The historical foundations of humanitarian action, part I: The religious influence', *International Review of the Red Cross* No. 298, 1994, and also 'Part II: Humanism and philosophical thought' No. 299.

4 See, for example, the *Code of Conduct for the Red Cross Movement and NGOs in Disaster Relief*, Geneva 1994; the Providence Principles from Brown University, 1991; and the Mohonk Criteria for Humanitarian Assistance in Complex Emergencies, World Conference on Religion and Peace, 1994.

5 The seven fundamental principles of the Red Cross and Red Crescent Movement were proclaimed by the Twentieth International Conference of the Red Cross in Vienna 1965.

They are Humanity, Impartiality, Neutrality, Independence, Voluntary Service, Unity and Universality.

6   See, for example, the *Code of Conduct, op. cit.*

7   Gallic debate on humanitarianism has tended to be particularly strident in recent decades, evolving around the notion of '*sans frontiereism*' and its conviction in the *droit d'ingérence*. While such robust relief ideology has its place alongside military intervention, it lacks a certain subtlety in situations where forceful intervention is not available or not necessary and where negotiation is inevitable and desirable.

8   See for example Article 23, IV Geneva Convention.

9   Norman Geras, 'Richard Rorty and the righteous among the nations', *Journal for the Society of Applied Philosophy* Vol. 12, No. 2, 1995. See also Mat Ridley, *The Origins of Virtue*, Viking, 1996.

10 Idriss Jazairy, *An Expanding Role for ACORD in the Face of Wider Conflict* London: ACORD Annual Report, 1994.

11 Albert Nolan OP, *Taking Sides*, London: Catholic Institute for International Relations, 1984.

12 Iain Levine, 'Humanitarianism and humanity', *DHA News* No. 19, Geneva, August 1996.

13 In the extensive literature on the Jewish Holocaust, the word 'by-stander' has emerged as one of the most damning. The particularly odious image of a by-stander thus seems to make it an appropriate term to express relief workers' fears.

14 Effective action is not always to be equated with speaking out. Much can be achieved in silence. Indeed, discretion and secrecy may be the optimal strategy in many particular situations.

The author

Hugo Slim is Director of the Complex Emergencies Programme at the Centre for Development and Emergency Practice (CENDEP) and Senior Lecturer in International Humanitarianism at Oxford Brookes University. He is also an international adviser to the British Red Cross Society, and has extensive prior experience in the NGO sector.

The humanitarian responsibilities of the United Nations Security Council: ensuring the security of the people[1]

Juan Somavía

Introduction

The question of the humanitarian responsibilities of the Security Council is for me a natural sequel to the 1995 World Summit for Social Development, of which I was Chair. It concerns the challenge of putting people at the centre of development and international cooperation, this time in a different sphere of action within the United Nations (UN). Humanitarian tasks and development objectives continually intersect and reinforce each other. They are not sequential, but different dimensions of an integrated understanding of how to promote the security of people. A comprehensive and integrated view of these questions goes far beyond the scope of this paper. Rather, I shall limit myself to matters that the Council should deal with more urgently.

Conceptual framework, definitions, and key issues

The UN Charter confers on the Security Council prime responsibility for the maintenance of international peace and security. Until recently, this has been understood basically to mean disputes among States with international consequences. Yet these two concepts — peace and security, the very conceptual foundations for the UN's mission — are undergoing a radical change in the way they are perceived.

Peace, as we know, is much more than the mere absence of war. It has come to mean harmony within as well as among nations. Countries which are not actively 'at war' with other countries are not necessarily at peace with themselves. In an era when individual people and communities struggle to hold their own against seemingly insuperable odds, peace increasingly means more than the absence of

threats and discrimination. It means freedom from fear and want. For people everywhere, the heart of peace is peace within our own hearts, within our families, our schools, our workplaces, our communities. Peace has acquired a human dimension far larger than the original State-centred notion of the UN Charter; and we have learned that its absence at the local and national levels can have multiple international implications.

The concept of security is also evolving. Today it means inclusion, cohesion, and integration — a sense of belonging to a society and a prevailing order within and among nations that is predicated on fairness and respect for differences and human dignity. The only legitimate (and lasting) security is security rooted in the well-being of people. We have all observed that you can have a secure State — in the traditional sense — full of insecure people who face poverty, destitution, and threats to their integrity. The security of people has thus emerged as a complementary and distinct notion from that of the security of the State.

Another important evolution has been the growing presence on the Security Council agenda of internal conflicts in which the 'parties to a dispute' are not sovereign States but rather groups or factions within a State, sometimes mere warlords, most of whom do not represent an entity with the attributes of a State as defined by the traditional norms of international law.

The first ten years of the Security Council's activities were marked by State conflicts arising out of Cold War situations, the initial tensions of the decolonisation process, threats of external aggression, and traditional frontier-disputes among countries. In each, the humanitarian dimension existed but was not a central feature of the dispute.

In the last ten years, by contrast, the agenda of the Security Council has been fraught with civil wars in which the threat to civilian lives looms paramount. Suffice it to mention Namibia, Cambodia, El Salvador, Guatemala, Afghanistan, Georgia, Angola, Mozambique, and Liberia — as well as Somalia, Rwanda, Burundi, and the Former Yugoslavia — to know what we mean. In these types of conflict, it is increasingly civilians (unarmed and unprotected) who are the principal victims. During World War I, five per cent of all casualties were civilians; in Cambodia and Rwanda, almost 95 per cent were.

Further, it is understood that the Security Council operates under the aegis of the basic principles of international law, a central tenet of which is non-interference in the internal affairs of States. Yet, if the Council is to be effective in promoting solutions and agreements to end this type of conflict, it inevitably becomes deeply involved in the internal affairs of the society in question. Moreover, if the crisis is serious enough, there are, understandably, strong public calls for the Council to 'do something' to prevent death and destruction.

Recently, the Security Council has repeatedly been told: 'Look at the horrible tragedies that are going on in the world. Do something about them!' But the whole tradition of diplomacy leads elsewhere. It is difficult to apply classical diplomacy to these new conflicts.

The evolution of the concepts of peace and security — against the backdrop of mainly internal conflicts posing grave threats to civilians, and an international public opinion that demands action — raises new issues and requires the Council to re-examine the appropriateness and effectiveness of existing instruments and traditional diplomatic courses of action. This suggests that a stronger link must develop between the UN, the Security Council, and organisations like Oxfam which are on the ground, doing humanitarian work, touching those societies, looking into the eyes of the people in danger, learning who they are and what is going on, who the factions are, and what relations people have with their leaders — much of which never gets to the table of the Security Council.

A window on civil society

Maintaining peace and security must take into account the underlying causes of conflict, often development-related, as well as the expressions of power-struggles among leaders and factions. The nature of preventive diplomacy, conflict-

resolution, peace-making, and peace-building, however, is still too State-centric. Together, governments and civil society must evolve a more dynamic concept and praxis, within which non-government actors play a key role. The notion of what some of us call 'preventive development' is crucial: conflicts often have their origins in socio-economic conditions, but are too often dealt with as if they were exclusively political problems. We need to link analysis of the development causes to the actual political processes under way. We can also build upon the lessons learned from experiences of conflict-resolution efforts at the inter-personal level and within divided communities, which are sometimes more relevant than classical dispute-resolution tools.

The tendency to think of peace and security in State-centric terms also fails to take into account the multiple social and economic factors which underpin the security of people, or the vital need to safeguard and support individual actors in civil society, whose energy and mutual confidence are essential to maintaining peace and security in the long term.

A critical feature of the last decade is the civil-society movement, which is burgeoning all over the world. The impact of non-government actors of immense variety — representatives of trade unions, churches, voluntary groups, and grassroots organisations — has been tremendous. It is now generally acknowledged that together they have helped to shape our contemporary definitions of sustainable development, population, gender, and human rights, and in their characteristically practical style they have pushed governments to develop the means to translate these concepts into action.

But they are also centrally involved in humanitarian relief, thus helping to increase the chances of conflict-resolution. The essentially internal dimensions of contemporary crisis — and the increasingly central role played by non-government actors in forging a culture of sustainable peace — have brought NGOs and other non-government actors much closer than before to the analysis and action of international political affairs. This is happening *de facto*, but, in my view, it is insufficiently recognised by the Security Council. Consequently, the experience of humanitarian organisations is being under-used.

The Council's method of work and mandate are sufficiently broad to incorporate, in an appropriate way, inputs from civil-society organisations within its scope of operations. However, these elements are less than broadly interpreted — and much less than flexibly applied. Indeed, while acknowledging the highly sensitive nature of the Council's work, more widespread consultation and transparent decision-making is necessary, not only to enhance accountability *vis a vis* the General Assembly, member governments, and public opinion, but also to provide a broader basis of information, experience, and professional advice for its decision-making.

Given that so many non-government actors are now involved in assisting, safeguarding, and enhancing the security of people threatened by conflict, it is only logical that their role should be fully acknowledged and that they should be enabled (safely and successfully) to make their specific humanitarian contribution. It is thus in practical terms that I wish to consider the Security Council here.

I am convinced that the Security Council itself could be better organised to this end. Here, I would refer to several provocative suggestions set forth in an excellent report entitled *The International Response to Conflict and Genocide: Lessons from the Rwandan Experience*.[2] It contains a number of practical suggestions, highlighting a re-invigorated role for the Department of Humanitarian Affairs (DHA), as well as the role of regional organisations and NGOs, the military, the judiciary, and the media, which are well worth considering.

I would add that what the Council truly needs is an additional mechanism to raise the political profile of humanitarian coordination, to put it on a par with military coordination. Let me offer a practical example: Chile and other countries have advocated that troop-contributing nations be directly privy to Security Council deliberations over where and how their soldiers will be deployed in peace-keeping operations. A special provision for consultation has been approved for this purpose.[3]

Similarly, there should be regular consultations with external actors who have a unique and often first-hand perspective on the specificity of a given conflict, and on where and how humanitarian operations can most safely and productively be undertaken. Such background information and exchange would enhance the decision-making capacity of the Council. However, I should interject a note of caution, to urge that the autonomy and independence of humanitarian work must be safe-guarded in all circumstances.

The consultations could evolve from existing contacts with humanitarian NGOs undertaken by the DHA, and have an informal character.

Security of humanitarian relief

What forms of protection exist for the non-government community in situations of armed conflict and in complex emergencies threatening the lives of large numbers of civilians?

As we have seen, with the end of the Cold War, the UN has become increasingly involved in resolving conflict within States in crisis. Calls upon the UN to take a proactive role in responding to complex emergencies have increased apace. In this context, the safety on the ground of UN and non-UN personnel alike has become a pressing issue. Staff of Oxfam and other NGOs have fallen victim to brutal attacks and harassment over the past year. In addition to the Oxfam worker recently killed in Angola, three Red Cross workers were murdered in Burundi in June 1996. The irony is that, while their loss was mourned among many in the non-government community, it provoked nowhere near the response that the loss of uniformed military personnel has elicited in connection with UN peace-building operations elsewhere.

Indeed, sometimes governments appear more willing to sacrifice the lives of relief workers than they do those of their own troops: the former serve out of the conviction that their presence builds peace; the latter accept participation in the dangers of conflict as part of their terms of service. Yet it is often non-uniformed relief and development workers who are on the front-lines of conflicts in which some governments are reluctant to commit their own troops.

This situation is quite incredible: one group are the professionals — instructed and trained to deal with danger — and yet, for various internal political reasons, governments are unwilling to place them at risk. The other group are there out of conviction, out of their beliefs and values, and are prepared to face the dangers and difficulties. Yet relief and development workers operate with far fewer resources or forms of protection, and stay long after the active fighting has ceased — often remaining until security in its fullest sense is assured, or until it is patently impossible for them to stay.

Some would argue that relief and development workers have become *de facto* advance troops in conflicts where States parties have no real political intent or practical means to guarantee their safety — let alone to achieve peace. Others allege that the political and humanitarian dimensions of complex emergencies are poorly understood, and that lack of coherent assessment, priority-setting, and field operations on the part of the international community not only prolongs the agony of people living in countries in crisis, but puts at risk those trying to help them.

The Security Council itself, in light of the tragedies which have unfolded over the course of the past five years in Afghanistan, Angola, Bosnia, Burundi, Georgia, Haiti, Lebanon, Liberia, Rwanda, Somalia and elsewhere, has begun to refer explicitly in its decisions to the role of non-government humanitarian actors in peace-building and emergency situations. A recent statement on Somalia by the President of the Security Council reflects this trend: '*The Security Council considers the uninterrupted delivery of humanitarian assistance to be a crucial factor in the overall security and stability of Somalia*'. I consider this to be a very significant political recognition of the role that humanitarian agencies are playing in situations of conflict.

Humanitarian concerns have indeed become central to the calculus of whether and how the UN's continued (official) presence in a country can advance the peace-building process. On Liberia, statements by the President have been equally direct, noting that, as of early April 1996, 'factional fighting, the harassment and abuse of the civilian population and humanitarian and relief workers' had increased to the point that the country's political leaders 'risk[ed] losing the support of the international community'.[4]

The challenge is to develop a series of interlocking legal and logical safeguards that are shored up by the political will of countries to enforce them, and operationalised through a coherent UN system that functions in tandem with regional, national, and local institutions.

The ultimate responsibility for peace, however, rests with those in power in a given country. I deliberately avoid the use of the word 'government', for often those in power have not necessarily been elected, nor do they conduct themselves with any sense of civic obligation towards majority rule, or the capacity to govern effectively. Their claim to legitimacy often rests on nothing more than having gained physical control of the capital city and seat of govern-

ment through force. Pressure can nonetheless be brought to bear upon those in power: pressure not only to resolve a conflict, but to respect the humanity of individuals engaged in building the foundations of a sustainable peace, whether formally in partnership with the UN or independently.

I also believe that the Council should consider the compelling issue of strengthened legal provisions for the protection of humanitarian workers. This is an extremely complex issue, but we know that law is only as vigorous as its application. We must address the challenges of implementing international humanitarian law (IHL). Discourse on this subject has occupied policy-makers and academics for the better part of the past century; however, I raise it here because of the compelling nature — indeed, the urgency — of the subject, given the proliferation of highly complex conflicts in which the principal disputants appear increasingly dismissive of these fundamental anchors of global order. Given, too, the multiplicity of agents involved in relief work, we must find new ways to strengthen the legal safeguards available.

There is a *lacuna* in international law today, where non-government workers act more or less autonomously in a conflict situation, unprotected. All there is at present is a UN convention that safeguards those who perform humanitarian work done in agreement and under the aegis of the framework of the UN — but no-one else.

Oxfam and others in civil society might press for the creation of a separate convention which *explicitly* protects non-government personnel and others affiliated to UN relief efforts — whether or not they operate directly under the umbrella of UN control. I believe we should explore what kinds of protection and enforcement should be guaranteed by such a convention. Who would adjudicate it? and how could reporting and related enforcement be expeditiously and effectively ensured?

What can be done to strengthen the mechanisms for the implementation of IHL? As we know, signatory States are enjoined, under the Geneva Conventions, to respect core provisions concerning the protection of the sick and wounded, prisoners of war, and civilians. Through a mix of injunctions and prohibitions on contracting parties, the Conventions seek to protect 'undefended localities' from attack, while at the same time forbidding murder, torture, collective punishment, and hostage-taking — all of which are woefully common in contemporary conflict.

However, as argued in Oxfam's September 1995 position paper prepared on the occasion of the UN's 50th Anniversary (provocatively entitled 'A Failed Opportunity?'),

international humanitarian law, including the Geneva Conventions, [is] upheld in very few modern conflicts ... the debate about addressing the problem concentrates more on limiting the rights of States, rather than seeking to enforce the rights of individuals.

This is a very apt assessment.

The fact that sanctions on States in breach of the Conventions are extremely problematic has led some to suggest that individual reprisals are preferable. The recent tribunals established to address war crimes in the Former Yugoslavia and genocide in Rwanda, respectively, offer a useful example of mechanisms for punishing individuals who violate the rules of IHL. It is encouraging to recognise that people throughout the world are saying: 'enough — an end to impunity'. Think about the difference in our collective consciousness from the days of Pol Pot — and the genocide of millions in Cambodia, where there were no tribunals — and our efforts today.

However, the operational (and financial) challenges faced by these tribunals is sobering. And even if an individual approach is pursued, there are blank spots in the Geneva Conventions; for example, they do not cover 'gender crimes', like large-scale and individual rape as a method of torture and intimidation.

Herein, States can and must exercise their responsibility to ensure that IHL is respected and rights observed. The difficulty in bringing to justice the Serbian leaders Karadzic and Mladic, together with less visible Croatian and Bosnian personnel indicted, is a clear example: a painful reminder of the separation between the notion that becomes law, and the capacity to make the law become reality.

Above all, the importance of international NGO contributions to humanitarian efforts cannot and should not be allowed to substitute for political will on the part of governments. Neither reforms in the organisation of the Security Council and its consultative mechanisms, nor the creation of additional legal protections for humanitarian workers, can substitute for what governments and governments alone can do. Governments have the responsibility to use their political clout, military capability, financial means, and diplomatic capacity to help to solve these conflicts. The increasing role of humanitarian agencies is no excuse for their inaction. Highlighting the role of NGOs should serve to *reinforce* the responsibility of governments in this field.

Making sanctions more humane and effective

How does the international community engage itself in addressing the consequences of sanctions for civilians? The consequences of conflict include large numbers of refugees and displaced persons; famines and shortages of food and water; prisoners of war and combatants missing in action; violations of human rights; genocide and gross breaches of international humanitarian law; and also the effects of economic sanctions.

With limitations, there exist international mechanisms to address some of these consequences: among them, the office of the UN High Commissioner for Refugees (UNHCR); the World Food Programme (WFP); the Geneva Conventions; the human-rights mechanisms of the UN system; and the international criminal tribunals for the Former Yugoslavia and Rwanda, as well as the Commission of Inquiry for Burundi.

By contrast, economic sanctions are a rough, blunt, and extremely unsophisticated measure. We need to develop policies and instruments to make sanctions more humane and, at the same time, more effective. Both the underlying concepts and the implementation mechanisms need to be reviewed, taking into account the fact that in some instances (such as in South Africa and Burundi) some local and regional actors themselves felt that sanctions were necessary.

I am not asserting that sanctions are *a priori* illegitimate. On the contrary, the foundation of every national legal system is the notion that breaking the law incurs a sanction. So it should be for the international system. There is no quarrel over the principle; that is why the Security Council has the authority to apply sanctions. The problem lies in the effects of applying these measures in practice.

A close read of the UN Charter reveals that sanctions essentially aim to condition the behaviour of a State which poses a threat to international peace and security — not to punish or otherwise exact retribution,[5] and even less to contribute to a crisis for the civilians of the nation affected. Sanctions must be based on fundamental respect for human dignity. Indeed, the aim is to bring a State that has violated justice into good working relations within the community of nations, to cite one thoughtful interpretation.[6]

Chapter VII of the Charter thus empowers the Security Council to use both military and non-military measures to maintain or restore international peace and security. Article 41 outlines the nature of non-military sanctions — specifying that the Council may call upon the member States of the UN to apply 'complete or partial interruption of economic relations and of rail, sea, air, postal, telegraphic, radio, and other means of communications, and the severance of diplomatic relations' in order to give effect to the Council's decision.

Yet the conceptual basis for sanctions is flawed, in that they are premised on implicitly democratic assumptions, but are normally leveraged upon more or less authoritarian regimes. It is assumed that the people in a targeted country who will first feel the negative impact of sanctions are sufficiently empowered to pressure the government to cease the aggression or offence which triggered the sanctions. This is seldom the case in an undemocratic setting. Moreover, Johan Galtung and others have argued that sanctions can disempower and weaken the opponents of a regime by offering a common, external enemy against which to rally collective opposition — thereby distracting attention from domestic problems.[7]

Sanctions normally fail to affect the lives of the leaders of such regimes; instead they hit the most vulnerable the hardest; in that sense, they are highly disproportionate. While 'humanitarian exceptions' can be made to allow the targeted country to receive or purchase medical or food supplies, for example, there are no set guidelines for regulating when and how humanitarian assistance is to be provided.

Iraq is a good case in point. After the Gulf War, wide-ranging sanctions were applied by the Security Council in 1991, including a humanitarian exception.[8] At the same time, a trade embargo was imposed. Iraq's means to make use of the exception became severely limited, and the government did not give priority to food and medicine in the use of its internal resources. When data from FAO, WHO, UNICEF, and private organisations began to reveal the terrible consequences for ordinary people, the Security Council approved in 1995 the now well-known Resolution 986, which permitted the sale of oil for food and medicine. In 1996, an agreement was reached between the Secretary-General and the Government of Iraq to implement this resolution.

This situation begs the obvious question: did the Security Council have to wait until 1995, and Iraq postpone its response until 1996, to alleviate the suffering of the more destitute of the Iraqi people? Shouldn't the 'oil for food and medicine' agreement have been a part of the initial sanctions resolution? Were all the deaths and infirmities necessary? What political purpose of the international community was served by them?

Furthermore, practice has shown that the targeted government will prefer to use any resources available to prop up its own power through military spending, and disbursements for the elites and the groups and factions that give it political support. The well-being of the general population (which, under authoritarian conditions, has little ability to react) has not proven to be accorded priority. Iraq is a textbook case. So is the Former Yugoslavia, which chose to use existing resources to wage a regional war and support its regime and its Serbian allies, while under-reporting the impact of sanctions on civilians, so as to avoid international pressure and scrutiny.

Ultimately, sanctions as currently practised produce large-scale insecurity for ordinary people, the opposite of their intended effect. The Security Council should address the issue promptly. The principal objective would be to make sanctions regimes both more effective and more humane.[9]

As a first step, the Council should adopt a resolution approving a set of humanitarian norms, standards, and practices applicable to any sanctions regime to be established in the future. Such guidelines should bear in mind that humanitarian requirements may differ according to the stage of development, geography, natural resources, and other features of the affected society.

A clear position by the Council would have a number of advantages. It would avoid double standards and be a practical response to a real problem which the Council was facing, and should be flexible enough to encompass different realities. Its end result would be to ensure that the Security Council would act in such a way as to ensure that civilians did not suffer the consequences of sanctions regimes. This approach goes much further than the General Assembly's normal method of dealing with the matter (namely, by stating that 'unintended adverse side effects on the civilian population should be minimised' by appropriate humanitarian exceptions).[10]

It is disingenuous to talk of 'unintended side effects', when everybody knows that the sector most affected by sanctions, as presently applied, is precisely the civilian population. There is nothing surprising or unintended about it. That is how economic sanctions actually operate in practice. We are all perfectly aware of it.

A clear position by the Security Council could address or provide a framework that would achieve the following:

• *Establish that the purpose of sanctions is to modify the behaviour of any party, not only a government, that is threatening international peace and security*, not to punish or otherwise exact retribution and even less to impose hardships on the population at large. Sanctions regimes should be commensurate with these objectives, and proportionality should be a guiding criterion.

• *Ensure that sanctions are primarily addressed to the leaders in conflict*, by targeting them on the military and civilian structures that support the regime, and on the factions, groups, and warlords that are parties to a civil-war type of conflict. The impact of sanctions could be shifted from the people at large to the leaders in particular, through measures related to bank accounts, commercial interests, stocks and properties in foreign countries, and applications for residence status and visas.

Indeed, the broader challenge is to develop effective sanctions which wholly avoid punishing civilians. One example is to place sanctions on transit rights, along with selective air and sea boycotts (except for transport of essential humanitarian goods). Other examples might be to pose limits on representation in inter-government forums; or cancel military cooperation agreements, including training and representation abroad. Yet another involves the refusal to provide arms to sanctioned regimes — including the shipment of arms already sold or promised. To date, the practical effect of arms embargoes has simply been to raise the price of arms. We must move

towards commitment on the part of arms-producing countries to improve significantly the monitoring of arms transfers — in effect, to police their own dealings rigorously.

• *Include a provision for humanitarian exceptions in any sanctions regime*, together with the means to make it effective. No exception will work if there are no national or international resources to draw upon. The processing of requests under the exception should be much more expeditious and contain some elements of automaticity for UN agencies, the ICRC, and reputable humanitarian NGOs. A review and evaluation of the work of the Council's sanctions committees in relation to the impacts on civilians should be undertaken. In general, methods and procedures should be expedited.

• *Undertake a regular evaluation by the Council of the potential and actual humanitarian effects of sanctions on the country*. Rigorous criteria must be developed for judging their impact, particularly on the most marginalised and vulnerable members of society. The UN Secretary-General should also make available the following mechanisms:

a. Prior to imposing sanctions, an appraisal of their potential effects on ordinary people, and suggested measures to avoid them.
b. After the entry into force of the sanctions regime, a regular evaluation of its impact on civilians and the changes necessary to counter negative impacts.
c. To carry out such assessments and/or evaluations, the assistance of concerned international and financial institutions, relevant inter-government and regional organisations, and NGOs, should be sought.

To this end, appropriate systems must be developed for regular, unimpeded monitoring, evaluation, and dissemination of data concerning the social and economic impact of sanctions.

When a crisis affecting the ordinary population is about to arise within a targeted country, it is essential that such situations be brought immediately to the attention of the Security Council, and that specific corrective steps be outlined; uniformity of assessment criteria and of sanctions rulings is vital.

• In conflict-ridden societies, humanitarian activities are often under way before sanctions were applied. The right of the general population to bodily integrity and subsistence goods should not be violated. Thus, *the authorities of the targeted country and of the different factions and parties to the conflict must commit themselves to ensuring a continuous, impartial, and expeditious delivery of humanitarian assistance.* This includes the following:

a. Access to the necessary information required by UN and non-government humanitarian agencies.

b. No action to obstruct the day-to-day activities of relief workers.

c. Guarantees of the security of humanitarian personnel, their offices, homes, and operational sites.

d. Unimpeded access to conflict areas, and the use of ports, airfields, roads and other infrastructure.

The sanctions regime should consider strict measures to ensure compliance with the above.

• More generally, *sanctions regimes should have clear objectives for regular review, and precise conditions for being lifted.* These could entail clear warnings that sanctions are likely to be applied as a consequence of specific actions; specifying an agreed time-frame for evaluating the extension, modification, or lifting of the sanctions; and outlining provisions for progressive, partial, or early lifting (including the precise steps required from the target country).

Conclusions

Even with strengthened protections on paper for humanitarian workers, and even with the involvement of humanitarian agencies in measures to ensure that sanctions do not become 'the enemy of the good', the Security Council is ultimately a tool of governments. It can play a strong humanitarian role only at their behest.

Without the political will truly to avoid conflict, or to make the hard sacrifices necessary to preserve peace and promote long-lasting security, there is little guarantee that humanitarianism will not become deeply mired in its own inherent contradictions. For much of humanitarian 'relief' today appears even to its most ardent supporters to be a sticking plaster over the scars of years of social and economic decay, which have festered to the point that open wounds confront us with the raw reality of women, children, and the elderly alike becoming the targets of snipers — along with the people seeking to assist them.

What can we do to stem the tide of brutality and impunity? How can we heal the wounds of conflict that tear apart even societies which appear to be 'at peace'? Taking note and calling upon our governments to make human concerns central to statecraft is the first and most important step. Only when we are truly able to ensure the security of people will the Security Council itself have succeeded in its mission.

Well beyond the Council's immediate reach are the societies of its member States — indeed, all members of the family of nations. The challenge is to find ways to enthuse civil society with a renewed understanding of the contemporary means to pursue peace and security — beyond the sometimes cynical and narrowly political aims of 'diplomacy' as traditionally practised.

Among the most committed people working to achieve these aims are, in fact, individuals such as Jimmy Carter, Julius Nyerere, and Oscar Arias — all of whom have actively participated in politics at the highest level, none of whom has lost sight of the humanism which must be at the heart of humanitarianism.

If I end by mentioning outstanding personalities, it is because there is no substitute for the commitment of individual human beings within government and civil society who *want to make a difference,* who are prepared to act on the basis of values and vision that are rooted in the belief that human beings can ultimately find solutions to seemingly insoluble problems.

Cynics would have us believe that there is no space for values in the globalised world of today — cynics who, in the words of Oscar Wilde, 'know the price of everything and the value of nothing'. Yet we know from historical experience that humanitarian agencies in the past have always had to swim against the current, in a never-ending struggle to promote and protect the dignity of people. We know that we will not give in to the moral indifference of our days and that our ethical convictions and political decision to act are far from being exhausted. We are many and enough with the passion to make our world a better place to live.

Notes

1 This is a slightly edited version of the Gilbert Murray Memorial Lecture delivered at the Sheldonian Theatre in Oxford on 26 June 1996. Professor Gilbert Murray was a

founder of the Oxford Committee for Famine Relief (Oxfam) in 1942. In 1957, a lecture fund was established in his memory.

2 *The International Response to Conflict and Genocide: Lessons from the Rwanda Experience — Synthesis Report*, vol. 5 in a series commissioned by the Steering Committee of the Joint Evaluation of Emergency Assistance to Rwanda (Dense, Denmark: Strandberg Grafiisk, 1995); ISBN: 87-7265-335-3.

This report was prepared collectively by, among others, 19 OECD multilateral donor agencies; nine multilateral and UN agencies, representatives of the International Red Cross and Red Crescent Movement, representatives of major NGO networks worldwide, as well as expert advisers from regional diplomatic and policy circles. Among the many policy recommendations advanced in the report, I would make emphasise the idea that the Security Council '[should] establish a specialised humanitarian sub-committee [whose purpose] would be to inform fully the Council of developments and concerns regarding humanitarian dimensions of complex emergencies linked to conflict, and to make appropriate recommendations' thereupon. It could be sent up as a Joint Committee with ECOSOC under Article 65.

3 See S/PRST/1996/4 of 24 January 1996.

4 See S/PRST/1996/16 of 9 April 1996.

5 See the report of the Informal Open-ended Working Group of the General Assembly on an Agenda for Peace, Sub-group on the Question of United Nations-imposed Sanctions, dated 10 July 1996.

6 Sister Mary Evelyn Jegen, 'Towards a Framework for International Sanctions Policy', Memorandum prepared 18 April 1996.

7 Unpublished working paper by David Cortright, submitted in May 1996; see also D. Cortright and G. Lopez (eds.), *Economic Sanctions: Panacea or Peace-building in a Post-Cold War World?*, Boulder, CO: Westview Press (1995).

8 See SC/RES/687 of 3 April 1991.

9 Many of the suggestions below are mentioned in a 'non-paper' on the humanitarian impact of sanctions, circulated among the members of the Security Council (S/1995/300) in April 1996, and in corresponding individual country responses. See also a Report of the Inter-Agency Standing Committee (XIV meeting, 19 April 1996), prepared in conjunction with the DHA (Geneva).

10 Ibid, see footnote 2.

The author

Ambassador Juan Somavía is the Permanent Representative of Chile to the United Nations, and served in this capacity on the UN Security Council during 1996-97. He was Chair of the 1995 World Summit for Social Development, and is Chairman of the Board of the United Nations Research Institute for Social Development (UNRISD).

For better? For worse? Humanitarian aid in conflict[1]

David Bryer and Edmund Cairns

Introduction

The future of humanitarian aid is now perhaps more in question than at any time since 1945. The providers question whether the abuse of their aid outweighs its benefits; while the donors, at least the official ones, reduce their funding. Yet the need for aid continues; the number of people who suffer needlessly for lack of it rises. Here, we consider some of the practical difficulties and ethical choices involved in judging the 'net impact' of aid that is provided in armed conflicts, where its abuse has become a certainty. It is not offered as Oxfam's last word on the subject, but as the perception of two individuals who are keenly aware that the state of modern war is likely to demand difficult choices of Oxfam and other aid agencies for years to come.[2]

Some of the difficulties in providing aid are created by the nature of most contemporary internal conflicts. Some are created by the providers themselves. But we shall argue that it is a failure of will on the part of both the combatants and of most governments to protect civilians that lies at the heart of most of the difficulties in providing humanitarian aid. A solution needs all of us, from the staff of humanitarian agencies to the Permanent Members of the Security Council, to recognise that we have *responsibilities* under international humanitarian law (IHL) to uphold the *rights* which civilians in internal conflicts can justly claim. Aid agencies could do more to fulfil their responsibility to implement minimal standards of humanitarian performance; and governments could do more to fulfil theirs. Few Northern governments yet show much will to do so; part of the reason is that any major 'engagement' that involves the delivery of significant resources is still largely seen in the North by those on the right of the political

spectrum as 'charity', and by those on the left as top-down redistribution. The case for 'internationalism' — the sense that we all have a responsibility to other human beings anywhere in the world — is seldom seen as a *parallel* responsibility to those who are already helping themselves and others.

We shall suggest that a focus upon what civilians in conflicts are doing for themselves and others, the responsibilities which they fulfil themselves, will present a more accurate portrayal of the world in which aid agencies work. This should perhaps be the analytical basis for a more effective attempt to persuade donor publics and politicians of the merits of supporting people who live in countries that they regard as being of little geo-economic importance.

Aid and rights

Observing the state of humanitarian aid in internal conflicts in the second half of the 1990s, we can say that two things are clear: that humanitarian aid remains vital; and that the difficulties faced in providing it are largely caused by the disregard of combatants and the 'international community' for much of the applicable international law.

Humanitarian aid remains essential to save lives and to help people to enjoy the most basic rights to shelter, water, and enough to eat. It may also help people to survive for long enough to enjoy their equally important rights to health and education, equal opportunity, and a say in their future. Since 1995, Oxfam has described its work as support for all people to enjoy ten such 'basic rights'; this stance depends on Oxfam's moral conviction that all human beings are entitled to these rights.

But it is also important that these rights are all, more or less perfectly, reflected in

27

international law. International human-rights law sets out the indivisible rights of individuals and groups, both economic and social, and civil and political. (That the violation of both sets or 'generations' of rights has much to do with increasing the risk of conflict is beyond the scope of this article.) In the case of armed conflicts, they are set down in IHL — the Geneva Conventions — and refugee law; and, as we shall outline, these most crucial rights for civilians cannot be legally suspended in any circumstance. It is part of the rationale for IHL to set down the absolute minimal rights which all civilians have, even when conflicts destroy their normal means of ensuring them.

Such destruction may leave people in need of emergency assistance to claim those moral and legal rights to water, food, and so on.[3] Humanitarian agencies respond to such needs, using their competences to help uphold people's basic rights. Their performance is neither perfect nor consistent, but it is beyond doubt that tens of thousands of lives are saved every year, and an enormous amount of human suffering is avoided, by the combined efforts of humanitarian agencies. Despite serious criticisms, the 1996 official evaluation of the international response to the genocide in Rwanda,[4] set up by a number of OECD governments, underlined how vital humanitarian aid had been. In Bosnia too, the aid effort was successful, despite the chaos and tragedy of the war.

Rights to material assistance and to protection

Seeing humanitarian aid in terms of international law — as well as the moral belief in rights or broad humanitarian principles — offers two advantages. For non-government organisations (NGOs), it shows that they are not above or outside the law. They choose to operate in a situation governed by international law and are therefore responsible for upholding those parts of it that are relevant to them. If NGOs are to be more accountable, they must be so on the basis of a universally accepted yardstick, which is what the law provides. In the final part of this article, we shall outline how relief practitioners in Oxfam and other NGOs are working to define precise standards of performance that draw on the broad precepts of international law.

Oxfam presents its work in terms of law and the rights it guarantees, in order to debate the ethical choices in providing aid, rather than to encourage a false contest between 'human rights' and 'humanitarianism'. Human-rights law and IHL alike include rights both to protection and to material assistance. Both are vital, and to recognise this is to lay the basis for making the tough choices about how to achieve them in practice. A real woman in a real conflict needs food as well as some means to stop combatants shelling her. If the combatants are taking some of the food aid, and perhaps even selling it to buy guns, there comes a time when the humanitarian agencies who provide that food aid must ask themselves whether it is doing more harm than good.

Legal responsibilities

Before making such choices, we must be clear what the relevant legal rights are. The right to protection is universal and absolute, because Common Article 3 of the 1949 Geneva Conventions sets down the minimum rights for civilians in conflicts 'not of an international character'. They should be 'treated humanely' and protected from 'violence to life and person ... [and] outrages to personal dignity, in particular humiliating and degrading treatment'.

The Conventions' Second Protocol, agreed in 1977, relates entirely to 'non-international' conflicts. It reiterates these rights and, in Article 4, includes specific prohibitions, including injunctions against rape and threats to commit any prohibited act; and, in Article 13, against 'acts or threats of violence the primary purpose of which is to spread terror among the civilian population'. Article 14 then sets out an unconditional prohibition on deliberate starvation and on the destruction of food, agricultural areas, crops, livestock, and water supplies. On these points, both the individual's right to protection and the combatant's obligation not to violate it are equally absolute.

The Second Protocol covers all civilians who are not taking 'a direct part in hostilities'. In most armed conflicts, while they may have a strong ethnic loyalty or other allegiance, the great majority of civilians take no such part. Civilians have played an *indirect* part in hostilities throughout recorded history, but have not on that account been considered legitimate targets of war. It would be quite wrong, for example, to afford less protection to civilians within an enclave or camp, on the grounds that combatants are also there.

Nevertheless, IHL recognises a balance between the rights of civilians and the military purpose of the combatants, including the provisions on forced displacement. More positively, there has been a recent trend on the 'right to assistance' in customary law to tilt the balance more in favour of the civilian. Though the Second Protocol left access for humanitarian supplies conditional upon the consent of the relevant State, the series of Security Council resolutions on this subject, beginning with those on Iraq in 1991, shows that accepted practice is developing towards effectively placing the rights of civilians above all else. Though tragically far from being consistently applied, this trend is much to be welcomed.

The rights which can therefore be claimed under IHL cover both protection from violence — to personal and physical security — and to humanitarian relief. Many NGOs have long shared this twin ambition, recognising that aid alone is not enough. *The Oxfam Handbook of Development and Relief* states clearly that Oxfam's 'fundamental principle for dealing with emergency situations is *the safeguarding of human life*. This involves protection and assistance ...' (original italics).[5] That principle remains as strong as ever. What may have increased is the awareness that war presents painful choices between the two. Strategies to provide assistance may undermine rather than support strategies for protection.

Negative impact

Humanitarian aid can prolong internal conflicts, and thereby cause a level of human suffering which, in some circumstances, is greater than the suffering which the aid is directly relieving. Mary B Anderson's work at the Local Capacities for Peace Project has identified some of the ways in which aid can have such negative, as well as positive, 'by-products'.[6]

One example of negative impact which has been influential in NGO thinking was when factional fighting in the Liberian capital, Monrovia, escalated in April 1996. The subsequent looting by warlords of more than 400 aid vehicles and millions of dollars of equipment and relief goods led several NGOs to

agree to minimise their assistance until guarantees to respect civilians' right to humanitarian assistance were forthcoming. The looting had not only blocked aid to people in need, but also contributed to the war, because vehicles and radio equipment were used, among other things, for military purposes.

Twelve international NGOs, including Oxfam, thus decided to limit their work, using only locally available equipment, with no new resources going into Liberia which could fuel what had become known as its 'war economy'. However, the NGOs still sought to respond where the lack of aid would have threatened human life. Consequently, in September 1996 in the face of new evidence of starvation, Oxfam set up a feeding programme which sought to meet urgent needs, while keeping to the principle of 'minimum inputs' (of lootable goods) in order to achieve 'maximum impact' (for the vulnerable population).

Oxfam decided not to provide dry rations, which were felt to be more susceptible to abuse by the Liberian factions, despite the fact that the feeding programme might have reached more people if it had done so. Doing nothing to encourage further violence against these civilians was judged to outweigh the provision of relief to the greatest number.

Liberia is not atypical. Similar military strategies — to use aid both as a reward for combatants and as a resource for the war — have been present in most other internal conflicts. In November 1996, when the *génocidaires* of Rwanda's former army, militia, and extremist political parties were routed, they left documents confirming that *Opération Insecticide* — the plan to complete the 1994 genocide through insurgency and the re-invasion of Rwanda — was well advanced. That *Opération* would have been fed in part by international humanitarian aid to the 1.2 million refugees controlled by the once and future killers. In Somalia in the early 1990s, the rents and payments for the so-called 'technicals' — the package of vehicles and armed guards which aid agencies bought — provided hard currency for arms, while the factions fought over food aid and water points.

In Bosnia from 1993 to 1995, aid for the 'safe areas' was clearly an obstacle to the military strategy of the Bosnian Serbs, and of benefit to the Bosnian government. Nearly every able-bodied man was mobilised. While much of Oxfam's aid could have been of no conceivable benefit to the combatants, it would be unrealistic to think that none of the supplies, which were directed largely to the 'safe area' of Tuzla, went to the fighters. For instance, UNICEF said that 30 per cent of the aid to Sarajevo was siphoned off by the Bosnian Serbs besieging the city, as payment for allowing it through — inevitably, since aid was the only thing with which the UN had to negotiate.

Oxfam and other aid agencies in Bosnia were accused both of indirectly feeding the government forces and thereby maintaining the war, and of prolonging the suffering of the civilian population by, for a time, sustaining the 'safe areas'. Would it have been better to help those people being 'cleansed' to flee more quickly, as UNHCR did in other parts of Bosnia?

Net impact

It would be wrong to say that the abuse of humanitarian aid necessarily means that agencies should provide none. The question is whether such abuse means that the net impact of that aid enables civilians to receive their material necessities and be protected from violence. Overall in Liberia, and perhaps in Somalia, the answer is on one side. In Bosnia and in Zaire, it was probably on the other.

An earlier case of Oxfam's deciding not to provide aid in an internal conflict was when it chose not to work with the Cambodian refugees on the Thai border in 1979, because it judged that the diversion of aid, including to the Khmer Rouge, was unacceptably high; and because the refugee crisis was in some ways being deliberately maintained for political purposes. What became the unintended consequence of international aid to Rwandan refugees in Zaire — the sustaining of a military force determined to regain lost power — was, in the case of aid to the Cambodian border, the strategic *objective* of the US administration and allied governments.

Yet Oxfam's expertise in the provision of water and sanitation might have improved the conditions for the 'hostage' refugees, had it supplemented the heavily criticised water-trucking operation run by the UN from Thailand. At the same time, the withholding of most official international aid from Cambodia, including even the most direct emergency aid between 1979 and 1981, meant that NGOs became involved in unusual major program-mes. Oxfam's water engineers were put to work

renewing the water system of Phnom Penh, the capital city.[7]

There can be positive as well as negative side-effects of humanitarian aid. Being an obstacle to 'ethnic cleansing' was not the *objective* of Oxfam's aid to Tuzla — but Oxfam would not mind admitting that this may have been a consequence, and in that sense its presence in the region was not precisely 'neutral'. Speaking in Tuzla a few days after Srebrenica fell in July 1995, the UN High Commissioner for Refugees, Sadako Ogata, said that 'ethnic cleansing' was the purpose, not just the result, of the Bosnian conflict. Humanitarian aid should always be driven by the impartial assessment of need, unbiased by either the host government or its opponents, and regardless of the race, creed, nationality, or politics of the intended recipient. But this does not mean that humanitarian agencies can be 'neutral' about whether atrocities are good or bad; sometimes they should say that the combatants who commit them are the main cause of the suffering which they seek to relieve.

The real victims of internal conflicts are not helped by addressing the question of the 'net impact' of aid from either of two extreme viewpoints: either that 'human rights', narrowly defined, are superior to the right to humani-tarian aid, or that no ethical consideration should ever outweigh the normal obligation of humanitarian agencies to deliver aid to those in need. The Rwanda evaluation was heavily critical of some of the plethora of NGOs who were at one time present in Goma, often uncoordinated with each other or with the UN system; a number of them do not seem even to have asked themselves the question. Though media criticisms of NGOs are not always just, we welcome the fact that aid agencies must now work in a world which no longer sees us as doing a simple job beyond reproach. Every agency must be able to demonstrate that it is not working in a particular conflict simply to gain the profile to raise funds from official donors or publics who generously respond to media coverage.

Conditional aid

The impartial provision of aid does not mean providing aid to everyone or without conditions. The 1951 Refugee Convention excludes from its protection those guilty of serious crimes,[8] and the 1949 Geneva

Conventions draw the clear distinction between combatants and non-combatants; accordingly we see no obligation to provide relief for those who have been convicted by a proper judicial process of grave abuses of human rights, or who are likely to use that aid to commit atrocities.

Hence, many NGOs sought from 1994 to persuade Zaire and the 'international community' to separate the genuine Rwandan refugees in eastern Zaire from the minority among them who were suspected of having participated in the genocide. That the call went unheeded left hundreds of thousands of refugees as virtual captives of the extremists, until the action of Tutsi rebels at the end of 1996; even now, the Hutu militia keep a hold over many.

In southern Sudan, NGOs have been closely observing how UNICEF and the Sudan People's Liberation Movement (SPLM) have agreed and are implementing so-called 'ground rules' to protect both aid and civilians from some of the worst ravages of the long-running war. Drawing on the Geneva Conventions and the 1989 Convention on the Rights of the Child, they essentially say that aid will be delivered through the SPLM's relief wing only if the combatants meet the condition of upholding the pertinent international law. Though some have criticised this 'conditionality' of emergency aid, it is difficult to see how else aid agencies in southern Sudan can seriously judge the 'net impact' of their work, and strive to reduce the abuse.

Though the 1996 review of Operation Lifeline Sudan (OLS) was heralded as a model for ethical behaviour in other wars, some aid agencies have feared that the practice has not been as effective as the theory.[9] It is perhaps obvious that at times of high military tension combatants are less willing to abide by the rules; but the rules agreed here seem to have had some effect in making fighters more conscious of the rights of civilians to protection, and perhaps greater impact in making them more conscious that aid should not be diverted for fighting their war.

In these ways, aid agencies do make a distinction between those who do and do not deserve aid, based ultimately on whether they too are fulfilling their responsibilities under international law, which in their most direct form prohibit any attack on the 'security and welfare of others'.[10] They recognise that the vast majority of individuals in emergencies are fulfilling this responsibility and doing much

more: in fact they provide relief, as the local health workers of the *Comité de Crise* did in Goma in eastern Zaire, and often prove the most effective agents of reconciliation. They see the purpose of humanitarian aid as being more than merely meeting immediate needs, but also supporting people in being socially responsible.

Beyond these most direct ethical choices, others have also arisen in many contemporary conflicts. Can aid agencies reach those who are in most need, or only those whom the combatants allow them to? Can they provide the type of aid most needed, or only that which the combatants permit? UNHCR devoted 70 per cent of its trucking capacity in Bosnia to food aid, not because that was the right proportion in terms of humanitarian need, but because other relief inputs — water pipes, fertiliser, seeds — were less tolerated by the combatants who controlled access.

When aid agencies cannot operate without the protection of UN peace-keepers or others, do the benefits they bring outweigh the disadvantages? With such UN military protection, they lose much of their claim to impartiality. In Somalia this was hardly surprising, given the *partial* actions of UNOSOM. But even in Bosnia, where UNPROFOR could perhaps be criticised for being too *impartial*, it and nearly all the aid agencies were perceived at times as partisan. The reality is that each party to a conflict may seek to manipulate humanitarian aid for its own ends. So does UN protection, and working in internal conflicts at all, actually demand unacceptable risks from humanitarian workers?

Mary Anderson's work on how aid can support or undermine local peace-making initiatives also broadens the direct ethical choice. Her *Local Capacities for Peace Project* seeks to bring NGOs and donors together to find ways to provide aid in conflicts in ways that help local people to 'disengage and find alternatives' to the violence. Anderson offers aid agencies structured questions to help them decide whether a particular input is more likely to support those who have a stake in continued war, or those who are struggling to end it.

Declining moral standards in armed conflict

These difficult choices arise from two linked developments. The first is the failure by the parties to virtually all current internal armed conflicts to respect the rights and obligations contained in international humanitarian and human-rights law. The suffering in modern wars is *their* prime responsibility, a point repeatedly made in Oxfam's accounts of the wars in which it has worked, from Cambodia to Rwanda. An Oxfam book on Rwanda, published six months after the genocide began, argued: 'Those extremists who sought to sabotage the Arusha Accords ... bear prime responsibility ... However, the international community, and in particular the most powerful states of the United Nations, have, through their complacency and inaction, contributed to the slaughter.'[11] Indeed, the second major trend is that such criticism of the 'international community' could be made in most recent conflicts.

None of this is meant as a shocking revelation. We all know it, but it is important to recognise it before we can seek any improvement. However, in the behaviour of combatants, and of States outside the regions in conflict, we see a decline in what has been judged as decent.

Among the 30 or so current armed conflicts (the exact number depending on how these are defined),[12] none is being waged between States. An equally important fact, perhaps, is the trend in the *purpose* of many internal conflicts, to which Sadako Ogata referred in Bosnia. Though terrorisation of civilians has been an aspect of war since ancient times, the strategic purpose of most internal conflicts until very recently appeared to be the removal of the government for the alleged benefit of the whole population. For this reason, the Viet Cong fought the South Vietnamese Government, and the Tigrayan People's Liberation Front (TPLF) eventually overthrew the Ethiopian Derg. This did not stop Mengistu exacerbating the Ethiopian famine of 1984–85, but what did survive was some semblance of respect for civilians in the territories controlled by opposing sides. This made it possible to negotiate access for humanitarian aid to cross the front lines, and for the same agencies who had major operations in Addis Ababa to run large cross-border programmes from Sudan with the humanitarian wings of the Tigrayan and Eritrean rebel movements; each side being aware of and even giving tacit approval to the NGO actions.

Is there today even the semblance of that respect for the status of immunity which the Geneva Conventions are meant to guarantee

for civilians? Is it because the purpose of many current internal conflicts appears not to be to change the government within an accepted State, but to carve out a new State or quasi-State on behalf of only one ethnic group — and/or to 'cleanse' the State of all but members of that group? That this is usually done for the benefit of a comparatively small elite within the ethnic group only makes it worse.

No one template explains all modern conflicts. The pursuit of power remains the goal of some wars, and the pursuit of profit in others, such as the 'war economies' of Liberia or Cambodia. But it is in this environment of 'total war' against the 'other' that aid agencies have been working in central Africa, the Caucasus, and the Balkans. Combatants have no respect for civilians, because they are not 'theirs'. Their objective is to remove them from a territory, and the way to achieve that is precisely to violate IHL by any means from killing, to the destruction of property and livelihoods, to rape: the specific suffering of women is another characteristic of most contemporary conflicts.

International response

Sadly, it is not only the combatants in internal conflicts who show an unhealthy disrespect for the consistent fulfilment of civilians' rights. So too have many governments of neighbouring countries, and even of the countries which contribute the bulk of humanitarian aid and dominate the response of the multilateral agencies to 'complex emergencies'. Humanitarian aid is used, in the words of the European Commission speaking at the June 1996 EU Summit, as a 'fig leaf', behind which governments can hide their inaction in seeking other means to protect civilians and build sustainable peace. The Polish journalist Konstant Gerbert, who has covered the Bosnian conflict since its beginning, said in June 1996 that 'humanitarian aid has been a solution to a problem *created* by humanitarian aid'.[13] It is at least arguable that the conflict could have been resolved before most of its 200,000 victims had died, had the members of the EU and the US government resolved on firm diplomatic and security measures.

A critical analysis of the series of EU and UN diplomatic efforts which took place until the fall of Srebrenica is beyond the scope of this article. Suffice it to say that they did not succeed either

For better? For worse? Humanitarian aid in conflict

in ending the conflict or in protecting civilians. In summer 1995, a different strategy was adopted; this did work, at least for a while. Part of the failure of the international effort from 1992, when the conflict moved to Bosnia after its independence referendum, until 1995 was that the humanitarian operation was presented as *the* overriding purpose. Its inviolability was frequently invoked as an excuse not to adopt the use of force.

In the 1990s, the humanitarian response — at varying levels of generosity — has been the only meaningful expression of most governments' concern about internal conflicts. As the Rwanda evaluation put it, we see a 'policy vacuum' in which aid policy becomes not part of a coherent international response, but almost the entire response. Aid policy replaces foreign policy towards those countries in which donor governments perceive little geo-economic interest. Indeed, the deepest problem of humanitarian aid in internal conflicts is that it may let 'the international community' off the hook of its responsibilities to uphold international law.

Humanitarian aid is essential, both to save lives and to provide minimal welfare for the most vulnerable. Funding for emergency assistance is money well spent, and in almost all internal conflicts has been too little to save as many lives as might have been saved. But humanitarian aid does not protect people from violence; it is not alone the solution to the flouting of humanitarian law.

Towards a stake in peace

What would it take to help fill the 'policy vacuum'? What, for example, would constitute better development assistance? We suggest that it would mean aid focused upon those countries (and the regions within them) where tensions are greatest, targeting those who may find a stake in the 'war economy' if they cannot find one in peace, ensuring that inputs support those who seek peace not war, and learning the lessons of what kind of development cooperation actually works.

If people are denied access to legitimate livelihoods, and to peaceful means to challenge that denial, they may have an incentive to support violence. The OECD's 1997 report on how development cooperation could better support 'structural stability' rightly points to the need to reduce poverty, to support *equitable*

development and the legal and political means for peaceful change.[14] Since only a small proportion of official development assistance (ODA) is currently devoted to these purposes, a significant improvement in how it is used to reduce the risks of war could be gained within existing resources.

For donors to do as much as possible to improve stability will, however, also require a reversal in the decline in official development spending, which at US$58.2 billion in 1995 was at its lowest level since 1970. But increased development aid should not be at the expense of humanitarian relief, which still accounts for only nine per cent of official aid. If governments take their global responsibilities seriously, there is no alternative to an increased investment in aid which, if it helps to prevent future conflicts, will be repaid many times over in savings on peace-keeping or receiving refugees.

A coherent policy to help to prevent internal conflicts would also see the better use of human-rights conditionality on the use of development funds. Why did the EU halt its development programme to the former Rwandan Government in late 1993, on the grounds of *accounting* problems, even when it was aware of appalling abuses of human rights and government plans for further violence?

Still more importantly, international financial and trading policies should take account of their effects on reducing or increasing poverty, and thereby reducing or increasing the risk that people on the economic margins of their societies will see their future stake in a 'war economy'. Was it with foresight that the debt burden on Algeria was not reduced until 1995, by when the 1995 Euro-Mediterranean Conference in Barcelona signalled recognition of the threat of increased violence, which was spreading beyond Algeria's borders? Would it not have been wise to do this before the *Front Islamique du Salut* triumphed in the quickly annulled 1992 elections?

Acting more preventively should also apply to the deployment of peace-keepers, modelled upon the success of the operation in Macedonia. Once more, it is fair to ask what would have happened if UNAMIR in Rwanda had in 1993 had both the mandate and strength to act on their intelligence of plans for what was described (by an informer to Force Commander Romeo Dallaire) as 'extermination'. A former Political Director of the British Foreign Office wondered in December 1996 whether some of the slaughter in Bosnia might have been avoided, had the outside world stepped in more decisively in January 1992, when Croatia's 'protected areas' were declared, and three months before the war spread to Bosnia.[15]

That there are costs incurred by accepting direct military protection for humanitarian aid does not mean that it is not sometimes needed. We see far less enthusiasm by governments for the still more important task, when necessary, of protecting the civilians who claim humanitarian aid. It is clear from what was done by Dallaire and some members of UNAMIR at the height of Rwanda's genocide that, even in the most ghastly circumstances, lives can be saved; with more resources, the UN could have saved more lives.

How such protection is achieved, and how much can be achieved, depends on each conflict. What is vital is that UN peace-keepers must have the resources and political will from their own governments and from the UN Security Council to do all that they can. What cannot be acceptable is to promise civilians that they will be protected and then not do it. As UNHCR's Karin Landgren wrote in the *International Journal of Refugee Law*,[16] every example of 'safe areas', under different names, from Iraqi Kurdistan from 1991, to Bosnia between 1993 and 1995, to *Operation Turquoise* in south-west Rwanda in 1994, has had only limited success in reaching the intended goal of protecting all the inhabitants. None has been backed by the will of governments to make that protection effective.

Protection, particularly in a fragile embryonic peace, does not always require soldiers or soldiers alone. As the 1995 Dayton Peace Agreement outlined in the case of Bosnia, there should be more use of police from donor countries, and support for building the capacity of impartial local police forces. Less happily, the implementation of Dayton has seen the slow and inadequate funding of the International Police Task Force; responsibility to deal with serious abuses has fallen between the protection functions of the Task Force and its military equivalents, I-FOR and S-FOR.[17] Perhaps there is as much need for some form of international police capacity as there is for the type of permanent peace-keeping force for which the 25 governments who call themselves the 'Friends of Rapid Reaction' have been calling since 1995.

Containment or resolution of conflicts?

Are there signs that governments will pursue a more coherent response to internal conflicts? If the new British Foreign Secretary, Robin Cook, can deliver a foreign policy with a moral mission, as he aims to, it will be a remarkable change from the standard practice of most Western governments in the 1990s. The norm has been a consistent desire to *contain* conflicts, not to resolve them, nor to provide adequate protection to civilians caught up in them. In most cases, only when conflicts threaten areas within what is perceived as the global economy, or areas of geo-economic interest, has any serious engagement beyond humanitarian aid come about; and that leaves out a lot of the world. UNDP's 1996 *Human Development Report* estimated that the growth of the global economy had by-passed one-quarter of the world's population, 1.6 billion of whom are now poorer than they were in 1980.[18]

Overall, there also seems to be less tolerance for refugees from internal conflicts. In Europe, we have seen the involuntary return of some refugees to former Yugoslavia, and the harsher treatment of asylum-seekers, in the United Kingdom and elsewhere. In Africa, refugees from Rwanda and Burundi are finding less than the traditional hospitality, and Liberian 'boat people' have been turned away from a number of countries. In part, this is because the cost of hosting refugees is not being equitably shared between poor host governments, such as Tanzania, and Northern donors.

Advocacy against abuse

Can we see the beginning of a solution? There are problems in providing humanitarian aid that are almost inherent in the nature of current conflicts: for the civilian has become the target, and aid has become one of the resources which fuels the conflict. There are also problems which come from the competitive nature of many humanitarian NGOs and UN agencies. But we have argued that much of the problem comes from the failure of governments around the world to undertake a wide range of conflict-prevention policies, and to protect civilians who are affected by conflict — instead using humanitarian aid, vital as it is, as an excuse for not doing more. Most donor governments appear to see aid as the whole, not merely a part, of the means to uphold the rights enshrined in international humanitarian law.

This leaves NGOs with the exacerbated difficulty of how to provide aid without its being abused. In our view, many aid agencies would be ethically compromised if they continued to do this without doing everything possible to advocate the types of policy we have mentioned — on behalf, as it were, of the civilians in conflicts who have a moral and legal claim for their right to protection to be upheld. (For agencies with very specific mandates, and for all agencies sometimes, such advocacy may need to be free of publicity.) In some circumstances, such advocacy may be incompatible with the continuation of an NGO's programme in any reasonable degree of safety. Combatants do not like to be told that they are murdering civilians. In such cases, an NGO must judge whether the 'net impact' in protecting civilians' rights is advanced more by its continued presence or by speaking out — even if it requires getting out.

And it is only with such advocacy that NGOs, who are ever more dependent on official donors, can demonstrate their independence and integrity. Even Oxfam, which receives a smaller proportion of its funds from governments than most other major international NGOs — due to the British tradition of private funding, not to our particular virtue! — should always remember this challenge.

Conflicts yet to be

Internal conflicts in the future look set to produce even more unnecessary suffering, and still more compromised aid. NGOs may continue to respond, judging in most cases that their aid produces a net benefit; but they will feel with good reason that they are being increasingly used as the main instrument of international engagement with internal conflicts, for the purpose of keeping refugees away from donor countries, and their suffering off the television screens. The British academic Mark Duffield argues that, for donor governments, humanitarian aid now effectively has the prime purpose of propping up an unjust international economic order.[19] If those governments regard this as too cynical, it is in their power to pursue what might fill the 'policy vacuum', which could begin both to make the economic order a little fairer and offer more protection to civilians in conflicts.

At present, it seems that most governments do not do this, because they do not perceive that they have to meet the cost of internal conflicts. Would the finance ministries which govern the Bretton Woods institutions prescribe structural adjustment programmes that took more account of their effect on poor people if those same ministries also had to pay the bill for humanitarian aid or peace-keeping, when excessively austere programmes helped to push a country into conflict? Similarly, would private corporations — currently responsible for 60 per cent of capital flows to the 'developing world' — be better employers, and less keen to ally themselves with corrupt and abusive governments, if there was a global tax regime which charged corporations for, say, UN humanitarian operations?

Beyond such specifics, we would argue that we all have humanitarian responsibilities. The real individual in the real internal conflict has a claim on us all to uphold the rights enshrined in humanitarian law. The claim is also on humanitarian agencies, because they put themselves forward, in a situation in which international law applies, as providers of some of the things to which that individual has rights. Their responsibility covers their obligations to perform well, and they should be held to account for the consequences of any failure. Thus, though Oxfam does not have a role in directly protecting civilians from violence, it *does* have an obligation to report violations of humanitarian law to the State parties to the Geneva Conventions, and an ethical duty to advocate for those States to provide the necessary protection.

One way in which some NGOs are seeking to meet this responsibility is through agreeing minimum standards of shelter, food, water, and health care, perhaps educational and social support, which could provide the basis for a great improvement in the performance, transparency, and accountability of the humanitarian system. The Steering Committee for Humanitarian Response (SCHR) is a network including the International Save the Children Alliance, the Lutheran World Federation (LWF), Caritas Internationalis, Care International, Médecins Sans Frontieres International, the World Council of Churches (WCC), the International Federation of Red Cross and Red Crescent Societies, and Oxfam International. In 1994, it agreed with the International Committee of the Red Cross (ICRC) a Code of Conduct for Disaster Relief, which was welcomed by governments at the 1995 International Red Cross and Red Crescent Conference.

Now, putting into effect the Code's general principles, SCHR is working with the US NGO network, InterAction, and others including official donors, to agree minimum standards, setting out with some precision what every civilian in any emergency has a right to, and therefore what the international humanitarian system has a responsibility to provide.

More than NGOs, IHL also confers responsibilities on governments. If the relevant State in the internal conflict does not accept and implement the claim which a civilian makes on it for protection and assistance, then that person must turn to the wider authority of all States. Legally, all governments and all citizens share a global responsibility.

Why does this seem to have so little reality in the policies of many governments, and in the political debate of the societies which guide them? Is it in part because that debate is dominated by the perception that almost everyone in conflicts is either a killer, a 'warrior refugee', or a helpless victim? What is largely missing is an appreciation that most individuals who are suffering in conflicts take responsibility for their own lives. This is the experience of NGOs, but they have not been very effective at presenting it. If they were, it would be possible to present the responsibilities which we expect from the 'international community' as a parallel response, not a charitable offering, to the willingness of most civilians caught up in conflict to support themselves and other victims.

Notes

1 This article is based on 'Providing Humanitarian Assistance during Internal Conflicts: Dilemmas and Prospects', an address given by David Bryer at an International Peace Academy seminar in Vienna on 23 July 1996.
2 Throughout, 'Oxfam' refers to Oxfam GB, and not necessarily to Oxfam International or its other members.
3 *The Universal Declaration of Human Rights* (Article 25) and *International Covenant on Economic, Social and Cultural Rights* (Article 11) include the rights to enough food, and to the highest attainable standard of health, which is generally interpreted to include access to clean water. The right to water was explicitly included in the Vienna Declaration of the 1993 World Conference on Human Rights.

4 David Millwood (1996): *The International Response to Conflict and Genocide: Lessons from the Rwanda Experience*, Copenhagen: Steering Committee of the Joint Evaluation of Emergency Assistance to Rwanda.
5 Deborah Eade and Suzanne Williams (1995): *The Oxfam Handbook of Development and Relief*, Oxford: Oxfam (UK and Ireland), vol. 2, p. 851.
6 Mary B. Anderson (1996): *Do No Harm*, Cambridge, Massachusetts: Local Capacities for Peace Project.
7 Maggie Black (1992): *A Cause for our Times: Oxfam — the First Fifty Years*, Oxford: Oxford University Press.
8 1951 Convention Relating to the Status of Refugees, New York: United Nations.
9 A. Karim *et al* (1996): 'Operation Lifeline Sudan: A Review', commissioned by UNICEF.
10 This is one of the seven responsibilities which all people share, matching their rights, according to the report of the Commission on Global Governance (1995): *Our Global Neighbourhood*, Oxford: Oxford University Press.
11 Guy Vassall-Adams (1994): *Rwanda: An Agenda for International Action*, Oxford: Oxfam (UK and Ireland).
12 There are 32 current internal conflicts, according to Kumar Rupesinghe (1997): 'What can Britain do to prevent internal conflicts like Bosnia and Rwanda?' in J. Gittings and I. Davis (eds): *Britain in the 21st Century: Rethinking Defence and Foreign Policy*, Nottingham: Spokesman.
13 This comment was part of a contribution to the 20 June 1996 Florence conference on The Role of Humanitarian Aid in Conflict Prevention, organised by ECHO and the platform of Italian NGOs.
14 The OECD Development Assistance Committee approved guidelines on development assistance to prevent conflicts on 7 May 1997.
15 This comment was part of an on-the-record presentation by Pauline Neville-Jones at the Royal Institute for International Affairs, Chatham House, London on 3 December 1996.
16 K. Landgren in *International Journal of Refugee Law*, 1996.
17 NATO's Implementation and Stabilisation Forces.
18 UNDP (1996): *Human Development Report*, Oxford: Oxford University Press.
19 Mark Duffield (1995): 'The Symphony of the Damned: Racial Discourse, Complex Political Emergencies and Humanitarian Aid', unpublished paper.

The authors

David Bryer is Director of Oxfam GB and current Chair of the Steering Committee for Humanitarian Response. He managed Oxfam's programme in the Middle East and then Africa from 1975, before becoming Overseas Director in 1984 and Director in 1992. **Edmund Cairns** has been since 1992 a Policy Adviser for Oxfam GB, specialising in the role of humanitarian agencies in conflicts. Before this, he worked in Oxfam's Emergencies Department and in the former Soviet Union.

Dismantling former Yugoslavia, recolonising Bosnia

Michel Chossudovsky

Introduction

As armed NATO troops enforce the peace in Bosnia, the press and politicians alike continue to portray Western intervention in former Yugoslavia as a noble, if agonisingly belated, response to an outbreak of ethnic massacres and violations of human rights. In the wake of the 1995 Dayton Peace Accords, the West is eager to touch up its self-portrait as saviour of the southern Slavs, and get on with 'the work of re-building' the newly sovereign States.

But, following a pattern set since the onset of the civil war, Western public opinion has been misled. The conventional wisdom, exemplified in the words of former US Ambassador to Yugoslavia Warren Zimmermann, is that the plight of the Balkans is the outcome of an 'aggressive nationalism', the inevitable result of deep-seated ethnic and religious tensions rooted in history.[1] Likewise, much has been made of the 'Balkans power-play' and the clash of political personalities: 'Tudjman and Milosevic are tearing Bosnia-Herzegovina to pieces'.[2]

Lost in the barrage of images and self-serving analyses are the economic and social causes of the conflict. The profound economic crisis which preceded the civil war has long been forgotten. The strategic interests of Germany and the USA in laying the groundwork for the disintegration of Yugoslavia go unmentioned, as does the role of external creditors and international financial institutions. In the eyes of the global media, Western powers bear no responsibility for the impoverishment and destruction of a nation of 24 million people.

But through their domination of the global financial system, the Western powers, pursuing their collective and individual 'strategic interests', helped from the early 1980s to bring the Yugoslav economy to its knees, thus contributing to incipient ethnic and social conflicts. Now, the efforts of the international financial community are channelled towards 'helping Yugoslavia's war-ravaged successor States'. The international financial institutions are busily collecting former Yugoslavia's external debt from its remnant States, while transforming the Balkans into a safe haven for free enterprise.

With the Bosnian peace settlement holding under NATO guns, the West has unveiled a 'reconstruction' programme which strips that brutalised country of sovereignty to a degree not seen in Europe since the end of World War II. It essentially makes Bosnia a divided territory under NATO military occupation and Western administration.

The shape of things to come

Multi-ethnic, socialist Yugoslavia was once a regional industrial power and economic success. Between 1960 and 1980, annual GDP growth averaged 6.1 per cent, medical care was free, the literacy rate was of the order of 91 per cent, and average life expectancy was 72 years.[3] But after a decade of Western economic ministrations and five years of disintegration, war, boycott, and embargo, the economies of the former Yugoslavia are prostrate, their industrial sectors dismantled.

Adopted in several stages since the early 1980s, the reforms imposed by Belgrade's creditors wreaked economic and political havoc, leading to disintegration of the industrial sector and the piece-meal dismantling of Yugoslavia's welfare state. Despite Belgrade's political non-alignment and extensive trading relations with the USA and the then European Community, the Reagan Administration targeted the Yugoslav economy in a 'Secret Sensitive' 1984 National Security Decision Directive (NSDD 133), entitled 'United States Policy towards Yugoslavia'. A censored version of this document, declassified in 1990, largely conformed to the 1982 National Security Decision Directive (NSDD 54) on Eastern Europe. Its objectives included 'expanded efforts to promote a "quiet revolution" to overthrow Communist governments and parties', while reintegrating the countries of Eastern Europe into the orbit of the world market.[4]

Secessionist tendencies that were drawing strength from social and ethnic divisions gained impetus precisely during a period of brutal impoverishment of the Yugoslav population. The first phase of macro-economic reform, initiated in 1980, shortly before the death of Marshall Tito, 'wreaked economic and political havoc ... Slower growth, the accumulation of foreign debt and especially the cost of servicing it as well as devaluation led to a fall in the standard of living of the average Yugoslav ... The economic crisis threatened political stability ... it also threatened to aggravate simmering ethnic tensions.'[5] These reforms, accompanied by the signing of debt-restructuring agreements with official and commercial creditors, also served to weaken the institutions of the federal State, creating political divisions between Belgrade and the governments of the Republics and Autonomous Provinces. 'The Prime Minister Milka Planic, who was supposed to carry out the programme, had to promise the IMF an immediate increase of the discount rates and much more for the Reaganomics arsenal of measures ...'[6]

Following the initial phase of macro-economic reform in 1980, industrial growth sank to 2.8 per cent in the 1980–87 period, dropping to zero in 1987–88 and to -10.6 per cent in 1990.[7] The economic reforms reached their climax under the pro-US Markovic government. In autumn 1989, just before the collapse of the Berlin Wall, the federal Premier travelled to Washington to meet President George Bush. A 'financial aid package' had been promised, in exchange for sweeping economic reforms which included a new devalued currency, a wage freeze, a drastic curtailment of government expenditure, and the abrogation of the socially owned enterprises under self-management.[8] This 'economic therapy' contributed to crippling the federal State system. State revenues which should have gone as transfer payments to the Republics and Autonomous Provinces were instead channelled into servicing Belgrade's debt with the Paris and London Clubs. The Republics were largely left to their own devices, thus

exacerbating the process of political fracturing. In one fell swoop, the reformers had engineered the demise of the federal fiscal structure and mortally wounded its federal political institutions. The IMF-induced budgetary crisis created an economic *fait accompli* which in part paved the way for the formal secession of Croatia and Slovenia in June 1991.

The agreement with the IMF

The economic package was introduced in January 1990 under an IMF Stand-by Arrangement (SBA) and a World Bank Structural Adjustment Loan (SAL II). The budget cuts to enable the redirection of federal revenues towards debt-servicing were conducive to the suspension of transfer payments by Belgrade to the governments of the Republics and Autonomous Provinces, thereby fuelling the process of political balkanisation and secessionism. The government of Serbia rejected Markovic's austerity programme outright, leading to a walk-out protest of some 650,000 Serbian workers, directed against the Federal government.[9] The trade union movement was united in this struggle: 'worker resistance crossed ethnic lines, as Serbs, Croats, Bosnians and Slovenians mobilised ... shoulder to shoulder with their fellow workers ...'.[10]

The 1989 enterprise reforms

The 1989 enterprise reforms adopted under Ante Markovic played a central role in steering the industrial sector into bankruptcy. By 1990, the annual rate of growth of GDP had collapsed to -7.5 per cent.[11] In 1991, GDP declined by a further 15 per cent and industrial output by 21 per cent.[12] The restructuring programme demanded by Belgrade's creditors was intended to abrogate the system of socially owned enterprises. The 1989 Enterprise Law required the abolition of the Basic Organisations of Associated Labour (BOALs).[13] These were socially owned productive units under self-management, with the Workers' Council constituting the main decision-making body. The 1989 Enterprise Law required the transformation of the BOALs into private capitalist enterprises, with the Workers' Council replaced by a 'Social Board', under the control of the enterprise's owners, including its creditors.[14]

The objective was to subject the Yugoslav economy to massive privatisation and the dismantling of the public sector. Who was to carry it out? The Communist Party bureaucracy, most notably its military and intelligence sector, was canvassed specifically and offered political and economic backing on the condition that wholesale scuttling of social protections for Yugoslavia's workforce was imposed.[15]

Overhauling the legal framework

A number of supporting pieces of legislation were hurriedly put in place, with the assistance of Western lawyers and consultants. A new Banking Law was enacted, with a view to prompting the liquidation of the socially owned Associated Banks. More than half the country's banks were dismantled. The emphasis was on the formation of 'independent profit oriented institutions'.[16] By 1990, the entire three-tier banking system, consisting of the National Bank of Yugoslavia, the national banks of the eight Republics and Autonomous Provinces, and the commercial banks, had been dismantled under the guidance of the World Bank.[17] A World Bank Financial Sector Adjustment Loan was being negotiated in 1990, to be adopted by the Belgrade government in 1991.

The bankruptcy programme

Industrial enterprises were carefully categorised. Under the IMF/World Bank-sponsored reforms, credit to the industrial sector had been frozen, with a view to speeding up the bankruptcy process. So-called 'exit mechanisms' had been established under the provisions of the 1989 Financial Operations Act.[18] The latter stipulated that if an enterprise remained insolvent for 30 days running, or for 30 days within a 45-day period, it must hold a meeting with its creditors within the next 15 days in order to arrive at a settlement. This mechanism allowed creditors (including national and foreign banks) routinely to convert their loans into a controlling equity in the insolvent enterprise. Under the Act, the government was not authorised to intervene. If a settlement was not reached, bankruptcy procedures would be initiated, in which case workers would not normally receive severance payments.[19]

In 1989, according to official sources, 248 firms were steered into bankruptcy or were liquidated, and 89,400 workers had been laid off.[20] During the first nine months of 1990, directly following the adoption of the IMF programme, another 889 enterprises, with a combined workforce of 525,000 workers, were

subjected to bankruptcy procedures.[21] In other words, in less than two years 'the trigger mechanism' under the Financial Operations Act had led to the laying off of more than 600,000 workers (of a total industrial workforce of about 2.7 million). The largest concentrations of bankrupt firms and lay-offs were in Serbia, Bosnia-Herzegovina, Macedonia, and Kosovo.[22]

Many socially owned enterprises attempted to avoid bankruptcy through the non-payment of wages. Half a million workers, representing some 20 per cent of the industrial labour force, were not paid during the early months of 1990, in order to meet the demands of creditors under the 'settlement' procedures stipulated in the Law on Financial Organisations. Real earnings were in a free fall and social programmes had collapsed, while unemployment, with the bankruptcies of industrial enterprises, had become rampant, creating an atmosphere of social despair and hopelessness:

When Mr Markovic finally started his 'programmed privatisation', the republican oligarchies, who all had visions of a 'national renaissance' of their own, instead of choosing between a genuine Yugoslav market and hyperinflation, opted for war, which would disguise the real causes of the economic catastrophe.[23]

The IMF-sponsored package of January 1990 contributed unequivocally to increasing enterprise losses, while also pushing many of the large electricity, petroleum refinery, machinery, engineering, and chemical enterprises into bankruptcy. Moreover, with the deregulation of the trade régime, a flood of imported commodities further destabilised domestic production. These imports were financed with borrowed money granted under the IMF package (the various 'quick disbursing loans' from the IMF, the World Bank, and bilateral donors in support of the economic reforms). While the flood of imports was helping to pile up Yugoslavia's external debt, the abrupt increases in interest rates and input prices that had been imposed on national enterprises speeded up the displacement and exclusion of domestic producers from their own national market.

Shedding 'surplus workers'

The situation prevailing in the months preceding the secession of Croatia and Slovenia in June 1991 points to the sheer magnitude and brutality of the process of industrial dismantling. The 1989–90 bankruptcy figures

40

provide only a partial picture, however, depicting the situation at the outset of the 'bankruptcy programme'. This process has continued unabated throughout the civil war and its aftermath. Similar industrial restructuring programmes were imposed by external creditors on Yugoslavia's successor States.

The World Bank had estimated that there were in September 1990 2,435 'loss-making' enterprises out of a remaining total of 7,531.[24] In other words, these firms — with a combined work-force of more than 1.3 million people — had been categorised as 'insolvent' under the provisions of the Financial Operations Act, requiring the immediate implementation of bankruptcy procedures. Given that 600,000 workers had already been laid off by bankrupt firms before September 1990, these figures suggest that some 1.9 million workers (of a total of 2.7 million) were classified as 'redundant'. These 'insolvent' firms, concentrated in the energy, heavy industry, metal processing, forestry, and textiles sectors, were among the largest industrial enterprises in the country, then representing 49.7 per cent of the total (remaining and employed) industrial workforce.[25]

Political disintegration

Supporting broad strategic interests, the austerity measures had laid the basis for 'the recolonisation' of the Balkans. In the multi-party elections in 1990, with economic policy at the centre of the political debate, the separatist coalitions ousted the Communists in Croatia, Bosnia-Herzegovina, and Slovenia.

Following the decisive victory in Croatia of the rightist Democratic Union under the leadership of Franjo Tudjman, the separation of Croatia received the formal assent of the German Foreign Minister, Hans Dietrich Genscher, who was in almost daily contact with his Croatian counterpart.[26] Germany not only favoured secession, it was also forcing the pace of international diplomacy and pressuring its Western allies to grant recognition to Slovenia and Croatia. The borders of Yugoslavia are reminiscent of World War II, when Croatia (including the territories of Bosnia-Herzegovina) was an Axis satellite under the fascist Ustasa regime: 'German expansion has been accompanied by a rising tide of nationalism and xenophobia ... Germany has been seeking a free hand among its allies to pursue economic dominance in the whole of Mitteleuropa ...'.[27] Washington, on the other hand, favoured 'a

loose unity while encouraging democratic development ... [the US Secretary of State] Baker told [Croatia's President] Franjo Tudjman and [Slovenia's President] Milan Kucan that the United States would not encourage or support unilateral secession ... but if they had to leave, he urged them to leave by a negotiated agreement ...'.[28]

Post-war reconstruction

The economic reforms now being imposed on the 'successor States' are a natural extension and continuation of those previously implemented in federal Yugoslavia. In the tragic aftermath of a brutal and destructive war, the prospects for re-building the newly independent republics appear bleak. Despite a virtual press blackout on the subject, debt re-scheduling is an integral part of the peace process. Former Yugoslavia has been carved up under the close scrutiny of its external creditors, and its foreign debt carefully divided and allocated among the Republics. The privatisation programmes implemented under the donors' supervision have contributed to a further stage of economic dislocation and widespread impoverishment, with GDP declining by as much as 50 per cent between 1990 and 1993.[29]

Moreover, the leaders of the newly sovereign States have fully collaborated with the creditors:

All the current leaders of the former Yugoslav republics were Communist Party functionaries and each in turn vied to meet the demands of the World Bank and the International Monetary Fund, the better to qualify for investment loans and substantial perks for the leadership ... State industry and machinery were looted by functionaries. Equipment showed up in 'private companies' run by family members of the nomenklatura.[30]

Even as the fighting raged, Croatia, Slovenia, and Macedonia had entered into separate loan negotiations with the Bretton Woods institutions. In Croatia, the Tudjman government signed an agreement with the IMF in 1993. Massive budget cuts mandated under the agreement thwarted Croatia's efforts to mobilise its own productive resources, thus jeopardising post-war reconstruction. The cost of rebuilding Croatia's war-torn economy was estimated at some US$23 billion, requiring an influx of fresh foreign loans. In return for these loans, the government of Croatia agreed to implement reform measures that were conducive to further plant closures and bankruptcies, driving wages to abysmally low levels. The official unemployment rate increased from 15.5 per cent in 1991 to 19.1 per cent in 1994.[31]

Zagreb also instituted a far more stringent bankruptcy law, together with procedures for 'the dismemberment' of large State-owned public utility companies. According to its Letter of Intent to the Bretton Woods institutions, the Croatian government had promised to restructure and fully privatise the banking sector, with the assistance of the European Bank for Reconstruction and Development (EBRD) and the World Bank. The latter also demanded a Croatian capital market structured to enhance the penetration of Western institutional investors and brokerage firms.

Under the agreement signed with the IMF in 1993, the government was not permitted to mobilise its own productive resources through fiscal and monetary policy. These were placed firmly under the control of its external creditors. The massive budget cuts demanded under the agreement had forestalled the possibility of post-war reconstruction, which could only now be achieved through the granting of fresh foreign loans. In the absence of 'debt forgiveness', Zagreb's debt burden will continue to increase well into the next century.

Macedonia has followed a similar economic path. In December 1993, the Skopje government agreed to compress real wages and freeze credit in order to obtain a loan under the IMF's Systemic Transformation Facility (STF). In an unusual twist, multi-billionaire business tycoon George Soros participated in the International Support Group, composed of the government of the Netherlands and the Basel-based Bank of International Settlements. The money provided by the Support Group, however, was not intended for 'reconstruction', but to enable Skopje to pay back debt arrears owed to the World Bank.[32]

Moreover, in return for debt-rescheduling, the Branko Crvenkovski government had to agree to the liquidation of remaining 'insolvent' enterprises and the lay-off of 'redundant' workers — who included the employees of half the industrial enterprises in the country. As Deputy Finance Minister Hari Kostov soberly noted, with interest rates at astronomical levels because of donor-sponsored banking reforms, 'it was literally impossible to find a company in the country which would be able to (...) to cover [its] costs (...)'.[33]

Overall, the IMF economic therapy for Macedonia constitutes a continuation of the 'bankruptcy programme' launched in 1989 within federal Yugoslavia. The most profitable assets are now on sale on the year-old Macedonian stock market, but this auction of socially owned enterprises has led to industrial collapse and rampant unemployment. Yet despite the decimation of the economy and the disintegration of education and health services under the austerity measures, Finance Minister Ljube Trpevski proudly informed the press that 'the World Bank and the IMF place Macedonia among the most successful countries in regard to current transition reforms'. The Head of the IMF mission to Macedonia, Paul Thomsen, concurs that 'the results of the stabilisation program [under the STF] were impressive', giving particular credit and appreciation to 'the efficient wages policy' adopted by the Skopje government.[34]

Rebuilding Bosnia and Herzegovina

Resting on the November 1995 Dayton accords, the USA and the European Union have installed a fully fledged colonial administration in Bosnia. At its head is their appointed High Representative (HR) Carl Bildt, a former Swedish Prime Minister and European representative in the Bosnian peace negotiations. The HR has full executive powers in all civilian matters, with the right to over-rule the governments of both the Bosnian Federation and the Bosnian-Serb Republika Srpska. The HR is to act in close liaison with the Implementation Force (IFOR) Military High Command, and also with donor agencies. To make the point crystal-clear, the Dayton Accords spell out that 'the High Representative is the final authority in theater regarding interpretation of the agreements' (Dayton Accord, Agreement on High Representative, articles I and II).

An international civilian police force is under the custody of an expatriate Commissioner appointed by the former UN Secretary-General Boutros Ghali. Irish police official Peter Fitzgerald, with UN policing experience in Namibia, El Salvador, and Cambodia, presides over some 1,700 police from 15 countries, most of whom have never before set foot in the Balkans, and were dispatched to Bosnia after a five-day training programme in Zagreb.

While the West has underscored its support to democracy, the Parliamentary Assembly set up under the 'Constitution' finalised under the Dayton Accords acts largely as a rubber stamp. Behind the democratic façade, actual political power rests in the hands of a 'parallel government', headed by the HR and staffed by expatriate advisers. Moreover, the Constitution agreed in Dayton hands over the reins of economic policy to the Bretton Woods institutions and the London-based European Bank for Reconstruction and Development (EBRD). Article VII stipulates that the first Governor of the Central Bank of Bosnia and Herzegovina is to be appointed by the IMF and 'shall not be a citizen of Bosnia and Herzegovina or a neighbouring State'.

Just as the Governor of the Central Bank is an IMF appointee, the Central Bank will not be allowed under the Constitution to function as a Central Bank: 'For the first six years ... it may not extend credit by creating money, operating in this respect as a currency board' (Article VII). Neither will the new 'sovereign' successor State be allowed to have its own currency (issuing paper money only when there is full foreign-exchange backing), nor permitted to mobilise its internal resources. As in the other successor republics, its ability to self-finance its reconstruction (without massively increasing its external debt) is blunted from the outset.

The tasks of managing the Bosnian economy have been carefully divided among donor agencies: while the Central Bank is under IMF custody, the EBRD heads the Commission on Public Corporations, which supervises operations of all public-sector enterprises including energy, water, postal services, roads, and railways. The President of the EBRD appoints the Chairman of the Commission, which also oversees public-sector re-structuring, meaning primarily the sell-off of State-owned and socially owned assets, and the procurement of long-term investment funds.

One cannot sidestep the fundamental question: is the Bosnian Constitution formally agreed between Heads of State at Dayton really a constitution? A sombre and dangerous precedent has been set in the history of international relations: Western creditors have embedded their interests in a Constitution hastily written on their behalf, and executive positions within the Bosnian State system are to be held by non-citizens who are appointed by Western financial institutions. There is no constitutional assembly, there are no consultations with citizens' organisations in Bosnia and Herzegovina, and there are to be no 'constitutional amendments'.

The Bosnian government estimates that reconstruction costs will reach US $47 billion. Western donors have pledged US$3 billion in reconstruction loans, yet only US$518 million dollars were granted in December 1995, part of which is earmarked (under the terms of the Dayton Peace Accords) to finance some of the local civilian costs of IFOR's military deployment, as well as to repay debt arrears with international creditors. In a familiar twist, 'fresh loans' were devised to pay back 'old debt'. The Central Bank of the Netherlands generously provided 'bridge financing' of US$37 million. The money, however, was earmarked to allow Bosnia to pay back its arrears with the IMF, a condition without which the IMF would not lend it fresh money.[35] But it is a cruel and absurd paradox: the sought-after loan from the IMF's newly created 'Emergency Window' for so-called 'post-conflict countries' was not to be used for post-war reconstruction. Instead, it was applied to reimburse the Central Bank of the Netherlands, which had provided the money to settle IMF arrears in the first place. While debt is building up, no new financial resources are flowing into Bosnia to rebuild its war-torn economy.

Multinational interest in Bosnia's oilfields

Western governments and corporations show greater interest in gaining access to potential strategic natural resources than in committing resources for rebuilding Bosnia. Documents in the hands of Croatia and the Bosnian Serbs indicate that coal and oil deposits have been identified on the eastern slope of the Dinarides Thrust, a region re-taken from rebel Bosnian Krajina Serbs by the Croatian army in the final offensives before the Dayton Accords. Bosnian officials report that Chicago-based Amoco was among several foreign firms that subsequently initiated exploratory surveys in Bosnia. The West is anxious to develop these regions: 'The World Bank — and the multinationals that conducted operations — are [August 1995] reluctant to divulge their latest exploration reports to the combatant governments while the war continues'.[36] Moreover, there are 'substantial petroleum fields in the Serb-held part of Croatia just across the Sava river from the Tuzla region'.[37] The latter, under the Dayton Accords, is part of the US Military Division with headquarters in Tuzla.

The territorial partition of Bosnia between the Federation of Bosnia-Herzegovina and the Bosnian-Serb Republika Srpska under the Dayton Accords thus takes on strategic importance. The 60,000 NATO troops on hand to 'enforce the peace' will administer the territorial partition of Bosnia-Herzegovina in accordance with Western economic interests. National sovereignty is derogated: the future of Bosnia will be decided upon in Washington, Bonn, and Brussels rather than in Sarajevo. The process of reconstruction based on debt-rescheduling is more likely to plunge Bosnia-Herzegovina (as well as the other remnant republics of former Yugoslavia) into the status of a Third World country.

While local leaders and Western interests share the spoils of the former Yugoslav economy, the fragmentation of the national territory and the entrenching of socio-ethnic divisions in the structure of partition serve as a bulwark blocking a united resistance by Yugoslavs of all ethnic origins against the recolonisation of their homeland.

Concluding remarks

Macro-economic re-structuring applied in Yugoslavia in line with the neo-liberal policy agenda unequivocally contributed to the destruction of an entire country. Yet since the onset of war, the central role of macro-economic reform has been carefully overlooked and denied by the global media. The 'free market' has been presented as the solution, the basis for re-building a war-shattered economy. A detailed diary of the war and of the 'peace-making' process has been presented in the mainstream press, while the social and political impact of economic re-structuring in Yugoslavia has been carefully erased from our social consciousness and collective understanding of 'what actually happened'. Cultural, ethnic, and religious divisions are highlighted and dogmatically presented as the sole cause of the crisis, when in reality they are the consequence of a much deeper process of economic and political fracturing.

This 'false consciousness' has invaded all spheres of critical debate and discussion. It not only masks the truth: it also prevents us from acknowledging precise historical occurrences. Ultimately, it distorts the true sources of social conflict. The unity, solidarity, and identity of the southern Slavs have their foundation in history, yet this identity has been thwarted, manipulated, and destroyed.

The ruin of an economic system, including the take-over of productive assets, the extension of markets, and 'the scramble for territory' in the Balkans constitutes the real cause of conflict. At stake in Yugoslavia are the lives of millions of people. Macro-economic reform destroys their livelihoods and derogates their right to work, their food and shelter, their culture and national identity. Borders are re-defined; the entire legal system is overhauled; socially owned enterprises are steered into bankruptcy; the financial and banking system is dismantled; social programmes and institutions are torn down.

Yugoslavia is like a mirror of similar economic re-structuring programmes applied not only in the developing world but also, in recent years in the USA, Canada, and western Europe. 'Strong economic medicine' is seen to be the answer. Throughout the world, people are led to believe that there is no other solution: enterprises must be closed down, workers must be laid off, and social programmes must be slashed. It is in this wider context that the economic crisis in Yugoslavia should be understood. Pushed to the extreme, these reforms are a cruel reflection of a destructive economic model imposed via the neo-liberal agenda on national societies throughout the world.

Notes

1   See Warren Zimmermann, 'The last ambassador, a memoir of the collapse of Yugoslavia', *Foreign Affairs*, Vol 74, Number 2, 1995.
2   Milos Vasic et al., 'War against Bosnia', *Vreme News Digest Agency*, 29, 13 April 1992.
3   World Bank, *World Development Report 1991*, Statistical Annex, Tables 1 and 2, Washington DC, 1991.
4   Sean Gervasi, 'Germany, US and the Yugoslav crisis', *Covert Action Quarterly*, Number 43, Winter 1992-93.
5   Ibid.
6   Dimitrije Boarov, 'A brief review of anti-inflation programs, the curse of dead programs', *Vreme New Digest Agency*, 29, 13 April 1992.

7 World Bank, *Industrial Restructuring Study, Overview, Issues and Strategy for Restructuring*, Washington DC, June 1991, pp. 10 and 14.

8 Sean Gervasi, op. cit.

9 Ibid.

10 Ralph Schoenman, 'Divide and rule schemes in the Balkans', *The Organiser*, 11 September 1995.

11 World Bank, op cit., p. 10. The term GDP is used for simplicity, yet the concept used in Yugoslavia and Eastern Europe to measure national product is not equivalent to the GDP concept under the (Western) system of national accounts.

12 See Judit Kiss, 'Debt management in Eastern Europe', *Eastern European Economics*, May-June 1994, p. 59.

13 World Bank, op. cit.

14 Ibid, p. viii.

15 Ralph Schoenman, op. cit.

16 For further details see World Bank, *Yugoslavia, Industrial Restructuring*, p. 38.

17 Ibid., p. 38.

18 Ibid., p. 33.

19 Ibid., p. 33

20 Ibid, p. 34. Data of the Federal Secretariat for Industry and Energy. Of the total number of firms, 222 went bankrupt and 26 were liquidated.

21 Ibid., p. 33. These figures include bankruptcy and liquidation.

22 Ibid, p. 34.

23 Dimitrije Boarov, op. cit.

24 World Bank, *Industrial Restructuring*, p. 13. Annex 1, p. 1.

25 'Surplus labour' in industry had been assessed by the World Bank mission to be of the order of 20 per cent of the total labour force of 8.9 million, i.e. approximately 1.8 million. This figure seems, however, a gross underestimate of the actual number of redundant workers, based on the categorisation of 'insolvent' enterprises. Solely in the industrial sector, this affected 1.9 million workers (September 1990) of the 2.7 million employed in enterprises classified as insolvent. See World Bank, *Yugoslavia, Industrial Restructuring*, Annex 1.

26 Sean Gervasi, op. cit., p. 65.

27 Ibid., p. 45.

28 Zimmermann, op. cit.

29 Figure for Macedonia, Enterprise, Banking and Social Safety Net, World Bank Public Information Center, 28 November 1994.

30 Ralph Schoenman, op. cit.

31 'Zagreb's about turn', *The Banker*, January 1995, p. 38.

32 See World Bank, Macedonia Financial and Enterprise Sector, Public Information Department, 28 November 1995.

33 Statement of Macedonia's Deputy Minister of Finance Hari Kostov, reported in *MAK News*, 18 April 1995.

34 Macedonian Information and Liaison Service, *MILS News*, 11 April 1995.

35 See International Monetary Fund, 'Bosnia and Herzegovina becomes a Member of the IMF', Press Release Number 97/70, Washington, 20 December 1995.

36 Frank Viviano and Kenneth Howe, 'Bosnia leaders say nation sits atop oil fields', *The San Francisco Chronicle*, 28 August 1995. See also Scott Cooper, 'Western aims in ex-Yugoslavia unmasked', *The Organizer*, 24 September 1995.

37 Viviano and Howe, op cit.

The author

Michel Chossudovsky is Professor of Economics at the University of Ottawa, and author of *The Globalisation of Poverty: Impacts of IMF and World Bank Reforms*, published by Zed Press with Third World Network in 1997.

Non-neutral humanitarianism: NGOs and the Rwanda crisis

Andy Storey

Humanitarianism, neutrality and NGOs

The closure of Rwandan refugee camps in Tanzania and Zaire from November 1996 onwards brought to a partial end a controversial period in the history of international aid, including aid supplied by non-government organisations (NGOs).[1] As the camps closed, the extent to which aid had helped to support the military and political aims of those who controlled those camps — soldiers and militias of a genocidal regime — was widely discussed. This article examines how (some) NGOs ended up playing the roles they did, and seeks to examine what lessons NGOs may learn from the experience.

A word of qualification is important at the outset: there is no such thing as an 'NGO community': different NGOs have different principles and practices. This article does not seek to brand all NGOs as uniformly good or bad; instead, it seeks to identify certain tendencies apparent in some NGOs which participated in the response to the Rwandan crisis. (We do not name individual NGOs in this article, on the grounds that a personalised debate tends to shed more heat than light and to distract from the more important, underlying issues.)

Aid and neutrality

According to African Rights, 'relief aid delivered by international agencies [including NGOs] has become integrated into processes of violence and oppression' (1994b: 3). The accusation is not new: for example, many NGOs are acutely aware of how international aid helped to buttress the forces of the Khmer Rouge on the Thai border with Cambodia during the 1980s. Similarly, those working with Afghan refugees in Pakistan operated within an organisational framework established by anti-Soviet guerrillas (Minear and Weiss 1995: 76-7).

If not original, African Rights' formulation of the central problem is nonetheless pertinent and succinct:

The central dilemma is whether it is possible to supply humanitarian assistance, under the auspices of a governing authority that abuses human rights, without also giving undue assistance to that authority, and hence doing a disservice to the people one is aiming to help. Any involvement by international NGOs in a political emergency brings benefits to the parties to the conflict. The search for a completely neutral humanitarian space is ultimately futile. (1994b: 4)

In seeming contrast to African Rights, Minear and Weiss argue that non-partisanship should remain a guiding principle of humanitarian action: 'The fact that the principle of nonpartisanship is regularly abused does not mean that it should be abandoned' (1995: 71). In fact, there is no necessary contradiction between these two positions: one can accept that NGOs and others should strive for non-partisanship, but it is quite another thing to claim or assume that their actual actions can ever be neutral in their impact. It is this question of the impossibility of neutrality in the context of the Rwandan crisis which is the theme of this article.

The importance of NGOs

With the end of the 'Cold War', Western governments are, for the most part, less interested in developing countries *per se*: the main impulse behind any action is more likely to be public relations than strategic interest. And, because of the generally positive image of NGOs, good public relations can often best be achieved by channelling resources through, or otherwise supporting, the voluntary sector. The tendency for Western governments to 'sub-contract' development activities to NGOs — the privatisation of overseas charity — also has the convenient effect of reducing direct State involvement (and often expenditure) on 'Third World' affairs, as well as linking NGOs to the neo-liberal shift in donors' policy agendas.

Robinson (1997) notes that NGOs have tended to take on the role of 'public service contractors' on a cautious and *ad hoc* basis, but the outline of the emergent relationship is nonetheless apparent: for many States, NGOs 'are seen as the preferred channel for service-provision in deliberate substitution for the state' (Hulme and Edwards 1997: 6). By the mid-1990s, approximately 30 per cent of NGO income came from official sources, compared with an estimated 1.5 per cent in the early 1970s (Hulme and Edwards 1997: 6-7).

A second reason for the growing importance of NGOs is the declining power and influence of 'Third World' governments, often due to the restriction in their economic power through the medium of 'structural adjustment' — a further link to the neo-liberal shift in global policy agendas. The State has been significantly 'rolled back' in most countries of Latin America and Africa, allowing private actors — both businesses and NGOs — much greater autonomy of action.

These changes have made international relief agencies not only larger and more influential, but have de facto expanded their mandate and role ... They may be the chief providers of public welfare, among the main sources of salaried employment and commercial contracting, but even more significantly they act as news agencies and diplomats. In short, relief agencies are expanding into a void left by the contracting power of host governments and the declining political interest of western powers. (African Rights 1994b: 6)

An example comes from Mozambique, where 'NGOs ... have used the freedom of movement allowed by the end of the war and the lowered authority of government ... to increasingly "do their own thing" — to go where they want to go and do whatever they wish' (Hanlon 1995: 13).

It is important not to exaggerate the importance of NGOs; for example, between April and December 1994, 86 per cent of all aid allocations to the Rwandan crisis derived from government sources (Joint Evaluation, 1996: 24-5). And it is government and inter-government agencies which bear primary responsibility for certain aspects of the Rwandan crisis discussed below, such as the failure to tackle abusive authority systems in the refugee camps:

The question of relief agency morality in Eastern Zaire cannot be answered in isolation from an analysis of the actions of other responsible actors in the international arena during and after the genocide. The United Nations and its member states are particularly mandated by international law to respond to genocide ... Essentially, they failed to do so and provided an 'aid only' response to the crisis without the requisite judicial response. Their failure left a notable moral vacuum on the ground in the refugee camps, where alleged perpetrators should have been sought out, denied refugee status and brought to justice. But the failure of international politicians should not mean that relief agencies ... somehow inherit moral responsibility for administering international justice, and in not doing so become tainted with the failure of other parts of the international system. (Slim 1996: 12)

However, despite these qualifications, the positions and practices adopted by NGOs are still of significant and growing importance.

NGOs and the Rwanda crisis

Background to the crisis

Between April and June 1994, the army and government-run militias of the then Rwandan regime initiated and led the massacre of up to one million Rwandan people. (This regime was, strictly speaking, an interim administration formed after the death of President Habyarimana; for ease of presentation, it is this government which is here referred to as the 'former/old regime', despite its short duration in power.) Most of the dead were from the minority Tutsi ethnic grouping, though members of the majority Hutu grouping who were opposed to Hutu extremists were also killed. A rebel army, the Rwandan Patriotic Front (RPF), which had been at war since 1990 with this regime and its predecessor, ultimately succeeded in defeating the government forces and taking power in July 1994. The RPF is Tutsi-dominated but does contain some Hutu members; the new RPF-led government also includes several non-RPF Hutu ministers, though their positions appear marginal and vulnerable.

As the RPF advanced across the country in 1994, millions of Hutus fled, mostly to camps in

Zaire. Some feared retribution for their part in the genocide, while many others were persuaded or intimidated to flee by the propaganda of the old regime, which, anxious to undermine the legitimacy of the new government, warned of indiscriminate revenge-seeking massacres by the RPF. The forces of the former government mostly fled with the civilians and quickly established themselves as the *de facto* rulers of the newly created exile camps. Other Hutus — 'internally displaced persons' (IDPs) — took refuge in camps inside Rwanda, in a zone where a French intervention force temporarily prevented the RPF from taking over the whole country; these camps were later closed (with varying degrees of violence) by the RPF. Despite the massive level of displacement, it is important to note that most Hutus did not flee from their homes.

In a number of ways, some NGOs (as well as official donors, such as the UN agencies) lent support to the forces of the deposed genocidal regime, especially after they had fled to neighbouring countries. This support was manifest in the following ways:

- the choice of where to work;
- the type of support offered, and the structures and people with whom the NGOs worked; and
- some public statements made by NGO representatives.

Where to work

Writing in April 1995, one journalist estimated that over US$700 million of aid had gone to the people who had fled from Rwanda, compared with less than US$300 million of support allocated for use within the country itself (Vidal 1995). This imbalance was confirmed by the 1996 Joint Evaluation of Emergency Assistance to Rwanda, which reported that, for 1994 as a whole, only 35.3 per cent of all aid had been allocated for use within Rwanda (25–6), and even this figure was artificially boosted by the inclusion of allocations prior to April 1994 (before the genocide and flight) and of later allocations to IDPs within Rwanda. By mid-September 1995, 20 times more aid had gone to refugees outside the country than to support the plan for refugee resettlement within Rwanda (Drumtra 1995: 17).

This imbalance had clear political implications. The camps to which most of the displaced had fled were, as mentioned,

predominantly under the control of the forces of the former regime, which had been responsible for the genocide. A World Bank mission to the camps in March-April 1995 noted that '[t]here is an underlying power structure based on a committee of fifteen or seventeen members, made up of former government, military and business leaders ... which still controls most of what goes on in the camps' (World Bank 1995: 10).[2] A later report for the US Committee for Refugees concluded that 'The exiled regime and its militia maintain control over the refugees through relentless propaganda' (Drumtra 1995: 7).

This is not to deny that the needs of the people who had fled were urgent and significant; but meeting those needs, while at the same time practising relative neglect of the needs of those who remained within the shattered State of Rwanda itself, sent a clear political message — whether an NGO thought it was sending it or not.[3]

Some NGOs did adopt a position of offering support within Rwanda, on the grounds that the needs there were being neglected by comparison with the attention afforded to the situation in the external camps. During late 1994, up to 180 NGOs were active inside Rwanda, compared with 100 in the Goma region (the site of several camps in Zaire) at the height of the crisis there (Joint Evaluation 1996: 152).[4] However, many NGOs inside Rwanda chose to work in the camps for the 'internally displaced' in the south which, as mentioned, had been established under the 'protection' of a French intervention force — at least part of the remit of which had been to prevent the RPF from taking over the whole country.

Again, this is not to imply that the needs in the IDP camps were not serious and pressing: indeed, it has been argued that NGOs were somewhat tardy in responding to them (Joint Evaluation 1996: 44, 55). This tardiness may have been due to the fact that 'Many NGOs were initially reluctant to commence operations in the area, being suspicious of the motives underlying Opération Turquoise [the French intervention] and reluctant to work with Hutu officials and IDPs who had been involved in the genocide'. However, 'In July, ECHO [the European Community Humanitarian Office] practically obliged NGOs it was funding to establish operations in the safe [French] zone' (Joint Evaluation 1996: 43). (The issue of how NGO responses were affected by funding pressures — both governmental and non-governmental — is discussed below.)

Another factor for some NGOs was the relative security afforded by the presence of French troops, again an understandable consideration. However, the point is that, given the history of these camps, and the fact that the army and militias of the former regime were also influential in them (though to a lesser extent than in the external camps), the decision to operate in them was very far from neutral.

The type of support offered

The decision adopted by a number of NGOs to focus solely or mainly on the external (and even internal) camps had clear political implications, especially in terms of the legitimacy it inadvertently afforded to the forces controlling those camps. The type of support offered — both inside and outside Rwanda — also had the effect of boosting those forces.

Massive material assistance was given to the killers, including food, transport and a secure base from which to launch attacks into Rwanda. Ironically, while the soldiers of the new government of Rwanda remain unpaid volunteers, the genocidal army of the former government, now in exile, is fed by international food aid. (African Rights: 1994b: 35)

There was not, for the most part, a deliberate policy to support the old regime. In many (probably most) cases, the forces of the former regime benefited from the diversion of aid, rather than being the direct recipients of it. But, in some cases, the relationship was more straightforward, as a report from Human Rights Watch (Africa) made clear in May 1995:

Essential services (food, water, blankets and tents) provided by the international NGOs to the civilian camps have been pilfered by the ex-FAR [government army] and militias for use at their own military bases ... [I]n at least two instances ... the ex-FAR has kept children, including child soldiers, on its military bases in order to retain access to NGO assistance which would otherwise be denied their camps because of their predominantly military character. In this way, some NGOs appear to be contributing indirectly to the ex-FAR's attempt to build up its military infrastructure. One international NGO ... has continued to provide supplies to two explicitly military camps ...; its staff ... claim that the organisation does not wish to distinguish between civilian and military recipients of its humanitarian aid. Another NGO ... provides medical treatment to sick and wounded soldiers at [a] ... military camp, where it runs a field hospital.

The ex-FAR also controls many predominantly civilian camps ... [M]ilitias operating under ex-FAR command have seized control of refugee camps ... The militias in these camps have taken control of food distribution, engage in theft, prevent the repatriation of refugees through attacks and intimidation, carry out vigilante killings and mutilations of persons suspected of crimes or of disloyalty, restrict the movement of persons in and out of the camps, recruit and train young men for incursions into Rwanda and Burundi, and actively launch cross-border raids. (Human Rights Watch 1995: 16)

One NGO official defended the feeding of soldiers on the grounds that 'no one else was prepared to feed these people' and 'they have to eat; they are not all murderers' (quoted in Human Rights Watch 1995: 16).

Other ways in which NGOs (and others) assisted the forces of the former regime included the recruitment of staff and the general organisation of camp life. The issue of recruitment was particularly sensitive, as it was widely accepted that many of the Rwandans employed by NGOs to control food distribution in the camps, for example, were people who occupied senior positions within Rwandan society before their flight. From the point of view of the NGOs concerned, this made practical sense: these people were usually well qualified and suited to leadership. However, the facts that they were highly placed in Rwandan society, that they were not targeted in the genocide (when most opposition activists were killed), and that they subsequently fled, all placed question marks over their suitability for such employment. Many, doubtless, were innocent, but many NGOs did not even address the recruitment issue, despite the troubling implications it raised. As a US Committee for Refugees report noted (in October 1995): 'Too many international NGOs in Goma ... continue to employ Rwandan individuals who are strongly suspected of participating in ... mass murder ... In many instances, the genocide participants are well-known and easily identified' (Drumtra 1995: 4).

The employment issue was especially important, because, when those employed were associated with the former regime, it directly boosted their income and reinforced their prestige and influence within society. But it was not the only practice through which some NGOs aided the perpetrators of the genocide. Procurement and other business arrangements sometimes had similar impacts. For example, one NGO working in Zaire chartered buses (marked as property of the Rwandan government) for staff transport from the man who was Minister for Transport in the former regime.[5]

Public statements by NGO representatives

While some NGOs were most clearly inadvertent parties to the conflict in their operational activities, partisanship (intentional or otherwise) was also evident in the public statements of NGO officials, both inside and outside Rwanda. This is understandable: NGOs which adopt a wider political analysis of their role, which seek to place their relief work in a broader context, must feel obliged to try to influence that context in what they see as positive directions. What was more troubling was the tendency for partisan positions to be disguised as simple humanitarianism, or for some NGO arguments based on ignorance, and tending to lend political support to one or other side, to be accepted as those of informed observers (a problem which poses at least as many questions to the international media as it does to the NGOs).

Perhaps the clearest example in the Rwandan context of assumed 'neutrality' were the calls, endorsed by many NGOs, for a cease-fire between the FAR and the RPF during April to July 1994. These calls seemed the essence of reasonableness: rival forces were urged to desist from hostilities, so that the innocent civilian population could receive humanitarian assistance. In fact, this was not a conflict about which one could be neutral: one side bore ongoing responsibility for the genocide of up to one million people, and the other side, although also guilty of abusing human rights, was trying to stop them. If there had been a cease-fire, the FAR would have been able to consolidate its control over at least parts of the country and, almost certainly, continue the massacres in those parts — massacres which predated the renewed RPF offensive and which were often at their most intense in areas far removed from the fighting. Had the RPF advance — which is ultimately what stopped the genocide — been halted by the imposition of a cease-fire, it is possible that many more lives would have been lost. (It is impossible to form a more definitive judgement on this subject as, in some areas, killings intensified as the RPF advanced towards them.) The 'neutral, humanitarian' demand for a cease-fire could have had the effect of preventing the defeat of a genocidal regime and, possibly, prolonged the genocide itself.

Those NGOs which called for a cease-fire to be accompanied by increased UN protection of civilians had a more refined and coherent position, though not necessarily a very realistic one, given the dim prospects for serious UN action at the time. It was probably also the case that some NGOs tended to support a cease-fire because that would have made it easier for them to operate — in which case, an implicit and questionable assumption was being made concerning the relative priority which should have been accorded to the freedom of NGOs to offer immediate relief.

To return to a point made in the introduction, statements made by NGOs are more important now than ever before, because of the increased role and influence of these agencies. Yet there has been very little analysis of why NGO statements should be particularly esteemed (by the media or by policy-makers), save perhaps for a vague perception that they are the ones 'on the ground', and therefore in the best position to assess developments. This perception may have little basis in fact: 'inexperienced relief workers ... are treated as experts by even more ignorant reporters parachuted in for the event' (Winter 1995: 15).

In Rwanda, 'with few exceptions, it is fair to say that the staff of international organisations and NGOs ... [did] not have a grasp of the political situation, let alone an incisive analysis' (African Rights 1995: 61). This, in some ways, is hardly surprising: NGO staff are not usually recruited for their political sophistication, but rather for their more specialist skills. This does not prevent them developing political viewpoints, though many of them will choose not to do so: as one aid official commented, 'There are hundreds of inexperienced kids [in aid organisations] running around here who know nothing about Rwanda. Worse still, they are not interested' (quoted in African Rights 1995: 61).

It would be fair to add that the pressures of relief work may mean that there is little time or energy to develop an informed view of the country. However, this did not prevent some NGO representatives, both inside and outside the country, being asked for, and offering, their views, however misguided. For example, the head of one large NGO analysed the Rwandan situation in a (European) newspaper article in the following terms:

Two groups [Hutu and Tutsi] are intent on destroying each other ... Last April, the Hutu tribe turned on their Tutsi neighbours and butchered 800,000 of them ... The Tutsis are now bent on revenge ... When the Tutsis subsequently took power, the Hutus fled.[6]

The article continued in the same vein. The facts (as stated earlier) are that the Hutus opposed to the old regime were among the first targets in the 1994 massacres; that Hutus and Tutsis share a common language and culture and have lived peacefully together in the past (though political manipulation does regularly whip up ethnic strife); that the genocide was not a spontaneous 'turning' of one group on another, but a carefully planned, officially sponsored programme; that the new government is RPF-dominated but also contains Hutu members (albeit in rather tenuous positions); that the Hutu flight referred to was instigated and forced by the defeated forces of the old regime; and, furthermore, that the majority of Hutus did not flee (which is not to deny that the human rights of some who stayed have since suffered abuse). All of these facts were completely ignored in this particular NGO contribution.

By no means all NGOs accepted this position, just as some NGOs chose not to work in the camps, and others took care to ensure that their recruitment and business practices did not lend support to the old regime's adherents. And many other NGOs repeatedly called for action by the UN to disarm the soldiers and militias controlling the organisation of the camps. But the piece just quoted reflected one strand of NGO thinking: a claimed 'neutrality' which lent support to the old regime by diminishing its responsibility for the genocide, and by justifying its keeping people in the camps (to protect them from those allegedly 'bent on revenge').

Why did some NGOs do what they did?

When people first fled to Zaire, the office of the United Nations High Commissioner for Refugees (UNHCR), together with some NGOs, insisted that they should return home as soon as possible and that the fears being cited as causes of flight were unfounded. One human-rights group, working closely with the UNHCR and the International Committee of the Red Cross (ICRC), established an independent radio station which broadcast factual information on the situation in Rwanda to the camp population, to counter extremist propaganda.

At the same time, the UNHCR and, again, some NGOs, refused to feed or otherwise assist fleeing soldiers who had established themselves in separate camps; they insisted that these people should first, at least, disarm. One NGO official went so far as to write an internal memorandum, recommending that continued assistance to the displaced be made conditional on action being taken to facilitate the arrest of leading criminals. This recommendation was rejected by the official's superior, who responded: 'Our remit is to provide humanitarian assistance. That is what we have to do. We are going to be feeding people who have been perpetrating genocide' (in African Rights 1994a: 655).[7] Later, some NGOs remained sensitive to the dilemmas involved in their work: prominent agencies pulled out of the camps in Zaire in protest at the extent to which the genocidal regime was drawing support and control from the operation.

Given the early awareness of the situation's complexity, why did the response often fall back on assumptions of 'neutrality' of impact and/or on relative disregard of whether the impact was neutral or not?

Some personal explanations

The personal experiences of agency staff in the refugee camps were deeply traumatic and shaped their thinking in fundamental ways — while there were many fewer staff members inside Rwanda whose personal outlook was moulded by the genocide. (African Rights 1994b: 28)

This observation does not explain why agencies concentrated staff and other resources on the camps in the first place (see below), but it does help explain why some NGO staff, appalled at the levels of suffering endured by the displaced, would, for example, readily work with officials of the former regime in order temporarily to relieve that suffering. It also helps to explain why the public statements of such NGOs sometimes seemed to under-emphasise the centrality of the genocide. A variant on this level of explanation was offered by a nurse, quoted as saying: 'It's too much to handle emotionally. I just concentrate on what I'm doing' (Vidal 1995).

Some politically aware workers, conscious of the dilemmas involved, still supported working in the camps. One very experienced worker (in this case with a UN agency in camps in

Tanzania) posed the question: 'If you were asked in 1945 to work in a camp for Nazi refugees, would your abhorrence for Nazism have prevented you?'. He concluded, 'when we acknowledge other people's humanity, we verify our own ... In the final analysis perhaps this is why I might have worked in a Nazi refugee camp' (Daly 1995: 30). This response does not distinguish between simply working in a Nazi refugee camp and working in a way which helps to restore Nazi power — which is the most relevant parallel in the case of the Rwandan camps. It is, nonetheless, a principled and defensible position. Such reasons go some way towards explaining why some NGO workers de-prioritised the non-neutral impact of working in the external camps.

Some institutional explanations

But the personal feelings and pressures of individual aid workers cannot explain the whole story. Most particularly, why did many NGOs choose to become involved in providing relief to the external camps to a greater extent than they sought to provide relief within Rwanda itself? Or why did some NGO spokespeople feel obliged to make public statements about situations of which they clearly understood little?

Part of the answer must lie in the institutional position of NGOs in terms of competitive fundraising: once a disaster (in this case, massive outflows of people) achieved international attention (through the media), all NGOs had to be seen to respond.[8] Failure to do so would have lost an individual NGO credibility and profile at home, even if it believed that such an intervention was misguided or not a priority. One NGO worker stated that, for reasons of publicity surrounding the cholera outbreak in the camps in Zaire, it was a case, for the NGO, of 'be there or die' (in Joint Evaluation 1996: 117).

The 1996 Joint Evaluation of Emergency Assistance to Rwanda commented:

Where media coverage is intense and such agencies [NGOs dependent on private funding] can literally 'buy a field presence' for the cost of sending a team to the area, then their ability to raise funds will be substantially increased. A field presence enables NGOs justifiably to claim to 'be there'; enables them to 'be seen' through the display of their logos; and increases their chance of benefiting from direct media coverage, particularly if they operate the type of programme that TV crews and audiences find appealing, such as unaccompanied children's centres and clinics. (p. 151)

One observer has identified the tendency for NGOs to 'become more and more alike so that no single NGO can move in and scoop the publicity and the funds ... [P]rofile is the key to success and the relationships entered into and the roles pursued will be determined by the necessity for profile' (Crowley 1995: 40). While, as has been seen, some NGOs responding to the Rwanda crisis sought to pursue a more innovative approach, '[i]n a context of severe competition it will be hard for any individual NGO to break ranks and set new standards - especially given the lower ... profile [such] ... standards would require' (Crowley 1995: 44).

As was noted earlier, official funding, on which NGOs are increasingly dependent, may also push NGOs towards a more homogeneous approach, as evidenced by the pressure from ECHO — the official emergency funder of the EU — on NGOs to become more involved with the IDPs in south-west Rwanda.

Policy implications

As mentioned in the introduction, different NGOs reacted differently to the Rwandan crisis. This suggests that change is possible and that lessons can be learned. For those NGOs which want to improve their performance and impact in this regard, the following is a preliminary list of questions which might usefully be asked before any intervention is launched. (For a much more comprehensive guide to good practice in humanitarian operations, see Minear and Weiss: 1995.)

Where should the intervention be made?

The temptation to follow the television cameras is probably one of the most difficult for an NGO to resist. As discussed above, this may lead to a concentration on refugee camps in particular. However, an NGO seriously trying to alleviate suffering could usefully ask:

- Where is the area of the greatest need? This may, as was partially the case in Rwanda, be inside a country rather than at border camps.
- Are the needs currently being addressed by others? Even if the needs at the high-profile locations are indeed the most pressing, it is often likely that a large number of other actors (official and private) will already be dealing with those needs, so that the requirement for an additional intervention there by the NGO may be limited.

On this last point, a World Bank mission to the camps in Zaire in March and April of 1995 found that '[t]he rise of women's associations has been one of the most important phenomena to occur recently. These "associations" work for the economic betterment of families in camps, while also providing a sanctuary to discuss a range of sensitive issues, including repatriation. Support for these groups should be a priority of any assistance programme' (World Bank 1995: 1). Searching out such alternatives to reliance upon the previously existing power structures is one way in which some NGOs might have avoided bolstering abusive authorities, difficult though this would have been in the absence of camp disarmament.

The development of information-dissemination capacities, along the lines of the radio initiatives mentioned above, constituted another potentially innovative response, recognising that a greater good may sometimes be achieved by a speedy closure of camps than by catering to their immediate needs.

What is the impact of public statements by NGO representatives?

Before commenting upon a situation, NGO representatives might ask:

- Is this statement based on a proper understanding and knowledge of the situation?
- Is the purpose of the statement to draw attention to a genuine problem, or merely to draw attention to the NGO?
- Who will benefit from this statement? Rather than simply claiming neutrality, has the statement been analysed to assess whether it will offer support to one side or other in a conflict?

Should the NGO intervene at all?

This, of course, is the most difficult question of all. One example of where an NGO intervention should perhaps have been opposed has already been cited: had the conditions (i.e. a cease-fire) been created for major humanitarian intervention in Rwanda before July 1994, then the genocide could have been prolonged. In situations such as this, NGOs must ask whether their perceived 'right' to intervene should not be subordinated to other priorities.

Unfortunately, it is often easier to brush aside reservations (where they exist) and concentrate on the high-profile work in hand, while ignoring or under-emphasising the far from neutral implications of the work done. It will be difficult for many NGOs to follow the example set by the Religious Society of Friends (the Quakers) in Britain in 1849, when they discontinued their relief efforts regarding the famine in Ireland, and in fact turned down official financial support offered to them for that purpose. Their reasoning was based on what they saw as the limitations of private charity and the need to assert governmental responsibility:

Seeing that the difficulty was so far beyond the reach of private exertion, and that the only machinery which it was practicable to employ was that under the control of the public authorities; and believing that the Government alone could raise funds, or carry out the measures necessary in many districts to save the lives of the people, we feared that if we ventured to undertake a work for which our resources were so inadequate, we might, through our incompetency, injure the cause of those whom we desired to serve.[9]

The admission of inadequate resources and incompetency, and the willingness to stand aside rather than 'injure the cause of those whom we desire to serve' are examples from which today's NGOs could yet draw inspiration. The Quaker purpose was to highlight the failings of official agencies, failings which remain depressingly familiar today. The strongest defence of NGOs in the Rwandan crisis is that they were asked to perform impossible roles in vacuums left by those agencies — such as the UN and governments — which had the power to frame and enforce an appropriate political response; the challenge for NGOs is to decide whether 'standing aside' is sometimes the best way of confronting and correcting the actions and inactions of others.

Acknowledgement

Thanks are due to Niall Crowley, Deborah Eade, Margaret Kelleher, Tim Meisburger and an anonymous referee for their comments on earlier versions of this article. Thanks also to the many NGO colleagues, especially Paul Ledwidge and Olga McDonagh, who shared in the discussions on and around the topic.

Notes

1 For ease of presentation, the term 'NGOs' here refers only to international NGOs; the role (often vital) of indigenous NGOs in

emergency situations is not the focus of this article.

2 This World Bank report, however, also noted that '[t]he control of the former leaders is not absolute' (1995:1), a point we return to in the concluding section of this article.

3 The Joint Evaluation points out that the tendency to favour those outside the country was evident in the fact that people who were displaced inside Rwanda on 13 July 1994 received almost no assistance, while the same people received very generous assistance when they crossed the border into Zaire on 14 July; this change was only partly explained by the outbreak of cholera in the newly formed camps in Zaire (1996: 117).

4 We should also mention the approximately 40 NGOs which had become involved in relief and rehabilitation work in RPF-held areas in northern Rwanda by June 1994 (Joint Evaluation 1996: 35).

5 As reported to the author.

6 As explained in the introduction, individual NGOs are not identified in this article.

7 The earlier discussion of promising initial aid responses to the crisis is also drawn from this source.

8 It is beyond the scope of this article to examine in detail the reasons why some disasters receive greater media attention than others, but one factor is clearly that it is easier for the media to cover a disaster which is concentrated in a small number of areas (border crossings, refugee camps) than one which is spread throughout a whole country (devastation, destitution, trauma). The former also makes for more spectacular footage and can be 'explained' through standard terms of reference: helplessness, flight, etc.

9 Letter from Jonathan Pim of the Religious Society of Friends to Sir Charles E. Trevelyan, Treasury, 5 June 1849.

References

African Rights (1994a) *Rwanda: Death, Despair and Defiance*, London: African Rights.

African Rights (1994b) *Humanitarianism Unbound: Current Dilemmas Facing Multi-Mandate Relief Operations in Political Emergencies*, Discussion Paper no. 5, London: African Rights.

African Rights (1995) *Rwanda: A Waste of Hope - The United Nations Human Rights Field Operation*, London: African Rights.

Crowley, N. (1995) 'The NGOs are really government', in *Pitfalls in Development Aid*, Dublin: Irish Mozambique Solidarity (1995).

Daly, G. (1995) 'Aggressors or victims?', *Focus on Ireland and the Wider World*, Dublin: Issue 52.

Drumtra, J. (1995) 'Rwandan Refugees: Updated Findings and Recommendations', site visit notes for US Committee for Refugees, 25 October.

Hanlon, J. (1995) 'The "success" of aid to Mozambique', in *Irish Mozambique Solidarity* (1995).

Hulme, D. and M. Edwards (1997) 'NGOs, states and donors: an overview', in Hulme and Edwards (eds.): *NGOs, States and Donors: Too Close for Comfort?*, Basingstoke/London: Macmillan in association with Save the Children.

Human Rights Watch Arms Project (1995) 'Rwanda/Zaire: Re-arming with Impunity: International Support for the Perpetrators of the Rwandan Genocide', New York: Vol. 7, No. 4.

Joint Evaluation of Emergency Assistance to Rwanda (1996) *The International Response to Conflict and Genocide: Lessons from the Rwanda Experience*, Vol. 3, Copenhagen: Joint Evaluation.

Minear, L. and T. G. Weiss (1995) *Mercy Under Fire: War and the Global Humanitarian Community*, Boulder: Westview Press.

Robinson, M. (1997) 'Privatising the voluntary sector: NGOs as public service contractors?', in Hulme and Edwards (eds.) (1997).

Slim, H. (1996) 'Doing the Right Thing: Relief Agencies, Moral Dilemmas and Moral Responsibility in Political Emergencies and War', draft background paper for the Scandinavian NGO Workshop on Humanitarian Ethics, Nordic African Institute, Uppsala, 24 October.

Vidal, J. (1995) 'Blood money', *The Guardian*, 5 April 1995.

Winter, A. (1995) *Is Anyone Listening? Communicating Development in Donor Countries*, Geneva: UNGLS Development Dossiers.

World Bank (1995) 'Evaluation of Current Rwandan Refugee Camp Conditions and Structures in Goma and Bukavu — Zaire', mission report, 5 March–5 April 1995.

The author

Andy Storey lectures at the Development Studies Centre in Dublin, and worked in Rwanda in 1995. He has published a number of articles on the role of NGOs, and also on wider development issues, including aid, trade, and refugee policy. His current research interests include the political economy of ethnic mobilisation.

Guatemala: uncovering the past, recovering the future

Elizabeth Lira

Editor's note: In early 1995, Dr Elizabeth Lira met with Guatemalan human-rights workers involved in the transition process which was being overseen by the UN (MINUGUA), and with the Human Rights Office at the Archbishopric.[1] In December 1996, the Peace Accords were signed, signalling the formal end to the 36-year war and, among other things, conferring amnesty on the military. The author's personal reflections on her visit are included here for the insights they offer into the human-rights dimensions of transition from war to peace.

Human rights: a numbing obsession

What does one expect of Guatemala, a country with one of the worst human-rights records in the western hemisphere? I had few preconceptions other than what I had learned through reading people like Rigoberta Menchu.[2] I knew that the military had pervaded all areas of life and expression, and I had an idea of the Guatemalan version of 'national security' and the policies emanating from this. I had listened to Guatemalan refugees in Los Angeles, Berkeley, and Boston, and read many accounts of human-rights violations, torture, assassinations, and political disappearances.[3] I knew the work of the historian and poet Eduardo Galeano, and had read poetry and stories of the Mayan culture. Yet, in spite of everything I thought I knew, I had no idea what Guatemala would actually be like.

My first impression of Guatemala City was the pollution. The traffic congestion is so severe that the city seems on the verge of collapse. Everything moves at a snail's pace. The constant racket is itself an assault on the senses: traffic, street vendors, music blaring out from stores and shops. This chaos is compounded by the posters, bill-boards, and signs of every shape and size hanging from every available space. The number of street sellers makes it impossible to move around. The beauty of the city is lost in the noise, the crush, the bustle, and the general disorder. But I saw no beggars, no violence. Everyone seemed friendly. The human climate was hard to gauge.

Some chance conversations gave some idea of what was going on in the country. A woman who was selling weavings began telling me about the pains in her heart, which she described as one might describe anguish. She told me about her insomnia, her fears, her psychosomatic illnesses. It was not easy to ask her what caused these pains. But she told me that they arose from profound fears and things to do with death concerning members of her family, 'things one cannot talk about'.

How many things can one not talk about in Guatemala? I tried to understand what was going on, but the newspapers gave very little idea. The television was the same. Though endless speeches by politicians appeared on the news, these were mostly repetitive and meaningless. Whatever their ideological persuasion, they seemed pretty much the same. Television itself seemed like a good way to create exactly the kind of confusion that would make sure that nothing ever changed.

Superficially, the issue of human rights seemed to be the most important subject in the public arena, given the exhaustive media coverage. It was disconcerting to see how 'human rights' could become so obsessively absorbing. Cases were denounced, extracts from reports on human rights in Guatemala were publicised, and so on. Many issues featured under 'human rights', from acts of violence attributed to the guerrillas, or the international report on human rights, to the discovery of clandestine graves or information about past violations. I wondered whether this almost indiscriminate coverage did not trivialise the problem, by making everyone used to hearing about atrocities that would be quite overwhelming if one stopped to listen, while at the same time mixing up politically motivated violence with acts of State-sponsored terrorism. A similar thing happened in Argentina, when it came to light that gross violations of human rights had been committed by the Alfonsin government. Information was prolific and constant. What it actually generated was a sense of banality; people became weary and uninterested. Thus the enormity of the horror went unheeded. Consequently, the information had no great impact on public opinion, and there was little pressure to go beyond a mere denunciation of events.

Yet in Guatemala I was impressed by people's sense that these crimes had been committed with impunity, that the threat is still ever-present. Fear is palpable, despondency as well as hope, and the impact of the violence is deeply personal. Given the scale of the atrocities, and how they are perceived by ordinary people, it is hard to understand how the peace process could be under way. Some say the transition began in 1985. But what can this possibly mean? The end of the repression? A transition to what? How can fear be eradicated? How can social peace be built? What social and cultural behaviour will be needed to make possible the changes in people's minds, alongside the political changes? What institutional changes will occur? How can the information to establish the yearned-for truth about what happened possibly be produced, given the impunity with which the abuses were committed? And what about the military? In other spheres, what would be the role of academics, what controls would be imposed on their teaching, and what type of ideological persecution might follow? What about the students or social organisations?

The signing of the Peace Accords will bring enormous consequences, especially for those who suffered most intimately during the four decades of political violence.[4] Fear lies behind every conversation, like something woven into the fabric of society, something one must live with. When i read the Archbishop's reports on human-rights violations since 1992, I was impressed by the thoroughness of the documentation. I also realised that, while the scale has lessened, grave violations continue. Fear becomes a chronic response to a situation that is constantly threatening, and where there

seem to be no boundaries. Arbitrariness is 'normal', even in a context that is supposedly democratic.

I was often told that the telephones were probably bugged, and correspondence intercepted. But it was far from clear what kinds of precaution one should take. Simply reading the denunciations made me feel that there were no adequate precautions, since political repression was characterised above all by being arbitrary and unpredictable. From what I could gather, the recent persecution had focused on people who had been trying to piece together the sheer enormity of the violence of the past, especially in the countryside. It was clear that some forces wished to stop cases reaching the tribunals, in spite of MINUGUA.

Breaking the silence

A central element in human-rights work is to contribute to peace through establishing what actually happened. Breaking the silence means creating the social conditions that enable the truth — 'the clarification of what happened in the past' — to contribute to a kind of subjective justice. This means that individuals must be able to see that their experience of pain and persecution is recognised by society.

For the Church, breaking the silence means restoring the value of human life, and re-weaving the social fabric so to include a collective memory of the past: a past that includes not only the repression, but also resistance, and the efforts of the dispossessed to bring about social and political change. The Church is therefore developing a history of the violence in order to help to build a Guatemala that can form a collective judgement about its past. This is not just a question of gathering statistics, but also of testifying to the ways in which the violence was experienced by individuals, families, and entire communities. This will in turn contribute to the work of the Truth Commission.

Basically, there two main aims to the ambitious task of recovering the collective memory. The first is to gather well-substantiated information that can serve as legal documentation, so that judicial proceedings may be initiated. The second is to obtain first-hand testimonies that register not only the concrete facts but also their psychological impact. The emphases are different. The rigour with which facts must be documented for strictly legal purposes may not generate the right conditions for recovering the collective memory, which is essentially intended to have a subjective and therapeutic function. Giving testimony is a chance to recount a history that has been silenced — and to do so in the presence of someone who represents that element of Guatemalan society which wants to acknowledge as fully as possible what really took place.

Giving testimony is an emotionally cathartic act. However, while it can be a huge psychological relief for the individual, it is also important to contain these emotions — something that places a huge responsibility on the one who receives the testimony. This person must demonstrate empathy, but also be skilled in conducting the interview, so that the witness is not re-traumatised. The interviewers themselves need to be trained and supported by a capable team. They need a high level of self-awareness, an understanding of what draws them to the work, their fears and vulnerabilities, and inner resources. It is important to bear in mind that, while the interviews are with individuals, the political repression was generalised, and much of the history is of wholesale massacres of rural indian communities.

The Church's task is then both social and political, but also potentially therapeutic. It is concerned with recognising and validating the experience of violence, of the pain and loss this caused, in a context that still cannot guarantee basic rights to all; a context in which the 'truth' is a repudiation of the military version of repression and the impunity enjoyed by the Armed Forces, and which is thus likely to generate intense emotional reactions. This remains an extreme experience that cannot be adequately symbolised.

At the same time, the interviewers are not immune to what they will be documenting, for the experiences and realities have been shared by almost everyone. Those who testify are likely to have needs that range from wanting to establish the truth and seek justice to simply having someone listen to them. Likewise, the interviewers will have their own needs and expectations of the process. These should be out in the open, so that they do not interfere with the work.

Who wants to hear about the past?

And what is this work? It consists in building up both a formal environment and the human relationships that will foster the gathering of reliable information. This means establishing a sense of trust, and a relationship that can 'hold' the torrent of emotional release. Fear will inevitably be present, since fear is a protective emotion, part of the protective baggage that is itself a response to the life-threatening reality in which everyone has had to function and survive for decades. At the same time, what people will describe is a history of unimaginable horror and suffering. Who wants to hear it? Who wants to tell it? What's the point of telling it? And why listen?

While all this can come to seem self-evident to those who are used to working with these issues, the answers are in fact not at all obvious. We need to be very clear with everyone concerned about why we are doing this work. We cannot deny the need for emotional release, but *catharsis itself is not enough*. People need support and feedback in various ways, which may include therapy or various forms of cultural expression. But what is needed is a space within which people can find some kind of symbol of what they know about what happened, and their feelings about it, and gain a public recognition of the experience. This is fundamental, given Guatemalan society's denial of what took place, and the impunity with which these violations were committed.

Victor Montejo's *Testimony: Death of an Indian Community in Guatemala*, published in 1993, is a first-person account of the obliteration of an entire community, and gives some insight into the emotional issues to be taken into account. The personal vulnerability, and the possibility of reprisals for giving testimony about the repression, must be considered. It is one thing for someone spontaneously to talk about some of what happened, as part of a discussion about the price of maize or whatever, because it is a very deep and significant part of their everyday existence. But it is quite another to talk about these terrible events in a formal and structured way, for this to be recorded in writing. People's reactions could be very different. For some, it will be something they have been longing to do for many years. Others may be more ambivalent. Language and the meanings of particular symbols will vary from one ethnic group to another, just as the reactions and needs of mothers and fathers, children, brothers and sisters, husbands and wives, will differ.

Assessing reality: risks and feelings

It is essential to have a realistic picture of the human-rights situation today, and the likely future scenario, in order to distinguish the real risks, as opposed to those perceived by people with long experience of repression and violence. This will provide the basis for a better understanding of the social conditions in which the work of collecting testimonies will be done. It will also assist in developing appropriate strategies for coping with the uncertainty and constant threat, the difficulties and risks inherent in a chronic emergency. Recognising one's own strategies gives insights into the defence mechanisms used by others — such as black humour, psychosomatic complaints, inter-personal conflicts, or specific psychological responses such as denial or dissociation. Such awareness makes it possible to give space to and validate other people's fears, their uncertainties, their anguish; and at the same time to recognise that everyone involved in this kind of work also has the right and the need to have their own feelings recognised — whether of tiredness, frustration, or impotence.

This calls for keeping one's feet firmly on the ground. There are ethical issues at stake, as well as subjective needs. In addition to training, those involved in gathering testimonies need a strategy of collective support. For many people, this work inspires great hope and represents something they have been longing to happen. But precisely because of these expectations, reality will be very hard: it is important to avoid unrealistic expectations, in order not to lose hope.

Training for human-rights workers

If the preparatory work is done collectively, it should be possible to anticipate specific situations, and predict the kinds of problem that will arise: difficulties affecting the individuals involved in the work, or the people they are interviewing; problems inherent in the situation, or the process itself. If we know that we will be dealing with pain — pain that will often resonate with our own — we need to learn how to offer support, acceptance, emotional limits, and help. These are part and parcel of the work, and we need to be clear and self-aware in order to function. We need to acquire some specific skills, like how to ask questions, almost as if one were taking a clinical history — which means being as objective as possible about what the patient says, without losing sight of the fact that it is pain that causes people to be concerned about themselves, and to seek and accept help. Taking a clinical history is a skill that must be learned, but in this case it also entails both the interviewer and the 'patient' using all the resources at their disposal to relieve the pain that is actually caused by giving the history.

When we talk about memory, we are using a concept that is sometimes a metaphor for unresolved personal or collective grief. We need to construct memory, to recall — 'feel it in one's heart again' — in order gradually to close the wounds. There are two elements here: the history of the 'patient', and that person's history in his or her wider social context. That is, the history of the community, the family, the social group to which they belong. Therapy is often a process of restoring the link between an individual's grief and their collective experience. It is like finding some sense of what happened, whether as a way of understanding the past, or of projecting into the future. It does not depend on an outsider, but on each particular individual.

It is far from easy to see how to design an appropriate training programme for human-rights workers in this context. Clearly, the legal requirements are real, but have somehow to be combined with interviews which are intended to gather many hundreds of profoundly painful experiences. The task of preparing people to deal emotionally and professionally with this is daunting. The needs of the coordinating team will differ from those of the people working on the ground, but there will undoubtedly be a need for some kind of counselling support for everyone in what cannot but be a gruelling experience. There is also the question of how to recognise psychological and psycho-social trauma, and how to formulate specific recommendations in response.

Underlying everything is a need to reflect on the wider implications of a 'transition' which seems to be focused on establishing peace and respect for human rights. This reflection should draw on a range of backgrounds and disciplines, and promote a meaningful exchange of experiences of other post-war transitions in order to get a sense of what is really possible, and where the problems lie. Perhaps the problems to concentrate on relate to political transitions, which depend on achieving peace. The calls for peace have many different origins, each posing a different challenge. In Guatemala, memory, history, truth, justice, reparation, and reconciliation have particular significance. Experiences of transition elsewhere would need to be set within the Guatemalan context, where real advances in the area of human rights are taking place, and where it has been the military who have been primarily responsible for political repression. Any such exchange should be within a framework for mutual learning from the experience of people elsewhere.

Human rights and mental health

Many Guatemalans have for years been involved in mental-health work as well as human-rights work. One NGO began working in the early 1990s in areas that suffered badly in the war, using a small technical team and a larger group of community-based health workers. For them, mental health has nothing to with classifying people as mad and shutting them away. It has to do with living communities, with collective identity, and with day-to-day survival. In this, small production projects play an important role.

The organisation CONAVIGUA (a war widows' rights organisation) was formed as a direct response to the repression. It provides a forum within which bereaved women 'can say what we feel, talk about our fears, our mistrust, as well as domestic violence, and alcoholism'. Alcoholism has increased in the rural areas, which the army occupied and controlled for 15 years. CONAVIGUA's festival of community mental health is aimed at helping people to see alcoholism as a collective problem that needs some public expression.

The case of the Nebaj area of El Quiche is telling. High in the mountains, about 250 km from the capital, it suffered terribly from army repression and brutality. The military destroyed many homes and settlements, and then forced people to live in 'model villages', in each of which is a monument to military achievements — in what? creating peace? promoting education? repression? Given the lack of land in these 'model villages', the army eventually began to allow resettlement in the surrounding areas. The people of Nebaj, mainly young adults, began to return to their places of origin in the early 1990s. They did go back, while other communities were still resisting in the mountains. They had been forced to leave because of the massacres. They are dignified, interested in the world around them (for example, about events in Chiapas, Mexico), but do not place their trust lightly. The men urge the women to speak out, while the women hide behind their lack of Spanish, at least when they are addressing a group. Speaking to them individually is easier. Gradually, these people open up enough to speak about what they have been through: about how they are frightened to set down roots, because who knows whether the violence is really over, or whether it will return? They are afraid, and yet they seem quite calm under the protective shield of their own language. To see where these people are living now, to view the 'model villages', to understand something about how they organise themselves, and how they see their lives — all these details give shape to the personal testimonies of repression.

Back in the capital, some church-based human-rights workers are holding a workshop to look at the problems they face. One group mentions people's fear of denouncing any form of violence, whether personal or structural. They may show apathy and lack of interest in the institutions that are meant to deal with the problem. Other reactions range from timidity to aggressiveness, from despair to obedience, resignation, or passivity among those who have directly experienced political repression. 'They seem to have no recollection of what has happened, saying "I don't want to remember", while what one sees are signs of anguish, stress, disbelief, and despair.' A second group displays a range of reactions and behaviour patterns. People are afraid of widespread criminal violence. Some people are against human rights. Many of those who come to the human-rights office are aggressive, violent, and expect to be given everything on a plate. But some become enthused, and start getting involved. A third group of workers describes how, when people come to file a denunciation about a human-rights violation, they often find themselves weeping. Some fear that this may affect their capacity to work; others fear that they are not affected at all. The last group talks about violence in all its forms — economic, political, and social — seeing poverty as a consequence of this. 'People feel marginalised, and violence causes psychosomatic problems', they say.

In summing up, one worker says that many of the things they have described are things they feel themselves: 'We feel frustrated, impotent in the face of a situation of no change'. The group jokes about impotence, taking it to mean sexual impotence. Then someone comments that this is not so far from the truth, and that sexual impotence is one way in which people respond to their feelings of helplessness. 'We reproduce the authoritarian system as a kind of defence mechanism. We become withdrawn and express things through black humour and booze. Liquor is the people's psychiatrist' — a comment that causes ripples of nervous laughter — 'and may be a personal response to pressure.'

We need to be on constant alert, not on the defensive, but ready to fight back. It is something we get very sensitive about, and sometimes aggressive, when we feel impotent, when we feel helpless and yet responsible for raising others' expectations. We think about our work all the time, and lose sleep over it. We feel indignant about things that can't be changed. We are afraid that our impotence may make us indifferent. We sometimes over-identify with the problems we hear about, and feel isolated as a result. The work is stressful, especially since some of us have been the direct victims of violence. It can give rise to a wish for vengeance, and this can become a very strong feeling among human-rights workers. The problems we are dealing with affect us. And what we don't talk about can come out later in the form of aggressiveness. The sources of stress stimulate our own destructive capacities, and we seem unable to tap into our constructive potential.

Collaboration through difference

This is only the briefest glimpse of Guatemala. In everything I observed and heard, there were are things that are familiar — from the constant traffic jams to what these human-rights workers said. But many things are very different. Any serious efforts to collaborate in the area of human rights must be based on a recognition of our similarities and our differences, and on the possibilities that these offer. In all human experience we find some elements that are universal, and others that are unique: and we must learn to recognise these. Can we work together on human rights? Possibly, but precisely in those areas in which we can join in identifying our differences, so that these become the basis for a genuine exchange of experience.

Notes

1 The Catholic Church was embarking on a nationwide effort to recover and record the memory of the military atrocities that resulted in the deaths of 150,000 people during the 36-year war.
2 Rigoberta Menchu is a Mayan indian and human-rights activist, awarded the Nobel Peace prize in 1990.
3 As the opposition to the government represented by the URNG (Guatemalan National Revolutionary Unity) mounted in the late 1970s, the armed forces launched 'a campaign of terror that has rarely been paralleled for its savagery (and lack of publicity) in the history of Latin America. The resulting carnage was so vast that at least another 30,000 Guatemalans [had] been killed [by 1987], hundreds more [had] been "disappeared", 440 Indian villages [had] been wiped off the face of the map, and between 100,000 and 200,000 children [had] lost at least one parent' (J. Painter (1987): *Guatemala: False Hope, False Freedom*, London: Latin America Bureau).
4 Since the CIA-sponsored military overthrow in 1954 of Jacobo Arbenz, the democratically elected President of Guatemala.

The author

Elizabeth Lira is a Chilean psychologist and political scientist with wide experience in situations of repression and violence in Latin America and elsewhere, including Bosnia. She is the Director of the Latin American Institute of Mental Health and Human Rights (ILSA).

This paper was translated and abridged by Deborah Eade. The full version, in Spanish, is available on request.

Assisting survivors of war and atrocity: notes on 'psychosocial' issues for NGO workers

Derek Summerfield

Introduction

What has been generally labelled the 'psychosocial' dimension of the impact of war and organised violence has been of increasing interest in the development field, and in agencies like the World Health Organisation (WHO) and United Nations High Commissioner for Refugees (UNHCR). This offers some positive possibilities, but the danger is that a narrowly 'medicalised' and 'psychologised' view of 'trauma' will be imposed in diverse settings worldwide. This would constitute a typical North-South transfer of concepts and practices.

Because this issue has become fashionable, funding is being attracted to some highly flawed proposals. What are the issues for agencies which aim first and foremost for the fullest possible understanding of the experiences of war-affected peoples and of the factors which shape their responses over time, including the decision to seek help? Can such NGOs enrich the relationships they forge with those they seek to assist, and go on to highlight new possibilities for well-grounded interventions?

The following notes are not intended to be prescriptive, but to sketch out a framework to guide workers in whatever war-affected setting they are addressing. Actual approaches and solutions have to be locally tailored.

1 There is a set of themes running through most modern conflict. Violence is played out where people live and work; there is little distinction between combatants and others; and more than 90 per cent of all casualties are civilian. Exemplary brutality is often systematically used to create terror as a means of control of whole populations. Abductions, extrajudicial executions, and torture are frequently public and witnessed by families of victims. Sexual violation is a standard and under-reported element: women are exposed to this in prisons, in their homes in conflict zones, during flight, and in refugee camps. In twenty violent conflicts during the 1980s, children were not just passive bystanders, but also had active roles, including bearing arms — either as volunteers or through coercion. Damage, frequently intentional, to social, economic, and cultural institutions and ways of life takes place almost invariably. This may disrupt the way a particular people connect with their history, identity, and lived values, all of which define their world. Prominent and respected people — community leaders, health workers, priests, educated people — are often targeted. The neutrality of medical facilities is not respected.

The cumulative effect can mean that large numbers of civilians are rendered near-destitute, whether or not displaced from their communities. Modern conflict is frequently chronic and fluctuating, with hostilities varying in intensity and location. People feel besieged and threatened, even when their particular locality is quiet. Staying silent about what they have endured or seen may be important for survival. In many parts of the world, social tension and war are not extraordinary or 'abnormal'; their effects are so chronic that they have come to be incorporated into economic and social life; various groups, affected in varying ways, respond and adapt to the situation in diverse and shifting ways.

2 Thus survivors suffer multiple injuries, not just to life and limb but to the social fabric of their communities, which may no longer be able to play its customary protective and problem-solving role. They will be horrified and grieving, not just for what has happened to individual human beings, but to their community, society, and culture. Most will register the wounds of war in social rather than psychological terms. Those who are refugees must also contend with the insecurities and hardship of their new situation, including (for

61

some) a cultural gulf between themselves and the host society.

3 Fundamental to the human processing of atrocious experience is the subjective meaning it has or comes to have for those affected, the understandings and attributions they draw on in the struggle to encompass what has happened. These understandings, and the adaptations that flow from them, are drawn from society, its history and politics. People who have not been able to generate an interpretation of what has happened, and who find events incomprehensible, are likely to feel most helpless and unsure what to do.

Help-seeking behaviour will be determined by background, culture, and social norms. War-affected communities are heterogeneous, and there will not be one standard reaction to events. Those affected are not 'pure' victims, and even the most destitute still exercise active interpretations and choices. They are victims, but they are also survivors. It is important to know as much as possible about how the particular society functioned in the past.

4 The sense which people make of their predicament, and the priorities they nominate, are not static; they may shift with time, with change in the war situation, and as people adapt and reorganise.

5 Supportive interventions for war-affected people must ideally be based upon an accurate and comprehensive grasp of the complexities of what has happened. Naturally this starts with appraisal of the scale and nature of the material damage and upheaval which the war has wrought. But the experience of people on the ground also involves subjective, less material elements. War provokes states of feeling and thinking which to the people concerned are not necessarily any less 'real' as reflections of what has happened than, say, the total numbers of dead and injured. For them this is part of the story of the war and is destined to become part of social memory. These factors will influence what survivors say and do, and what they want, and thus shape short-term and, arguably, longer-term outcomes for individuals and for their society.

6 NGO workers must be aware of these issues, and pay attention to the ways in which they may be manifesting themselves in a particular setting, if they are to deepen their background knowledge and capacity for accurate empathy with those they seek to assist. This may generate new possibilities for creative intervention and provide more criteria for choosing between proposed projects. It may minimise misunderstandings, make survivors feel better understood, and thus improve the relationship between NGO and 'client' group, whether the project concerns emergency aid, agriculture, education, or whatever. Thus we are talking about *an approach*, about the way NGO workers engage with war-affected peoples, and not just about defined projects. The effectiveness of project evaluation will also be strongly influenced by the quality of this relationship over time.

7 NGO workers need first to reflect on their own assumptions and notions about the personal impact of war, atrocity, torture and so on. Do you think, for example, that someone who has been tortured is likely to be psychologically disturbed or damaged, if not overtly then under the surface? Psychological concepts are part of Western culture and thought and are thus not absolute or universal, though they are being increasingly globalised. 'Trauma', and a presumed need for psychological treatment, is a fashionable concept in the West, and there is a danger of inappropriate application to war settings worldwide. Every culture has its own constructions of traumatic events and recipes for recovery. Interventions aimed at alleviating the psychological distress of war-affected peoples may be simplistic and ignorant of local culture, and risk being experienced as insensitive or imposed. If this is so, they will fail anyway. Local workers can also feel undermined by imported concepts and 'experts' who implement them.

8 Wars cause distress or suffering, and this is of course understandable and 'normal'. We should not generally interpret and re-label this as psychological 'trauma', denoting a mental injury, analogous to a physical injury, needing treatment or 'therapy'. This basic error is already being made, at the risk of distortion in the wider debate about the effects of war and the prioritisation of resources to address them. Only a small minority develop a psychological problem which (if facilities permit) merits professional help. Expressions of distress, even when forceful, do not generally imply psychological frailty or damage, or nearness to breakdown. Survivors do not want to be psychologised or have some kind of 'sick' identity imputed to them. The few who do develop objective psychological disturbance generally show themselves by their inability to function properly in their situation. For this reason their family or community tend to identify them for themselves. It is not these few but the majority, and the processes which can sustain them, which will be the focus of interventions by the NGO field.

9 The narratives of survivors can give a graphic illustration of their experiences, what they mean to them, and the coping processes brought to bear on them. Some may seek to tell their stories to others, including NGO workers, to obtain ordinary human comfort and solidarity. However, we must not assume that this is what survivors *should* do if they want to get better; some cultures do not prescribe this, and even in the West individual needs vary.

10 What is fundamental is that suffering is a social experience and not a private one. What this suffering provokes in war-affected peoples is played out in public. They struggle to come to terms with their losses (which sometimes seem to amount to their whole world), engaging with their situation in what one hopes is a problem-solving way.

11 Provision of the essentials for daily living, and issues of physical security, obviously come first. Beyond that, the major thrust of NGO interventions will be towards the social world of survivor populations, for herein lie the sources of resilience and capacity for recovery for all. Thus the 'psychosocial' agenda is substantially a social one. Because of its association with the mental-health field, it might be better to drop the term 'psychosocial' in favour of one indicating that the core task is to address the social and collective wounds of war. *Interventions should not use a (mental) aid-and-relief model, addressing 'psychology', but a social-development model, addressing suffering.*

12 Most people endure war and recover from it as a function of the extent to which they can, firstly, regain a measure of dignity, control, and autonomy over their immediate environment. They will seek to reconstitute what they can of their family and other networks, so often splintered in modern conflict. Anything that generates a sense of solidarity or community, and bolsters the viability of local organisations and structures, must be helpful. Meaningful training and work can be one logical focus of

NGO efforts, allowing people to feel useful and effective again, as well as perhaps generating income or essential items for subsistence. Most people would rather be active citizens than mere recipients of aid. Involvement in projects can help people to sustain their weakened social relationships, or develop some new ones. In a partial way, such engagement can perform some of the functions which peacetime society used to do: helping people to generate a social meaning for events, to recognise, contain, and manage grief and its social face, mourning; to stimulate and organise active means of coping and problem-solving, individual and collective, in the face of continuing adversity.

And when in due course they get the chance, people will seek a substantial reconstruction of the damaged social fabric, including the economic and cultural forms and institutions which make sense to them. The restoration of health services and schooling are generally high priorities in all cultures. However, they will not necessarily seek just to restore to their old state what they valued before the war; they recognise that some things may have changed for ever.

13 NGO workers may represent a source of emotional support to war-affected people; but this is not, and does not have to be, 'therapy' or 'counselling', implying a professional activity with a technology. None the less, in some situations workers may feel empowered by some basic and contextualised advice on mental-health issues, either through contact with local professionals or from written material. An example of the latter are the succinct Save the Children Fund manuals on assisting children in difficult circumstances, notably war zones.

14 Those refugee camps which emphasise confinement and control, which provide residents with insufficient protection against further violence and abuse (often from within), or which do not involve them in decision-making obviously breach the basic principles outlined above. In some situations, NGOs also need to take account of the local people among whom refugees have come to rest. A good working relationship between them and the refugees may help both parties.

15 Much modern conflict worldwide is endemic, so that those affected have not even got to the stage of an aftermath and must keep up a kind of crisis-management response. NGOs need to support the structures which help these people to endure and keep going. A proper counting of the costs and a 'recovery' has to be postponed.

16 There are few prescriptions which can be carried from one context to another: solutions need to be local, drawing on survivors' resilience, skills, and priorities. War-affected peoples are often in fluid or evolving situations: with time, their perceptions and priorities may change, so their relationship with an NGO needs to be able to accommodate this. Will the NGO be able to detect and respond to such shifts, to join in their exploration of what is possible over time, without sacrificing clarity and rational planning?

17 While many of the experiences which war brings are shared by young men, young women and mothers, children and elderly alike, we may also identify differential effects in some circumstances. For example, the key role of women, both in relation to their increased vulnerability (particularly to sexual and other violence) and their responsibilities as providers and protectors of the children, should be recognised. They often constitute the majority of adult refugees. Time needs to be taken to establish the expressed needs of women, both in their own right and in respect of those for whom they care.

Women can be the focus of projects which generate community-wide benefits. The physical and emotional well-being of children in war is strongly dependent on the capacity of their principal care-givers to cope. Once this fails, their morbidity and mortality rapidly escalate. Orphaned and otherwise unprotected children are a high-priority group and urgently need reconnecting, if possible, with surviving family members or others from their original community. All children need as much day-to-day normality and structure as can be managed, inside the home and outside it — for example, through the restoration of some schooling. People with physical disability (frequently war-induced) represent another group who may have distinct problems.

18 When we are discussing 'targeting', we should also note that there have been projects which focused exclusively either on a particular event such as 'rape', or a particular group, such as 'traumatised children', and so imposed a simplistic and decontextualised view of the experiences of survivors.

19 Some survivors are aware that their experiences amount to testimony which may have a wider political and legal significance, and are a part of the history of the war and a counting of its costs. It may apply universally that victims suffer more over time when they are denied official acknowledgement or reparation for what has been done to them. NGOs could consider collation, publication, and dissemination of their testimonies. This is evidence which could be presented to war-crimes tribunals and other forums.

20 To summarise, it is pivotal to recognise that the social fabric is a core target of modern warfare and in its damaged state remains the context in which large numbers of people must manage their distress and cope with their fractured lives. A basic task is to help them to sustain some social 'space' within which they can foster their collective capacities for endurance and creative survival.

The NGO field should largely avoid Western approaches which presuppose the incidence of mental trauma and tend to take a simplistic view of the complex and evolving experiences of war-affected populations. Too often, such approaches ignore the way in which people's experiences are shaped by their background norms and current understandings; and too often such approaches merely assign people the role of client or patient. Instead, the basic framework should be based on the model of social development — a model which is already well understood by the NGO field. Actual projects should ideally be locally tailored, situation-sensitive, able to adjust as circumstances change, and capable of taking root and thus be self-sustaining.

The author

Derek Summerfield is a medical doctor with first-hand experience of war in Central America, Southern Africa and, via political refugees with a history of torture, in London. He has been a consultant to Oxfam GB since 1990. At the time of writing he was principal psychiatrist at the Medical Foundation for the Care of Victims of Torture, London, and a research associate at the Refugee Studies Programme, Queen Elizabeth House, Oxford.

Tensions in the psychosocial discourse: implications for the planning of interventions with war-affected populations

Alastair Ager

Introduction

Derek Summerfield's paper on psychosocial issues for NGO workers (Summerfield, 1995; reprinted here) raises a number of fundamental questions regarding the planning and implementation of programmes targeting war-affected populations. Principal among these is whether psychosocial programmes adopting a broadly clinical approach have any justifiable role in addressing the needs of populations facing the consequences of conflict.

Summerfield (1995, 1996) persuasively argues that it is the destruction of the social fabric of a society which is targeted in much contemporary warfare, for the very purpose of instilling fear, disorientation, and loss of identity. In such circumstances, it is plausible to argue that assisting in the reconstruction of social forms — through the swift re-establishment of structures of civil society — should comprise the dominant form of response from the humanitarian-assistance community. The more molecular, clinical approach of many existing programmes can be seen in these terms to conceive of the impact of warfare in an inappropriately de-contextualised manner. A focus on individual experience, adjustment, and coping capacity may be seen to result in programmes blind to the crucial issues regarding the social meaning of war experience within a disrupted cultural frame of reference (Stubbs 1996). Other workers, however, have continued to assert the value of clinically based programmes in war-affected areas, pointing to the complex psychological needs associated with traumatic experience and the effectiveness of therapeutic intervention in addressing them (Agger 1995, Orley 1996).

Tensions in the contemporary psychosocial discourse

This response argues that there is a fundamental conceptual tension underlying such debate regarding the appropriate form and focus of psychosocial programmes. Figure 1 attempts to represent this tension, by identifying three associated continua which reflect the bases of different conceptualisations of psychosocial programmes.

The first of these continua represents the judgement that is made regarding the generalisability of knowledge in the field. At one extreme, the circumstances of each population are considered quite unique. As such concepts of well-being, mental health, and adjustment are socially constructed, it is inappropriate to generalise understandings gained from other cultural settings. At the other extreme, core psychological functioning is broadly invariant across cultures, and thus programmes may safely be established on a basis of certain fundamental principles regarding psychosocial processes.

This first continuum illustrates the complexity of the problems faced by those planning psychosocial interventions (and, arguably, a broad range of other forms of programme). While cultural sensitivity is a broadly acknowledged goal of humanitarian-assistance agencies, few programmes (if any) can afford to be based upon a truly rigorous anthropological analysis of local meanings and structures. A degree of generalisability must be assumed, if lessons learned in one setting can be seen to benefit planning in another. Any tendency towards a 'one-size-fits-all' approach (Reid *et al.* 1995), however, leads to clear problems in programme sustainability.

The second, related continuum reflects the emphasis given to technical as opposed to

Figure 1: Tensions in the discourse of psychosocial programmes

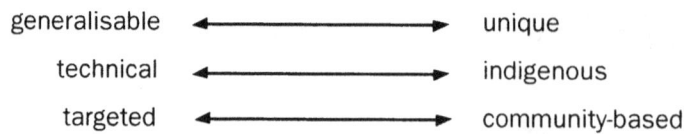

generalisable	←——————→	unique
technical	←——————→	indigenous
targeted	←——————→	community-based

indigenous understandings of trauma and difficulty. Summerfield's (1995) analysis encourages attention to 'the sense people make of their predicament, and the priorities they nominate'. Do such understandings drive the structure and form of the programme, or is there some technical, clinical framework determining the programme's fundamental nature? We may wish to avoid this question — as with the other continua — by saying that 'both' forms of understanding are valued. Nonetheless, in terms of structuring the debate regarding the appropriate forms of psychosocial intervention, the key question is: *which form of understanding exerts the dominant influence on programme goals, structure and reporting?* Local understandings may be captured in the course of assessment or intervention, but if overall programme strategy is set prior to implementation with regard to a Western, psychological framework, the latter remains the dominant discourse. Translation of elements of local understandings into external terms may appease sensibilities regarding cultural awareness, but it maintains a structural relationship between forms of knowledge which reinforces the dominance of the external discourse.

The third continuum reflects the extent to which programmes are targeted towards a particular client group or are community-wide in focus. This continuum may be seen to provide some insight into where a programme may be appropriately located on the previous two continua. Programmes that reflect certain generalisable principles of psychosocial functioning and respect technical understandings of potential intervention are, for instance, more likely to be those which specify a particular target group for whom the planned intervention is most needed and/or potentially effective. Specification of a programme targeting intervention for children traumatised by war, for example, will commonly bring with it assumptions of what has proved effective in previous 'war trauma' programmes for children, and be predicated on some technical

framework with respect to which children's vulnerability and means of readjustment may be conceptualised. On the other hand, programmes that focus on indigenous understandings of assumed unique circumstance are more likely to work on a community-wide basis. Community-wide programmes inevitably engage with dominant local understandings of circumstance, and are commonly fundamentally driven by them.

Implications for intervention

While it is tempting simply to propose a compromise between the two extremes of each continua, such a position is complex and necessarily dynamic. There is no comfortable ground in this territory. What follows is a personal appraisal of appropriate strategies for negotiating such difficult conceptual and pragmatic terrain.

A survey of the broad literature regarding the psychosocial status of populations following war and political oppression (see Ager 1993) supports the key role of a number of protective or ameliorative influences. These include, notably, family integration, social support, and personal ideology (the latter reflecting the potent benefits — see Punamaki's study of Palestinian women (1987) — of belief systems which provide a basis for constructing meaning for experienced trauma). Preserving and strengthening such influences *must* be the first line of psychosocial support — both in terms of practical resourcing and in terms of breadth and cultural contextuality of intervention. This affirms the value of generally beginning at the right-hand side of the continua portrayed in Figure 1.

So where, if ever, is there a place for more explicitly psychologically focused programmes? The key question here is whether 'technical' psychological understandings are purely Western cultural constructs, developed, in part at least, as a result of shifts in Western culture, where counselling and therapy have

66

increasingly replaced traditional mechanisms (the family, the church, etc.) of support and guidance. If therapy is no more than a Western mechanism compensating for the increasing failure of familial and social support in the developed world, it clearly has little place within more traditional societies, where such familial and social mechanisms are still operative, or at least arguably more readily restorable.

In these terms there can be only two justifiable bases for any form of psychosocial programme based upon some form of technical psychological understanding. The first of these is the circumstance hinted at above, where pre-existing cultural forms of support are so disrupted that facilitation of their reinstatement is not a realistic goal. Where civil society has been so disrupted by war and displacement that traditional mechanisms of community coping are not plausibly to be re-established in the short term, one can make a case for some form of 'compensatory support' as appropriate for some individuals. Such a justification can only be short-term, however, with the principal effort again being directed to the eventual establishment of traditional coping mechanisms.

The second basis for such programmes is that they do encapsulate some generalisable 'technical' understanding, which can be unpacked from the cultural baggage of Western psychology. Such a proposition is perhaps more readily acceptable in the case of Western medicine or agriculture. Such scientific enterprises reflect the values and concerns of the West, and yet have provided the basis for a wide range of development programmes with accepted local value within developing societies. The argument may be advanced that this process of sifting genuine technical understanding from cultural packaging is more achievable for the natural sciences (*Naturwissenschaft*) than the social sciences (*Geisteswissenschaft*). Nonetheless, a broad range of scholars from both developed and developing societies is currently engaged in work in the area of 'indigenous psychologies', with the explicit intent of identifying emic (generalisable) and etic (culturally bound) elements of Western and non-Western psychologies (Kim and Berry 1994).

The status of this developing field of work is currently such that it would be foolish to draw any firm line between emic and etic concepts within the Western psychological conceptual vocabulary. What is clear from such studies, however, is the value of the breadth of cultural background of those involved in the debate. Those indigenous to a given culture are in a far better position to identify potentially generalisable technical insight from Western cultural baggage than is a Western expatriate. For the latter, ignorance and insensitivity to cultural practice and custom are always likely to render the required 'conceptual sifting' too delicate a task to accomplish without extensive acculturation.

Given this circumstance, to the extent that psychosocial programmes based firmly upon psychological concepts are to have any place within development work, it is likely to be with indigenous psychologists (and other workers) very much to the fore. Concern over the lack of trained personnel required for such an approach can be overstated. Psychology is an established academic discipline in much of Africa, Asia, and Latin America. The peripheral involvement of untrained personnel within many existing psychosocial programmes seems to reflect more the nature of NGO project specification, planning, and implementation than any real constraint on their role. While many programmes can point to the training of local personnel as a key element of their strategy, there is a clear danger that such provision privileges external understandings, at the expense of local ones. Genuine empowerment of indigenous professionals in shaping programme goals, strategy, and methods is clearly warranted if the aim is sustainable, culture-sensitive intervention.

Phased response to psychosocial needs

Given the above analysis, it is proposed that the planning of psychosocial programmes be governed by consideration of four phases of potential response. These phases — while not formally identified with respect to this framework — may be identified in the work of an increasing number of NGOs working in the field (Ager 1995).

The first phase involves ensuring that humanitarian-assistance efforts in any given setting are planned in a manner which involves *minimal disruption of intact protective influences*. That is, where community structures, meanings, and networks have survived through conflict, assistance policy must explicitly seek to preserve such resources for community rehabilitation. Policies which threaten family integration (such as inflexible settlement and registration practices for refugee families separated during flight), social support (for example, discouraging community festivals and ceremonial adherence) or personal ideology (such as limiting public expression of religious or political beliefs) compromise the capacities of communities to rebuild a common sense of well-being. Where capacity to express religious or political ideology potentially provides a group with a sense of identity and purpose, at the cost of exacerbating inter-group tensions and precipitating further conflict (which is perceived by many as a major risk, for example, among Rwandan Hutu refugees), clearly some degree of cost-benefit analysis needs to be conducted. However, the basic notion remains that the first principle to govern psychosocial support must be not to threaten those adaptive structures which are already present.

The second phase of response in circumstances where protection of surviving protective influences is considered insufficient to ameliorate experienced trauma is the *re-establishment of protective influences*. Family reunification programmes, community-development initiatives, vocational training schemes, and so on can potentially serve as a means to strengthen family structures, social networks of support, and shared ideologies and understandings, each of which provides resources for communities to rebuild personal and social well-being. Much of this work may be seen as putting back in place structures which have been disrupted by conflict, though again there may be circumstances when re-establishment of structures may be seen to conflict with agendas for political development.

As noted earlier, there may be many circumstances where a strategy of reinstituting protective influences alone may be too long-term for the needs of particularly vulnerable groups. *Provision of compensatory support* may, as a third phase of response, be warranted in such circumstances. Here activities replicate not the form of pre-existing community patterns, but rather their function. Thus women's study groups may not be structures that were previously present, but they may represent the most effective way of re-establishing women's networks and support disrupted by the impact of warfare.

Only when the above phases have been implemented, and particular assessed needs have been shown to remain unmet, does there seem a clear case for considering a fourth phase of response: *targeted therapeutic intervention*. In most circumstances this would constitute the most culturally alien, and therefore unsustainable, form of response. It will also usually be the most costly. Nonetheless, if there is any acceptance of the existence of certain emic principles regarding human mental health, it must be acknowledged that clinical intervention plays a potential role in a comprehensive psychosocial programme. The delivery of such clinical intervention must clearly take due account of prevailing cultural norms; but, in terms of the preceding analysis, it is necessarily and fundamentally driven by external technical understandings of psychological process and function.

These four phases of response thus represent a strategic means of negotiating the conceptual space identified in Figure 1. Essentially, programmes begin with an explicit emphasis on unique, indigenous understandings and community-based support, only moving towards more generalisable, technical understandings and targeted support as evidence suggests this appropriate.

'Appropriateness' is another value-laden term, which is likely to be influenced both by judgements regarding unmet psychosocial needs and broader social, political, and ethical considerations. To illustrate the latter point, practices such as female circumcision may be considered to reflect existing indigenous understandings and, as such, potentially provide a mechanism for reinforcing patterns of meaning and identity strained by war. 'Reinstituting' such social practices, however, may be seen to contravene broader principles of human rights and thus be deemed 'inappropriate'.

The former point — regarding judgements of unmet psychosocial need — returns us to the heart of the conflict in the psychosocial discourse. Those advocating more generalisable, technical, targeted interventions tend to justify the demand for such an approach in terms of external technical assessments of need (Agger 1995); while those favouring unique, indigenous, community-based approaches consider the expressed needs of communities — 'the priorities they nominate' — the only justifiable basis for assistance (Summerfield,

1995). The presented analysis does not remove, therefore, the complexities of competing meanings and rationales for psychosocial programmes. Making the tensions in the psychosocial discourse explicit, however, may assist in their negotiation.

Note

An earlier version of this paper was presented at the Second International Conference, 'Palestinians in Transition: Rehabilitation and Community Development', Gaza Community Mental Health Programme, 13–15 September 1995, with support from the Refugee Studies Programme, University of Oxford.

References

Ager, A. (1993) *Mental Health Issues in Refugee Populations: A Review*, Working Paper of the Harvard Center for the Study of Culture and Medicine, Project on International Mental and Behavioral Health, Boston: Harvard Medical School.

Ager, A. (1995) 'Children, war and psychological intervention', in S. Carr and J. Schumaker (eds): *Psychology and the Developing World*, Westport: Praeger.

Agger, I. (1995) *Theory and Practice of Psycho-Social Projects Under War Conditions in Bosnia-Herzegovina*, Zagreb: ECHO/ECTF.

Kim, U. and J. Berry (1994) *Indigenous Psychologies*, New York: Sage.

Orley, J. (1996) 'Health activities across traumatised populations: WHO's role regarding traumatic stress', in Y. Danieli, N. Rodley and L. Weisaeth (eds.): *International Responses to Traumatic Stress*, New York: Baywood.

Punamaki, R.-L. (1987) 'Psychological stress of Palestinian mothers and their children in conditions of political violence', *The Quarterly Newsletter of the Laboratory of Comparative Human Cognition*, 9, 116-19.

Reid, M., A. Ager, O'May and D. MacWhannell (1995) *Towards a Health and Social Policy Research Agenda: A Background Paper Commissioned as Part of the ODA Social Policy Work Programme*, London: Institute for Health Sector Development.

Stubbs, P. (1996) 'Civil Society, Social Movements or Globalised New Professional Middle-class?: NGO Work with Refugees and Displaced Persons in Croatia', paper presented to the Conference of the American Sociological Association, New York City, August 1996.

Summerfield, D. (1995) 'Assisting survivors of war and atrocity: short notes on "psychosocial" issues for NGO workers', *Development in Practice*, 5, 352-6.

Summerfield, D. (1996) *The Impact of War and Atrocity on Civilian Populations: Basic Principles for NGO Interventions and a Critique of Psychosocial Trauma Projects*, Relief and Rehabilitation Network Paper 14, London: Overseas Development Institute.

The author

Alastair Ager is a Professor of Applied Psychology with a special interest in disability, refugee assistance, and psycho-social interventions.

Papers from a Symposium

Building Bridges in Southern Africa:

Conflict, Reconstruction and Reconciliation
in Times of Change

Sustainable peace-building in the South: experiences from Latin America

Jenny Pearce

Introduction: contextualising conflict

The 'peace industry' has grown enormously in the wake of the Cold War. The UN system, government and non-government aid programmes, and new academic research have focused their attentions on the complex and very violent internal wars which seem to have characterised the immediate post-Cold War era. The only area of overseas aid which has grown in recent years is that directed at disaster-relief and peace-keeping. According to the World Debt Tables 1996, aid levels in 1995 were 13 per cent lower than those recorded in 1991. Aid for disaster-relief and peace-keeping, however, had more than doubled from US$2.5 billion in 1990 to US$6 billion 1994-95.[1]

A new terminology has emerged. The UN Research Institute for Social Development (UNRISD) has focused its attentions on 'war-torn societies'; the UN has created a distinct group of conflicts, which it calls 'complex political emergencies'.[2] A new range of issues has come to preoccupy official and non-government donor agencies, such as the relationship of relief to development; peace-making and peace-building; the role of the military in humanitarian work; post-war reconstruction; and conflict prevention.

Attempts to generate universally applicable formulas collapse, however, when confronted by the huge range and complexity of the actual situations involved. 'Conflict' is not a very useful analytical category at all. Nor is it unequivocally negative: one of the conflicts examined in this paper was considered positive by a wide spectrum of international opinion and humanitarian agencies.

Much of the present concern with complex internal conflicts is in fact limited to certain recent and exceptionally violent conflicts which have attracted considerable media attention, notably former Yugoslavia, Central Africa, West Africa, and the Horn of Africa. Political imperatives and resource constraints place these major 'fires' at the top of the conflict-intervention agenda. The media tend to focus on these, making them real to millions of households, and in turn forcing politicians to respond somehow.[3] One could almost say that, whether media-determined or not, there is a threshold of what is not politically acceptable at the international or national level, and crossing it will provoke a response. Public and élite opinion tolerates 25,000 violent deaths in Colombia in 1995, but not the 800,000 which took place in Rwanda in 1994. Long-term conflicts with high accumulative death tolls (such as Guatemala, where between 1961 and 1997 an estimated 150,000, mostly poor indigenous peasants, were killed and some 45,000 'disappeared') attract much less attention than the massacre of thousands in a short period of time. An analogy might be the identification of the AIDS virus. The high loss of life resulting from the virus is appalling, but many more millions in the South have died and continue to die through avoidable illnesses such as diarrhoea, TB, and measles.

There is both a terrible reality to, and understandable preoccupation with, complex contemporary conflicts. At the same time, the focus on these distorts the real world, its many forms of violence, and the historic and developmental crises from which these emerge.

Non-government organisations (NGOs) concerned with longer-term development, for instance, find that it is the emergencies which raise the funds. The media-encouraged (or media-driven) public need for a 'quick fix', a 'result' commensurate with their donations, channels attention into certain kinds of operation and short-term vision. No cynicism is implied here. The desire to save lives is palpable. However, the logic of contemporary discourses on conflict is to extract the immediate and urgent from the long-term social realities in which they are embedded. The 'complex political emergency' becomes a phenomenon in its own right, requiring its own explanations, responses, and expertise.

It is not dissimilar to the debate on 'famine'. The image of mass starvation that shook the world in the mid-1980s similarly led policy-makers and much of the academic community to put aside studies of rural livelihoods and their macro-level environment. The words of my colleague, Donna Pankhurst, in her review of the literature on famine, could be used with respect to the 'complex political emergency':

Famine came to be seen as something separate and detached from the rest of history, requiring new explanations, which was reflected in the number of texts and commentaries on the subject ... Where famine is seen as the outcome and end result of many factors which make people poor and make them vulnerable to changes in their systems of production and reproduction (such as drought and war), then we can avoid seeking solutions to famine, or plans to ensure its prevention separately from all other analysis of how people become so vulnerable.[4]

The separation between the emergency and developmental wings of Northern agencies intervening in the South further encourages the decontextualising of conflict. The divide often reflects institutional separations (and some-times rivalries): for instance, at the international level between UNDP (United Nations Development Programme) and UNHCR (United Nations High Commissioner for Refugees); at the inter-agency level between agencies concerned with refugees and those concerned with development; and at the intra-agency level between the development and emergency departments within NGOs such as Oxfam GB. Increasingly, 'emergencies' become the headline-grabbing, fund-raising core of international assistance, as opposed to 'development', which is a more complicated process to explain, and beset with failures rather than clear successes. While individuals move between these various agencies and gain relevant and important experience of the connections between their activities, institutional dynamics often prevent the learning from these experiences at the institutional level. Time for reflection, analysis,

discussion, and systematising of experiences can be seen as an indulgence in the hectic and emotive world of relief and development.

But while the idea of a continuum between emergency relief and development, with clear cut-off points between the end of one phase and the beginning of the next, may be institutionally useful, in my experience it is a very poor way to conceptualise reality.[5] Most of the regions beset by conflict in the South never had 'develop-ment'; indeed, such conflicts often have their epicentre in the most peripheral regions of countries where development has been uneven, if at all. Failure to understand the socio-economic context of conflict seriously weakens the emergency effort, as well as the prospects for post-conflict peace-building.[6] There is a huge difference between peace-building in former Yugoslavia, for example, where there was a relatively highly skilled and educated population and level of economic development before the war, and much of Africa.

The reality of the world today, and notably in its Southern hemisphere, is that there is a spectrum of violent situations. There are the exceptionally violent conflagrations already mentioned, but there is a range of others. For instance, besides many protracted conflicts (such as Afghanistan, Sri Lanka, Colombia, or Angola), there are conflicts in a fragile transitionary phase from long-term conflict to peace (as in Guatemala, where the Peace Agreement was signed on 29 December 1996), conflicts which have formally ended but where social problems continue to threaten long-term peace (as in El Salvador or Mozambique), and situations that simmer on the edge of major conflict (as in Burundi).

The number of potential conflicts is great. Today's developmental crisis may be tomorrow's violent conflict; contemporary 'emergencies' all express deep developmental, social, and political crises. As Adams and Bradbury point out,

In 1993, when the UN designated 26 conflict-generated emergencies as 'complex', there were over 80 other violent conflicts recorded. In many countries not at war, violence and insecurity are daily realities in the private and public lives of many women, children and ethnic and religious minorities, with profound consequences for their physical, psychological, and material well-being. Insecurity and violence are development issues that have received little serious attention from the UN, governmental agencies, and NGOs working for poverty alleviation and justice.[7]

73

There is an urgent need to build up a body of authoritative knowledge about this range of conflicts and the social, economic, and political processes from which they erupt. We need to improve our conceptual tools for understanding them and their outcomes. In particular, we need to root conflict analysis, emergency intervention, and peace-building within specific socio-historical contexts. Conflicts have a social history: they are not abstract categories. Peace-building has a political economy. It also depends critically on human resources: most people will have been negatively affected by personal experience of violence, loss, and destruction, but also positively shaped by courage, new skills, and coping strategies. Peace-building should not become a set of abstract principles, unless they derive from careful study of a number of cases, take into account the range of contingent factors which affect post-war environment, and are then continuously revised in the light of experience.

Building a body of knowledge: the contribution of Latin America and Southern Africa

The recent internal wars of Latin America and those of Southern Africa are examples of conflicts which are not considered to be 'complex political emergencies'. These conflicts have disappeared from the headlines, but they have nevertheless had a devastating impact on their respective countries. Peace-building is taking place in a problematic macro-level environment in both regions.

The international dimension to these conflicts contrasts them with more recent ones. They were all in a sense 'Cold War' conflicts; the Peruvian conflict reflected Cold War ideologies, but did not involve the superpowers in the way that Central America did. But in fact the international influences only exacerbated and prolonged what were essentially internal conflicts. With the notable exceptions of Angola and Colombia, these largely came to an end in the last phase of the Cold War or in its immediate wake. Guatemala has been the most prolonged of the conflicts and of the peace processes, with an agreement signed only at the end of 1996. As the first examples of peace settlements with international supervision, they have been used as models of post-war reconstruction.

Long-term peace-building is the responsibility of local people, many of whom have been involved in the war in different ways: some as victims/survivors, some as protagonists, and some as relief workers and peace-builders. We need to understand these processes of local 'peace-building from below' and to learn what is and what is not effective.[8] But we also need to understand the factors operating at a broader level, including the external interventions, which facilitate or hinder local capacity to reconstruct societies from the devastation of war.

This article arises from my contribution to the Oxfam/CSVR Symposium, in which I described recent Latin American experiences of conflict and peace-building. It looks comparatively (and very schematically in such a short article) at two regions of conflict in Latin America: Central America (Nicaragua and El Salvador) and the Andes (Peru). The comparative method is used to draw out differences as well as similarities. It focuses on these countries because they are all in the post-war reconstruction phase. It is based on four years of research and fieldwork in most of the areas of conflict in Latin America except Chiapas in Mexico, with a particular focus on the problem of internal displacement.

The article begins with an analysis of each conflict, using a socio-historical approach. It subsequently tries to identify the critical social changes which took place as a result of conflict and how the humanitarian intervention responded to them. How did people cope with and survive the war, and what skills and capacities might they bring to the peace? Finally, it asks to what extent these local capacities have been able to influence the post-war situation and prospects for long-term and sustainable peace-building.

Conflict analysis

Violent conflicts appear to be cataclysmic events, but they are in fact the result of processes that have developed over time. They are rooted in some way in the interactions between identities of class, ethnicity, and sometimes religion (gender inequalities have not yet led to open warfare on gender lines!), and structural socio-economic factors. These identities are channelled, articulated, and politicised through the presence of some catalyst, and conflict is triggered by political acts or action of some kind.

The identities of any individual or subject are, as the post-modernists have taught us, multiple; they are neither fixed nor essential. In the conflicts examined below, for instance, most women have tended to suppress or play down their gender-related identity and concerns in favour of a sense of belonging based on class, ethnicity, or nationality, which cuts across gender; although gender-awareness has at the same time often grown stronger in the course of the war itself.[9] A vital question is why at any given moment one identity appears to predominate over others and even provides a reason for taking up arms. There is no automatic reason why any of these identities should result in conflict. Conflict analysis needs to understand how historically rooted injustices, exclusions, inequalities, and rivalries that exist in all societies turn into violent internal war in some.

Central America: Nicaragua and El Salvador

Long before the civil wars which tore this region apart in the 1980s, its socio-economic and political structures had developed along particularly exclusionary and socially divisive lines.

Common to both countries was the concentration of economic and political power in the hands of a mostly white or *mestizo* (mixed white and Indian) élite. Only a small, politically weak, professional middle class lay between the mass of the peasant population and the urban poor. The structural inequalities resulted in clear class cleavages in El Salvador (in the case of neighbouring Guatemala they were class and ethnic cleavages). In Nicaragua, however, class divisions were complicated by the fact that the élite itself was divided, with one dynasty concentrating power and wealth at the level of the State and alienating other sectors of the élite.

There were also significant spatial or geographical patterns to the deep social divisions in the two countries. In El Salvador, departments such as Chalatenango, Cabañas, and Morazán were the poorest, most ecologically damaged, and agriculturally unsustainable regions. Poor, land-hungry peasants struggled to sustain a fragile, vulnerable livelihood in these departments, which later constituted core regions of the conflict. In Nicaragua, there was also a geographic and ethnic divide between the Pacific and Atlantic regions of the country. The social structures of the former did not reproduce themselves in the latter, where indigenous Miskito and Sumo peoples had come under the influence of Britain and the Moravian Church, and had little communication or relationship with the Spanish-speaking Catholic population of the Pacific region.

More than any other structural inequality, the role of land distribution and use in the unfolding conflicts was probably the most significant. Inability to sustain the peasant economy on the amount and quality of land available to the poor majority was a core issue. Economic growth was nevertheless facilitated by the relationship between the agro-export and peasant economies: unable to live on the available land all the year round, peasants had to migrate and sell their labour cheaply at harvest time on the agro-export estates, in order to earn some cash to support themselves for the full year. The problem became ever more acute with population growth and the expansion of agro-export crops and concomitant expulsion of peasants from their land. The gravest situation was found in the smallest, most heavily populated country, El Salvador.

Many dispossessed people headed for urban areas, where they would once again end up on the margins of society, with relatively few gaining jobs in the small manufacturing sector. In Nicaragua, where there were still unsettled agricultural areas, colonisation schemes banished some of the land-hungry to remote areas in the 1960s and 1970s, where poor infrastructure and State neglect resulted in a difficult struggle for survival. Nueva Guinea in Nicaragua would later become one of the conflict-ridden regions of that country, for instance (the Ixcán in Guatemala would be another example of a zone of colonisation in Central America which subsequently became a centre of conflict). In Nueva Guinea, many peasants remained politically tied to *Somocismo* in gratitude for the former dictator's land grants, and this made them a fertile recruiting ground for the anti-Sandinista forces in the 1980s. Chalatenango in El Salvador was an area of unplanned colonisation. When thousands were expelled from the coastal regions to make way for cotton-growing in the 1950s, and thousands more were driven from their small subsistence plots on the coffee estates, they headed for the regions of little interest to the agro-exporters. In Chalatenango it was cattle ranching, not agro-exports, which predominated, and some land was available for rent.

The Andes: Peru

In Peru, class and ethnic identity overlapped in the highland departments of Ayacucho, Huancavelica, and Apurimac. These represented the poorest regions of the country and the epicentres of the conflict which erupted in the early 1980s.

Populations of alpaca herders and subsistence farmers and sharecroppers, some of whom paid labour dues up until the late 1970s to local landowners, lived in remote and desolate altitudes. The State showed little interest in the contribution that the region might make to the national economy, except insofar as the land reform which finally gave the peasants title to land in the late 1970s was aimed also at forcing expropriated landowners to invest their capital elsewhere. Ethnic identity among the peasants was culturally strong, with most still speaking primarily Quechua. Many women spoke no Spanish at all, and many men did so with difficulty. The problem of communicating with the wider Peru was an isolating factor, exacerbated by widespread racism towards the 'Indian'. Ethnicity was not an identity which the peasants and herders themselves valued or affirmed. Any action in the wider world taken by these people reflected their socio-economic position and not their ethnic identity; examples are the peasant movements which did emerge in the wake of the Velasco government's efforts to mobilise them 'from above' in the early 1970s.

In the valleys, such as that around Huanta in Ayacucho, where larger landowners and better-off peasants lived, the population was mostly *mestizo*, and strongly rejected the 'Indian' influence within it, although most also spoke Quechua as well as Spanish. Nevertheless, they would never be accepted into the same social élite as the Lima-based bourgeoisie. The frustrations of a generation of sons and daughters of peasants on medium-sized farms, with educational opportunities but few professional or social ones, would play an important role in the subsequent conflict.[10]

Catalysts of war

None of the conditions described leads invariably to war and/or violent conflict. Many parts of the world are characterised by deep class and ethnic divisions and a highly exclusionary distribution of political and economic power corresponding to them. Often these divisions, like the ones we are exploring, rest on a great deal of threatened or actual violence. The *status quo* is defended through a variety of coercive mechanisms from national to private armed force. Some writers have even identified 'structural violence' to describe situations of violence embedded in social relations but which do not manifest themselves in armed conflict between the parties.[11]

Affirming identity does not necessarily lead to conflict.[12] But there are situations where identity is mobilised in such a way as to challenge another social group or the State. It is the character of these catalysing factors which is critical to the analysis of conflict; they introduce new elements into an ongoing situation, and transform perceptions about the legitimacy of that situation and what can be done to change it.

Central America: El Salvador and Nicaragua

In **El Salvador** the catalysts consisted firstly of the radical Church and secondly of left-wing political movements. The fact that the Central American civil wars originated in the 1960s and 1970s meant that they were heavily influenced by the ideological currents that on the left made class an over-arching identity which could bring others, such as gender and ethnicity, under its umbrella. This produced a powerful mobilising tool to pitch against a State which also organised itself essentially around the interests of one class. A peasant movement began to emerge in the poorest zones of the country in the 1970s, linking up with other popular organisations in the urban areas, and articulated politically by the guerrilla movements that formed the FMLN (Frente Farabundo Martí de Liberación Nacional) in 1980. The class-based nature of this movement was a source of its initial strength, but it provoked a stronger class solidarity among the Salvadorean oligarchy who controlled the State and could call upon the armed forces, and ultimately the US government, for support.

In **Nicaragua** the success of the Sandinistas in overthrowing the Somocista dictatorship triggered the relentless hostility of the US Administration to what it perceived to be a revolutionary pro-Soviet government. While the revolution against Somoza had attracted a multi-class alliance, this did not survive the assumption of power by the Sandinistas, although the new government attempted to preserve it. Those who opposed the focus on social distribution and popular participation of the Sandinista government were the catalysts — with US backing — of an armed movement to overthrow it.

This armed movement was able to exploit the social discontent among sectors of the peasantry alienated by the Sandinistas' approach to the agrarian question. It also managed to mobilise the ethnic particularities of the Atlantic Coast communities, which were deeply disaffected by the Sandinistas' ill-conceived initial approach to a region used to virtual autonomy from Managua.

The counter-revolutionary movement grew with external support, but nevertheless exploited many internal social tensions and class and ethnic identities to bring down the first State in Nicaragua's history which proposed to base itself on the 'logic of the majority'. The historic weakness of a State which had developed around a dynastic dictorship could not be overcome very rapidly, however, and certainly not with sufficient speed to deal adequately with the social contradictions exposed by the overthrow of the old order.

The Andes: Peru

In **Peru**, the catalyst was a movement which emerged with a messianic Maoist vision which it attempted to apply to the most impoverished regions of the Andes. *Sendero Luminoso* ('Shining Path') set out to mobilise the peasants in a struggle against feudalism and capitalism. It exploited the abandonment of these regions by the State, an abandonment reaffirmed by the application of the agrarian reform to the Ayacucho region in the late 1970s. This gave peasant communities their land and freed them from servitude. But almost no other support was given to peasants struggling with an inhospitable terrain and lack of infrastructure to connect them either physically or socially to the rest of the country.

Indigenous communities responded initially to *Sendero* because the movement filled a virtual power vacuum in the area and sought to give them a wider vision of their role, although it

made violence a means for them to achieve recognition, status, and survival. *Sendero* had little interest in their ethnicity, much more in their class identity. Indeed, it was *Sendero*'s disrespect for their traditions and community structure which, among other factors, led the indigenous people to turn against the guerrilla movement. The imposition of a revolutionary committee structure, for instance, on the time-honoured community structure, and the killing of community elders and Presidents, were two such. But repudiation of *Sendero* was not enough to save the peasants from the vengeance of the Peruvian army. Peasants were killed in their thousands, either by *Sendero* for betraying them, or by the army for having given support to the guerrillas.

Similarities and differences

In analysing these three conflicts, some common threads are apparent amid many differences. A significant similarity is the way in which social marginalisation and exclusion could be mobilised by political forces in very divergent ways. In **El Salvador**, the popular movement of the 1970s was strong enough to create a social dynamic of its own. While it was closely linked to the political force which would lead it into conflict, there is sufficient evidence that a conscious movement of the poor had emerged and chose a revolutionary option. This would be a very important factor in determining the way in which the conflict took shape, and the humanitarian responses to it. Much support was channelled to the popular organisations and people's initiatives in this conflict. Only the USA and its agencies chose to put all their efforts into shoring up the Salvadorean State, both militarily and politically.

In **Nicaragua**, although the Sandinistas emerged from a multi-class alliance with strong backing from the urban poor, intellectuals, and significant sectors of the peasantry, they were not able to generate a national following behind their modernising and transforming governmental project. There was little history of popular organising before the revolution, and the lack of consciousness was apparent in the ability of external forces to mobilise social and political discontent around an anti-government initiative. However, the fact that the Sandinista State was committed to a socially radical and nationalist agenda would also influence the international humanitarian response to the conflict. A great deal of international support was channelled through the Sandinista State.

In **Peru**, social sectors isolated and neglected by a State with very little interest in the subsistence agriculture of the Andean highlands were mobilised by an ideologically rigid armed group. Although many abandoned this allegiance, they were already exposed to army revenge. It was only when subsequently the army began to arm them, and peasant militia were created, that the peasants gained a real protagonism of their own in this conflict. That protagonism has provided the basis for a humanitarian response now that the war has come to a kind of ending.

The impact of conflict

The particular character of each of these conflicts had a profound impact on their societies. Men and women changed their roles as they do in all wars; they may be victims of terrible things, but they also have to cope with the situation. Men tend to carry the guns and lead movements, while family survival comes to depend on women alone. Social and political change and economic destruction, unevenly spread and experienced, all characterise conflict. Only a careful analysis of this can provide the tools for understanding the challenges of peace, and in particular enable peace-building strategies to harness the positive energies and capacities developed to cope with and survive the conflict.

Central America: El Salvador and Nicaragua

In **El Salvador**, observers close to the popular sectors identified an impressive level of organisation among the most illiterate and marginalised social groups. An estimated 500,000 people were displaced inside the country by the war (10 per cent of the population), over 70,000 people were killed, and an estimated 68 per cent of the population were living below the poverty line in 1990.[13] But there is no doubt that the population most affected by army bombardment, State terror, and counter-insurgency showed an extra-ordinary protagonism at key moments.

In the zones of guerrilla control, they established their own local governments and

developed creative and courageous responses to the destruction and danger around them. In the refugee camps, they organised workshops and training; and, when the moment was appropriate for them (and in opposition to the wishes of international agencies such as UNHCR), they asserted their right to return in the manner they wished — openly. In the returned communities which were set up within the zones of conflict, they challenged the army through peaceful resistance to efforts to dislodge them from the civilian space they had won.

These activities opened up a political and civil space in the country, and enabled the popular movement to start re-grouping from 1986 onwards. Local NGOs were able to establish themselves and channel funds to the war-affected populations. While the guerrilla movements maintained political and military leadership, it was this grassroots organising that held people together in the face of relentless government repression, largely financed by the USA.

These capacities of the population had a big impact on international humanitarian NGOs. There was an understanding that an historic struggle was at stake for social and economic change in favour of the poorest. The humanitarian support from these NGOs was not neutral, but value-driven, and very much based on respect for the political options of the 'victims/protagonists' of the war. These international NGOs accompanied the popular organisations, lobbied their own governments to challenge the US role in the country, and provided an international umbrella of protection.[14]

In El Salvador, therefore, the history of the conflict is the history also of a social *and* political process, in which mostly illiterate or semi-literate men and women participated in a prolonged struggle to bring about a funda-mental transformation of their society. This they ultimately failed to do, however. But that population had gained an experience of protagonism that should have enabled them at least to influence the peace.

In **Nicaragua**, the conflict unfolded in a context where the State under the Sandinistas was itself the protagonist for a project of social change. The lack of tradition of independent popular organising, the weakness of political parties, and the culture of exclusion had to be addressed in order to mobilise support. At the same time, however, the Sandinistas had to channel that support into their national project, which included an alliance with the private sector. The Sandinistas did generate an enthusiastic following among a significant sector of the population. Many international NGOs, and Western as well as East European governments, gave the State strong support for what was seen as an historic opportunity for people-centred development. Humanitarian assistance during the war in Nicaragua encompassed a great deal of solidarity and political support for the project of the Sandinista State.

The military response organised by the USA and its local allies both undermined the social dimensions of the Sandinista project and exacerbated its contradictions. The Sandinistas were attempting to persuade the private sector to accept a loss of political power in exchange for retaining considerable economic power. Popular mobilising became increasingly organised around the defence of the revolution and support for the FSLN (Frente Sandinista de Liberación Nacional), weakening its capacity to generate autonomous and sustainable social action. In the conflict zones, the logic of war replaced the logic of the social processes.

The conflict in Nicaragua divided the majority population of poor peasants and indigenous peoples. It had high human, social, and economic costs for an already impoverished country; but it also contributed to the premature collapse of an attempt, however flawed, to harness popular energies into modernising the country and State.

The Andes: Peru

In **Peru**, the impact of the war was felt primarily in the three Andean departments referred to above.[15] An estimated 600,000 people were displaced within Peru during the conflict, 80 per cent of them from these departments, which also accounted for many of the 25,000 dead. However, the responses to the conflict among the population also demonstrated how 'victims' can also be 'actors', developing capacities to cope with the most barbaric and traumatic circumstances.

The conflict forced people to choose between fleeing the zone of conflict, dying at the hands of *Sendero* or the army, or staying and offering armed resistance. Many fled, either following historic migratory patterns and heading for Lima, or settling in the nearest urban centre.

But, unlike historic migrations, these were not planned population movements, but forced expulsions.

Unprepared and often traumatised, the displaced ended up on the periphery of towns and cities where they did not even speak the language. Many were widows or women left to cope with the children (including many orphans) alone, because their husbands had stayed to fight. Many displaced men were even less able to adapt from peasant life to urban environments, and found it more difficult to find work than the women, who could at least do domestic work. Nevertheless, the experience of urban life had a profound effect on these displaced people. Despite often appalling living conditions, the possibility of some schooling for their children, and the experience of modern communications and urban social life, have changed the expectations and aspirations of significant groups of Andean peasants.

Others stayed to resist, in some regions managing to preserve the community structure, but in others forced to move from isolated rural dwellings into virtual camps, from where they would venture out to farm their distant plots or to fight *Sendero*. It is the ill-armed peasant militia or *rondas*, rather than the army, which many believe to be responsible for the defeat of *Sendero* in the Andes.[16] This has given *ronderos* a sense of self-worth that was historically denied them.

The humanitarian assistance to the population affected by this war was very limited. Peru did not attract the international attention paid to the Central American wars, and *Sendero*'s hostility to international aid made it very dangerous to work in the war zones, although some agencies such as GB managed to maintain a flow of aid. Only with the capture of *Sendero*'s leader in 1992 and the virtual — though not complete — defeat of *Sendero* have the dimensions of the crisis affecting the displaced population become apparent.

The problem of sustainable peace-building

The impact of war was devastating for all three countries examined above. But social changes did take place, with some positive implications in terms of new capacities, skills, and expectations among the populations. These capacities are easily eroded in peace-time, as is well known in the case of women who take new public roles during war-time and return to private domestic ones subseqently. Indeed, the 'gendered' nature of peace agreements reflects this.[17] Fundamentally, however, the problem is that most peace agreements do not even purport to encompass or reflect social changes. They are political deals.

The discussion of peace-building is frequently confused by the different ways in which the term 'peace' is used. Some define it negatively as the 'absence of war'; others invest it with a positive content too: ultimately the 'peaceful' society is one in which there are no causes for violence and conflict. The mechanisms for achieving this and its precise content are much debated, and the debate centres around the concepts of justice, equality, liberty, and democracy. The debate about positive peace draws our attention to the apparently obvious: that the absence of war does not necessarily mean the absence of violence in a society, and it certainly does not mean an end to conflict. Socio-economic inequality, unequal gender relations, political exclusion, and racism are just some of the factors that fuel social and political violence in any society. For some, therefore, a sustainable peace is only meaningful and possible if steps are made to deal with these fundamental problems. Others prefer to focus on the immediately achievable, the by no means simple task of bringing parties to armed conflict into a negotiation which will at least allow for the 'management' of the conflict, or a decision by the parties not to pursue their differences through violence.

How can these two approaches be married? In practice, of course, a peace agreement may not deal with all the underlying causes of the conflict, but it might open up a political space to deal with them in another way. The problem arises if the peace agreement is treated as an 'ending' to something, rather than a 'beginning' in which the parties to conflict have formally agreed to address their differences in non-violent ways.

The process of peace-building — and it is by nature a protracted and complex one — will depend on the prospects for reconciling fundamental, often structurally embedded, differences through peaceful means. Given that conflicts are about attempts to change power relations in some way, their outcome will create an environment which negatively or positively affects this. The historical outcome of the conflict and the political economy in which the peace-building process takes place are critical factors for societies emerging from internal war. The conflict will have changed something in the society. But *to what extent* will these changes allow for the emergence of new social practices, the construction of accountable and representative government institutions, and inclusive economic processes? To what extent will the rule of law be legitimised, so allowing alternative means to violence for the redress of grievances, and the protection of basic rights of all the population? Will the cessation of armed conflict enable the victims of violence to write their history freely, and to deal with the trauma of bereavement? If the changes do not facilitate these things sufficiently, the ending of the conflict will simply bequeath a legacy of frustration and resentment to another generation.

'Peace-building' cannot be seriously discussed in the abstract, because armed conflicts end in so many different ways and offer such different possibilities. The social history of the pre-conflict period must be related to the political economy of the post-conflict context. If the reasons why people took up arms have not been addressed and there are no means of articulating them politically, how will they manifest themselves in the peace? Demoralisation and exhaustion may depoliticise aspirations and atomise individuals into seeking private solutions, giving the illusion of a 'stable peace'. But this will not be a society that has dealt with its past. In the short term, people are relieved that war is over, but the legacy of violence will imprint itself on the society and express itself somehow, in inter-personal relations, in levels of domestic violence, on children and, quite probably, eventually in the political arena once again.

The issue of 'impunity', truth, justice, and reconciliation remains one of the most problematic issues in the aftermath of conflict. In reality, most peace agreements are compromises or defeats/victories, rather than a joint attempt to redress the grievances of the past in order to build something new. The question of what is done to bring to justice perpetrators of extreme violence goes to the heart of the nature of the peace agreement and the power relationships it expresses as the conflict ends. Guatemala, for instance, is now beginning its transition to peace, following the signing of an accord. However, that accord was made possible by an agreement to an amnesty that protected the guerrillas from prosecution for political violence but also, far more significantly in terms of the scale of the violence they used, exonerated the army of responsibility for the mass and cruel violence it perpetrated against indigenous people and opposition groups. What kind of peace will emerge in Guatemala, where the rule of law has been practised so partially?

Realistic peace-building

Realistic peace-building must confront the flawed foundations of the peace agreement. It must take into account the power relations, persistent exclusions, and the social implications of the post-war political economy. The case-studies below suggest that the most important steps towards a sustainable peace are those which foster and strengthen local capacity to deal with the past, to engage with the present, and to shape the future in ways which do not exclude, oppress, or divide.

Central America: El Salvador and Nicaragua

El Salvador has been acclaimed as achieving one of the most 'successful' peace agreements. The are undoubtedly many significant features of the Salvadorean peace negotiations. But, in 1995, there were more killings each day through criminal violence than during the war.[18] Questions of land, poverty, and marginalisation are as much a concern as before the war. The difference is that the ability of previous leaders to articulate excluded groups politically is much diminished.

The protracted conflict wore people down; while the guerrilla movement remained militarily powerful, it was clear that they could not take power through arms. Sectors of the oligarchy meanwhile had also understood that they could not defeat the movement militarily. The price of peace would be to broaden the basis for political participation in the country, and this became acceptable to a sufficient sector. Meanwhile, the Cold War was ending and the USA was seeking to extricate itself from its military commitments.

Many other factors influenced the peace, but it is important to note that, in the end, and despite the mobilisation of civilian groups in favour of peace (through initiatives such as the *Debate Nacional*), it was negotiated between the élites of both sides of the war.[19] While the 'victims/protagonists' had high expectations of the outcome, the war did not transform the socio-economic basis of power in the society. It opened a political space for civilian government and free, contested elections, and most notably allowed for the political participation of the former guerrilla leaders. The international presence played a major role in guaranteeing the transition from war to peace.

International pressure ensured that local NGOs were given the space to participate in discussions about the post-conflict resettlement and reconstruction programmes, through what was called the CIREFCA (International Conference for Central American Refugees) process. But most of these NGOs had emerged during the war, closely tied to the FMLN and ill-prepared for the tasks of post-war reconstruction or working with people in a non-instrumentalist way. The popular sectors, despite their protagonism in the war, found it hard to adapt to the new discourse of electoral politics which relegated them to the role of voters, with little space to retain their political engagement. The demoralisation that resulted brought with it the dissipation of that creativity, courage, and energy with which people had responded to the revolutionary war.

The failure to transform the Salvadorean State would also have profound implications for the peace. A State which had historically served only one sector of society, and was very much weakened by the war, was in a poor condition to lead the post-war reconstruction; but above all it still fundamentally reflected the pre-war class structure. Issues such as the rule of law, accountability, and effective administration remain unsolved in El Salvador, although there has been a concerted international effort to address them and to support the modernising social and political forces. While these dominated the governing right-wing ARENA party (as they did under President Cristiani, 1989–1994), there were some prospects for progress. But his successor, Calderón Sol, proved ill-equipped to take the country forward. It is telling that the most searching analysis of the post-war reconstruction effort in El Salvador has drawn attention to the limitations of external post-war assistance where the national government lacks the political will to collaborate:

External assistance has played a critical role in El Salvador's peace process. Grants and loans from bilateral and multilateral agencies have been the main source of finance for many programs mandated by the Peace Accords, including the land transfer program, the reintegration of ex-combatants, poverty alleviation programs and infrastructure projects. External assistance actors have also influenced the political momentum of the peace process. Aid has affected not only the balance of payments, but also the balance of power. Aid can be an important complement to limited domestic resources. It can, however, also become a substitute for them ... This dilemma has been clearly apparent in El Salvador. External assistance unquestionably has contributed greatly to postwar reconstruction and to the consolidation of peace. But external assistance actors have been less successful in prompting the government to mobilize greater domestic resources to finance peace programs. Indeed, virtually no internal fiscal reforms were undertaken specifically with a view to financing the peace.[20]

The inability of former guerrilla leaders to provide political leadership to their supporters for the new agendas of the peace has had a very negative impact on the popular movement and its ability to influence that peace. There are some examples of successful interactions between NGOs and international agencies in the reconstruction, and some efforts to build accountable municipal governments, but they are relatively few and still not part of a systematic *government* project.[21] And while international agencies have stressed 'participation' in their interventions, time and attention must be invested in helping traumatised, impoverished, semi-literate populations to recover from war and respond to the often technocratic visions of professional external actors.

There is no plan to incorporate the former war zones into a national development plan. They are left to the projects of international financial agencies and international NGOs. Many of the urban and rural poor of El Salvador subsist on dollar remittances from relatives in the USA, rather than on their own productive capacity. The survival mentality today contrasts strongly with the creative mobilisations of the war period. Outstanding tensions over land and the future of demobilised ex-combatants continue to threaten the prospects for peace: the disaffection of the latter has already led to more than one violent incident.

In **Nicaragua**, the counter-revolutionary army was ultimately defeated militarily, but not politically — the reverse of the situation in El Salvador. The electoral defeat of the Sandinistas in 1990, just after the formal signing of the peace agreement, meant that the process of peace-building would take place without the commitment of a 'progressive' State. At the popular level, the legacy of Sandinista organising had left its mark, and there was much greater capacity to defend popular interests than otherwise. But much of this was still led and organised by the Sandinistas, now fighting to regain political power through electoral means.

The most vigorous and independent voices, many observers noted, were from the women's organisations that throughout the Sandinista period had defended both the revolution and also, increasingly, their gender interests. The other group which would emerge in the early years of the peace were the demobilised soldiers, peasants from both sides of the war who now identified common interests and who felt betrayed by their leaderships. The Foundation of Ex-combatants included former members of both the Sandinista and the counter-revolutionary or *Contra* armies.

The Sandinistas had not had the time or resources, particularly after the economy was put on a war footing, to modernise the State apparatus. The State they bequeathed was still prone to corruption and bureaucratism, tendencies enhanced by the weakness of the new Chamorro government. The government's main concern was to transform the macro-level policy environment from a State-led to a market-driven one. It was not concerned with systematic post-war peace-building. While the international financial community did contribute funds for this purpose, the lack of local capacity to administer them proved a major obstacle. Local NGO capacity was much weaker than in El Salvador. The Sandinista State had tended to dominate the associational sphere. While new NGOs emerged with the electoral defeat of the FSLN, they still mostly lacked the capacity and experience to make proposals relevant to the new conditions. A study of the search for peace and consensus in Nicaragua in the five years after the 1990 peace agreement concluded:

As a direct result of civil war fought within the context of the cold war, Nicaragua's peace process has been beset since 1990 by a sometimes violent array of conflicts over land, over economic policy and division of resources, over institutional power, and over quotas of power within and between a political class with many small parties and factions. For common citizens it has been a bewildering and dispiriting political scene they have viewed from an unsteady economic terrain which has deteriorated an already poor living standard.[22]

Again, the picture is not entirely negative. There have been some interesting local experiences. One of these is Nueva Guinea, where the Protestant Church had been very influential during the war in brokering peace between the *contras* and the Sandinista army. While it continued these efforts in the wake of the peace agreements, supported by international NGOs, these were continuously undermined by the economic marginalisation of the region. With little State investment in infrastructure and development, it is left to international and local NGOs and, in the case of Nueva Guinea, the peasant union, UNAG, to develop and implement projects. But often they do so with conflicting rather than common agendas. This tendency is sometimes fuelled by the increasing scarcity of funds and, therefore, competition among various organisations as Nicaragua moves from being a country of concern to the international community to one where 'peace' has been restored.

The situation is worsened by the neo-liberal national policy environment. A key ingredient of the peace-building in the zone, to encourage mostly *Contra*-supporting communities to accept Sandinistas into their midst, is economic reconstruction and improvement in the living standards of the people. The peasants in the zone, however, are moving desperately from crop to crop, as trade liberalisation brings in cheaper staples from neighbouring Costa Rica. As a new crop is tested for its market potential, so communities all turn to it, and the price collapses. The resolution of these problems is critical to sustaining long-term peace in a region where poor people in very recent memory took up arms against each other.

The Andes: Peru

In **Peru**, the war has never been formally brought to an end, and the State has felt no compulsion to invest in the reconstruction of the war-torn regions. Political parties have been much weakened in Peru over the last decade, in particular on the left. This has adversely affected Peru's historically strong non-government and popular organisations, which were mostly linked to the parties. President

Fujimori has claimed the credit for the victory over *Sendero* and has used this to launch his programme of economic modernisation. This does not include the Andean highlands, which according to the Peruvian anthropologist, Carlos Monge, are still seen by the government as *un gran comedor popular* (a big soup kitchen).[23] In other words, while efficiency, competition, and the free market are the agenda for the productive coastal export zone, the Andean highlands are still viewed as an unproductive region where State paternalism is the only economic hope.

As international and local NGOs struggle to develop an agenda for post-war reconstruction in the face of government indifference, so also their conceptions of what this should mean differ widely and often conflict with each other.[24] Technically competent NGOs lack sensitivity to the social dimensions of rebuilding communities devastated by violence and bereavement. The men who head the NGOs, for instance, do not know how to build on the capacities demonstrated by the women during the war years.

In El Salvador a highly politicised popular movement and NGO community found it hard to make the transition to a new role in the peace. In Nicaragua, the Sandinista State had not encouraged independent organising, and therefore the NGO and popular sectors were too weak to take full advantage of the post-war situation. In Peru, however, one of the most interesting developments is that of the organisational capacity of the displaced communities seeking support for a return programme or for permanent settlement in their places of refuge. With a new sense of protagonism inherited from their role in the war, these communities, particularly in the Ayacucho area, are embarking on an important attempt to influence the reconstruction programmes in the region. Their capacity to do so will greatly depend on the dynamics of their evolving relationships with the State and with the local and international non-government agencies which are currently supporting them.

Conclusion

This article has emphasised that 'conflict' should not be treated as an asocial, ahistorical category; nor should peace-building be understood without reference to the way in which power relationships have been reconfigured at the end of the conflict, and the nature of their impact on the political economy of post-war reconstruction.

At one level, these may seem very obvious points. However, a great deal of the debate on 'conflict', 'conflict-prevention', and 'peace-building' appears to treat them as if they have a reality of their own, divorced from their social context. The external agencies concerned with peace seem increasingly to focus the debate on *their* interventions (for instance, what *they* can do to articulate relief and development, what *they* can do to prevent conflict and build peace), and much less on the dynamic of *local* capacities and how they can shape the future prospects for peace-building. And where the discourse does focus on them, the practice of supporting the efforts of traumatised, poor, and ill-educated populations to re-build their lives is often insensitive and reflects unrealistic expectations of rapid results and achievements. For example, a real appreciation of how gender relations affect the ability of poor and powerless women to play their full role in the post-conflict situation (as opposed to a knowledge of the correct *discourse*) is essential. In my experience, few of the professional men involved in external assistance programmes have that real appreciation, and repeated gender-training workshops help only partly.

Latin America offers some useful case-studies of conflicts that have tended to be forgotten as international concern looks to the newly defined category of conflicts: the 'complex political emergency'. The Latin American examples, which are now in their post-war reconstruction phase, do nevertheless suggest some important topics that are worth exploring for their relevance to other conflicts and peace-building processes in the South.

The relationship between identity and structure is one such topic, which is critical to the analysis of conflict and for assessing the prospects for a sustainable peace. The case-studies reveal the importance of understanding the process of identity mobilisation in conflict, whether there is an 'empowering mobilisation', a 'manipulated mobilisation' (that is, one which seeks to manipulate exclusions for a political project which expresses the power rivalries of elites and leaders), or an 'affirmative mobilisation'.

In El Salvador, conscious movements emerged, linked by class interests, initially with the help of the radical Church, creating strong and combative popular organisations. This empowering mobilisation enabled ordinary peasants and workers to play an extraordinary role during the war, which was widely recognised by humanitarian agencies. These movements, which were closely tied to political leaderships during the war, have mostly, however, been unable effectively to influence the peace. Their leaders saw them in peace-time as a source of electoral support, not as a human resource for long-term peace-building. The rural and urban poor of El Salvador had demonstrated in the zones under guerrilla control, in the refugee camps and returned communities, their capacity for organisation and their readiness to learn new skills. But these have mostly not been harnessed for the peace.

In Nicaragua, poor peasants and ethnic groups were mobilised behind a counter-revolutionary project which was essentially about élites regaining political power and the USA regaining influence in the country. But the Sandinistas also mobilised 'from above' around their own agenda for government in an historical context of weak associational life, a tendency exacerbated by the demands of war. The reconstruction effort was weakened by the expectations among the population that the State or external agencies would provide solutions to their problems.

In Peru, there are signs that indigenous peasants have gained a sense of self-worth which could be the basis for an 'affirmative' identity for the peace. Indigenous women are potentially able to use their experiences during the war to play significant roles in the reconstruction of their communities. In this case, there is no 'mobilisation' around these identities, but a sense of self-value and a new sense of 'rights', which has emerged in the course of the conflict and which could be supported by humanitarian efforts in the post-war situation.

A second topic to highlight is the role of the State. In all three countries, the incapacity or unwillingness of the post-conflict State actively to promote the conditions for peace-building has seriously weakened the process. The three countries share a history of socially exclusionary, coercive, corrupt, and unaccountable States. The historic outcome of the conflicts in El Salvador and Nicaragua has placed the issue of State modernisation and legitimacy on the agenda, but has not brought about the shift in social and economic power which could force it through. Renewed polarisation into armed groups is unlikely, but the poverty and exclusion which led to war in the first place now fuel the non-political criminal violence of the desperate. In Peru, the historic outcome of the war has been to strengthen the modernising impetus of the State, albeit under the authoritarian leadership of President Fujimori. But here too, the distribution of social and economic power remains unchanged, despite the modernisation process afoot. It is too soon to judge the capacity of the victims of the war to claim State recognition that they bore the brunt of army and *Sendero* violence, as well as their rights as citizens in a country that has barely accepted its indigenous population in this way.

A third topic is the role of NGOs. There is much concern among the international community to build up local NGO capacity in the wake of war. This is not so much a recognition of the need to strengthen long-term, sustainable local peace-building capacity, as has been argued here. It is more about the macro-economic agenda of the international financial community, where NGOs are now seen as service-providers preferable to bureaucratic and corrupt States.

However, NGOs are not *necessarily* preferable to an effective, competent, and accountable State. And in order to enhance the capacity of NGOs to take on these new roles, the comparative advantages of NGOs — their cost-effectiveness, their closeness to beneficiaries, their lack of bureaucracy, etc. — often diminish. The NGOs in the three countries we have looked at are fragile institutions. To what extent will more sustainable peace processes be fostered by 'scaling-up' these organisations to carry out poverty-alleviation functions in the absence of State programmes? Experience from all three cases suggests that what is needed is indeed more effective NGOs, but ones that remain close to the marginal social groups caught up in the conflict, that can support not substitute for *their* efforts to articulate their needs better, to organise more effectively; NGOs which can assist them to make better use of the reconstruction funds available from international agencies, which can facilitate inter-community reconciliation, and so on.

Last, but by no means least, there is the topic of the post-war economy, and in particular the challenges of growth and equity which are both so critical to a sustainable peace. The main conflict areas of all three countries are characterised by their peripheral status in their national economies. The wars did not change that status. On the contrary, they further devastated and decapitalised them. While international institutions have poured money into these regions in the wake of war, in particular into El Salvador, there is no substitute for a national plan of socio-economic development which includes these regions.

However, these very same international financial institutions also promote the economic model of greater integration into the world economy on the basis of comparative advantage and a market-led approach to development. The export sectors are owned by the country's élites, and the main challenge for the national economy is to encourage greater efficiency, diversification and competitiveness in these sectors. There is real concern among the international financial institutions about the inequitable distribution of wealth in these war-torn countries, and much emphasis on how to build capacity to redress this imbalance and make the State more accountable and democratic. But in societies recovering from war, where the majority of the population lack basic services and minimal education, where bereavement and destruction have characterised their recent lives, their capacity to influence the State has to be nurtured and encouraged over time.

We return to the argument that if peace is not limited conceptually to 'the absence of war', then peace-building is a prolonged process which must incorporate concerns for development, justice, and equality. Emergencies are dramatic moments which affect public and political opinion and are capable of raising considerable economic solidarity. However, a serious commitment to peace requires much more than the rapid response to such emergencies. It requires an understanding of the historic social dislocations and divisions which, in the South in particular, have been exacerbated by external powers, poverty, and repressive exclusionary States. It also requires an honest appraisal of the impact of wars and their endings in particular cases. From what reality does the peace-building process begin?

It is likely that historic divisions have been only partly reconfigured, if at all, by the conflict, while economic destruction has further diminished the limited material capital of the society. But even a massive injection of dollars offers no guarantee for long-term peace-

85

building. An interim approach is sensitively and systematically to support the efforts of local people attempting to rebuild lives and livelihoods. Learning from their experiences and building on their capacities, rather than introducing quick-fix solutions dreamt up by outsiders, may be a longer path to peace, but a more sustainable one.

Notes

1 R. Ridell (1996), 'Trends in International Cooperation', London: ODI, mimeo.
2 '... the term "complex emergency" was coined in the United Nations to describe those major crises, which have indeed proliferated since 1989, that require a "system-wide response": a combination of military intervention, peace-keeping efforts, relief programmes, high-level diplomacy, and son on. In other words, the complexity refers to the "multi-mandate" nature of the international response as well as to the multi-causal nature of the emergency.' (Deborah Eade: Preface to *Development in States of War*, Oxford: Oxfam , 1996.)
3 The relationship of the media to conflict has been explored in Minear, Scott and Weiss (1996): *The News Media, Civil War and Humanitarian Action*, Boulder: Lynne Rienner.
4 D. Pankhurst (1989): 'Review article: Poverty and food — contemporary questions', *Journal of International Development*, Vol. 1, No. 4, p. 513.
5 Many fieldworkers recount anecdotes which reflect the artificial distinctions made by some donor agencies and governments. A former Oxfam fieldworker in Central America, for example, recalls how the Overseas Development Administration's distinction between relief and rehabilitation during the conflict of the 1980s meant that it was possible to secure emergency co-funding for housing materials for Salvadoran refugees returning from Honduras, but not to reconstruct their homes once there (unless they were bombed). The same nails and roofing sheets could be classified as 'relief' or 'development', involving distinct budget lines and grant processes.
6 Mary B. Anderson suggests that humanitarian intervention which is intended to provide relief to victims of war or to support the capacities of people to achieve economic and social development often ends up 'reinforcing or exacerbating conflict in the area where aid is given' (Mary B. Anderson, 'International Assistance and Conflict: an exploration of negative impacts', unpublished mimeo, p. 2.)
7 M. Adams and M. Bradbury (1994): *Conflict and Development: Organisational Adaptation in Conflict Situations*, Oxfam Discussion Paper 4, Oxford: Oxfam UK and Ireland, p. 36.
8 The Bradford University Department of Peace Studies is engaged in a collaborative research project on 'peace-building from below', aiming to identify its contradictions as well as its potential for long-term peace-building.
9 The extent to which women have kept alive their concerns about gender has often been under-estimated or simply ignored. A growing body of literature and testimony is now focusing on women's experiences of and perceptions of their role in conflict and war (e.g. Margaret Hooks (1991): *Guatemalan Women Speak*, London: CIIR; Emilie Smith-Ayala: *The Granddaughters of Ixmucané: Guatemalan Women Speak*, Toronto: Women's Press). That women experience war in ways that reflect gender-determined relations of power is beginning to be documented. The systematic rape of Bosnian women as part of a strategy of war caught the headlines, but rape is increasingly understood to be a strategy of war over the centuries. The extent to which women experience violence in their daily lives in contexts that the world has not yet recognised as a 'conflict' situation is also only recently being acknowledged. The 1995 *UNDP Human Development Report* (p. 7), for instance, reported that two-thirds of married women in countries as varied as Mexico and Papua New Guinea experience domestic violence, one woman in six worldwide is raped at least once in her lifetime, and over half of all murders of women in countries ranging from Brazil to Bangladesh are committed by husbands or partners.
10 The history of this process is only now being seriously researched. An important example is José Coronel: 'Violencia politica y respuestas campesinas en Huanta', in Carlos Ivan Degregori *et al* (1996): *Las Rondas Campesinas y la Derrota de Sendero Luminoso*, Lima: IEP Ediciones.
11 J. Galtung (1990): 'Cultural violence', *Journal of Peace Research*, Vol. 27, no. 3, pp. 291–305.
12 The concept of 'affirmative ethnicity' was raised at the Johannesburg Symposium, and emphasises the positive dimensions of

awareness of one's difference or specialness, such as a sense of self-worth. There is no implicit or inevitable translation of such affirmation into the denigration of others or into actual conflict with others. Why this happens and when has to be researched.

13 CEPAL (1990): *El Salvador: El Estado de la Pobreza y Lineamientos de Política para Afrontarla*, Santiago: CEPAL.

14 M. Thompson (1996): 'Empowerment and survival: humanitarian work in civil conflict' (part 1), *Development and Practice*, Vol. 6, No. 4, pp. 324–33.

15 The war did of course have a national dimension, particularly after *Sendero* had partially shifted its theatre to Lima. The jungle areas were also badly affected by the war, though the extent is less known, given the isolation of the region and the fact that *Sendero* still operates there.

16 The controversial role of the *rondas* is explored in Degregori *et al.*, *op. cit.* 1996.

17 See D. Pankhurst and J. Pearce, 'Engendering Conflict Analysis', in H. Afshar (ed): *Women and Empowerment*, London: Routledge (forthcoming).

18 The Human Rights Office of the Central American University (UCA) in El Salvador estimates that crime figures for 1995 included 24 murders and 500 robberies and muggings a day.

19 Geraldine McDonald conducted a series of interviews in 1993 for her PhD in the Dept of Peace Studies, University of Bradford, on 'A Comparative Analysis of Peace-building from "Below" in Colombia and El Salvador'. In assessing the impact of the popular sectors on the Salvadorean peace process, she records her interview with Salvador Samayoa of the FMLN: 'Salvador Samayoa explains that the FMLN argued for the establishment of a participatory mechanism for social sectors in the Geneva agreement as a means of improving the balance of forces in its favour. The "consultation" of so-called social sectors was in reality a means for both sides to gain legitimacy for their positions at the negotiating table. These organisations didn't exist autonomously. We knew that their entire social base was made up of FMLN supporters. They received political lines from us, we organised them, but we did it clandestinely ... this was a game we had to play and the government played it too ... Who accepted that the *Instituto de Libertad y Democracia* (Institute for Freedom and Democracy) was autonomous? Nobody did, and yet we still had to pretend that it was. In fact it was an organism of the right, of the ARENA party and it was at the service of the government' (G. McDonald's translation, from draft thesis chapter, 'Elite-led negotiations in El Salvador: perpetuating the legacy of exclusion', 1996 mimeo).

20 James Boyce (1995): 'External assistance and the peace process in El Salvador', *World Development*, 23, no. 12, p. 1201. The potential contradiction had been noticed for some time by international NGO workers with long experience in the country. Pauline Martin and Francisco Alvarez noted in 1992 that 'the National Reconstruction Plan of the Salvadorean government does not in our view inspire much hope that it has the will or the ability to go beyond party-political interests to build a broad-based consensus around rebuilding the country' (*Development in States of War*, Oxford: Oxfam 1996, p. 58).

21 The reconstruction processes taking place at local, municipal level are beginning to be documented. Even where there are FMLN mayors, however, many difficulties remain. See for example, M. Lungo (1995) 'FMLN mayors in 15 towns', *NACLA: Introduction to Hope: The Left in Local Politics*, Vol. XXIX no. 1, pp. 33–7.

22 David Dye *et al.* (1995): *Contesting Everything, Winning Nothing: The Search for Consensus in Nicaragua 1990–1995*, Cambridge, Massachusetts: Hemisphere Initiatives.

23 Interview with author in Lima, May 1996.

24 For instance, there is a debate between the 'modernisers' and the so-called *Andinistas*, who aim to preserve something of the indigenous skills and way of life. These comments are based on the author's discussions with local NGOs, academics, government officials, and the displaced and returned communities of the Ayacucho and Huancavelica areas in 1993 and 1996.

The author

Jenny Pearce currently lectures in the Department of Peace Studies at the University of Bradford. She was previously Director of the Latin America Bureau, and has published extensively on development and politics in Latin America.

87

Transition in El Salvador: a multi-layered process

Martha Thompson

Introduction

I have a snapshot in my memory of the main square of San Salvador on 16 January 1992 — the day the Farabundo Martí National Liberation Front (the FMLN) signed the Accords with the Salvadoran government that put the peace process in motion. The setting up of the joint decision-making body, CONPAZ, ended the eleven-year conflict that had claimed over 75,000 lives, displaced 500,000 people, and pushed almost one million more Salvadorans to flee the country.

That sunny January day, the square was jammed with people celebrating. Late in the afternoon, the FMLN directorate — all in jeans, white shirts, and red kerchiefs — mounted the platform to wild applause. Everyone lifted linked hands and sang the Spanish version of Beethoven's setting of the Ode to Joy. The happiness, the fountain of euphoria, the avalanche of hope seemed unstoppable. A Salvadoran friend, a worker in the repatriation movement, said, 'The impossible was becoming possible before everyone's eyes. These people who had fought so long in the mountains could now stand on a platform in the central plaza of the capital city, and share in our celebration of peace.'

Four years after that afternoon of hope, the right-wing ARENA party was in power, having been re-elected a scant 15 months after the Accords were signed. The FMLN, although a political party with representation in the General Assembly, had split; and its support base was shrinking. Violence was rampant. The government-appointed National Ombudsman for Human Rights had received multiple death threats. The NGOs and popular organisations were divided, with serious problems in their vision, their internal organisation, and their relationship with the grassroots.

The NGOs, popular organisations, and churches who had played such a vital role on behalf of those who were suffering the brunt of the war had seemed well placed to play a similar role in the physical reconstruction programme and in the process of social reconciliation. Grassroots groups and NGOs which had been decimated in the early 1980s had re-formed a popular movement in the midst of the war, even in the face of steadily increasing repression. They had a large base of support, and many had considerable experience in re-building the communities in the conflict zones, seeing grassroots empowerment as the key to social change. They also had widespread contacts and credibility among international funding agencies. Yet by 1993–94, many of the groups which had functioned so well in adversity now seemed to be losing their clarity and going through division and turmoil. It was not then clear why they were finding it so hard to adjust. No one had really foreseen that they might have such difficulty in making the transition from working in wartime to their new role in reconstruction and reconciliation. This paper explores some of the reasons for this phenomenon by looking at the problems and challenges suffered by the NGOs and popular movement in the transition from war to peace.[1]

The war in El Salvador was basically about the poor fighting for structural change, and the elite and the military resisting it. The FMLN wanted to win State power to bring about changes that would achieve justice for millions of dispossessed people. During the war, justice was more important than peace. When it seemed that this could not longer be achieved by armed struggle, the FMLN agreed to negotiate.

It could be argued that the war ended for four inter-linked reasons. Firstly, the FMLN, an armed group of 8,000, demonstrated enough military might to continue the war against an army of 40,000, despite the implications of the fall of the Berlin Wall and the Sandinistas' electoral loss in Nicaragua. Secondly, the new generation of Salvadoran elite, trained in US business schools and interested in regional commerce and international investment, saw that neither could happen while the country was at war. Thirdly, the 1989 urban offensive, when the FMLN took and held the northern belt of the capital, convinced many of the elite that the military could not win the war, and that a negotiated peace was their best solution. And it was clear that, with the end of the Cold War, the USA would no longer underwrite the government's war effort.

While the fighting has ended, we must remember that El Salvador has not swung like a pendulum between the state of being at war and the state of being a peaceful democracy. Rather, deep societal conflict has been forcibly suppressed until it erupts into armed warfare. The pattern is not that of a see-saw so much as a circle, which explains why social and political institutions have been geared to control and to preserve privilege, rather than to serve all citizens of El Salvador.

With the advantage of hindsight, this paper offers reflections on the obstacles facing NGOs in the transition from war to peace. First, it looks at the difficulties which were part of the broader framework of the Salvadoran peace process, but which affected the NGOs in particular: insufficient structural change through the Accords; getting drawn into electoral politics as the vehicle for change; the trap of a transition process that was too narrowly defined; and the impossibility of reconciliation without addressing the need for establishing collective memory, public responsibility, and justice. The second part covers the difficulties peculiar to NGOs and popular organisations in El Salvador: the difference between the skills and resources they had developed in war and those needed in peace; their problems in establishing their role in the national reconstruction plan; and the fact that they themselves consisted of people who were still wounded by loss, grief, fear, and anger from the war.

Inadequate structural change

Many Salvadoran organisations and NGOs believed that the war grew directly out of the historic legacy of massive inequality. They saw structural change as the only way to achieve a social equilibrium based on justice that could bring permanent peace to El Salvador. As the negotiations began, many believed that for the first time ever the balance of both internal and external forces could support a process that would lead to real structural changes.

The main points of the Accords, to be implemented under UN observation, were:

• a physical reconstruction process funded by the international community;
• a Human Rights Commission;
• a Truth Commission to collect and publish evidence about the human-rights abuses during the war;
• an institutional re-building process focused on the judicial and legal structures;
• a re-structuring of the military, including dismissal of the high-ranking officers;
• the disarmament of the FMLN combatants, and the dissolution of the Treasury Police and the National Guard (two security forces deeply implicated in human-rights violations);
• the gradual dissolution of the national police force, which was under military authority, and the establishment of a national civilian police;
• the re-integration of the FMLN into national political life as a political party.

These were important steps, but it cannot be over-emphasised that they were being taken in a country still in trauma from a cruel civil war. The war had indelibly marked those touched by it. Tens of thousands of civilians had been killed or disappeared, and thousands more tortured. Human-rights abuses were legion; of them, about 92 per cent were attributed by the Archbishopric's Office on Human Rights (*Tutela Legal*) to the military and para-military. The government's counter-insurgency strategy had sought to split Salvadoran society in two: those allied with the government, and those who questioned it in any way. To express criticism or dissent was to become immediately identified with the FMLN — that is, the subversive illegal forces — and so be subject to the kinds of military measure taken against them. There had, of course, never been a peaceful democracy in El Salvador. Rather, an uneasy *status quo* had been maintained by State and para-statal violence. This history of desperate inequality and State-sponsored brutality constituted a daunting challenge to a nation embarking on post-war reconstruction and reconciliation.

In a country with a population of five million, living on 800,000 sq km, with no major natural resources besides land, the elite had traditionally concentrated as much as possible into their own hands. They owned most of the land and controlled the financial institutions. They built the country's infrastructure to support their own export-oriented agriculture, relying on a pool of landless people to serve as cheap casual labour. There had been formal political structures such as parties and elections, but the government was used to legitimise the power of the wealthy. The major social and political institutions were extremely weak and controlled by the oligarchy. This is critical, since it is impossible to 're-build civil society' without some political space.

In addition, the war had so structured reality that the difference between supporting the government and even sympathising, however remotely, with the FMLN, was the cost of one's life. In December 1991, a person in the urban slums could be hauled off to jail and beaten just for saying that the FMLN were not subversive terrorists, let alone for having any connection with them. In January 1992, the FMLN were honoured guests at embassy receptions, addressed the peace celebrations, were interviewed on television, and talked of opening an office. Such a complete reversal from the weeks before, when survival meant taking the most extreme forms of security measure, caught people off balance. Looking back, it seems that the immediate changes with the end of the war were *so* visible and *so* powerfully symbolic that we believed they meant that deeper change was possible. To see the FMLN leap instantaneously from being cast as 'illegal terrorists' to being a legitimate force within the Peace Accords seemed miraculous.

Unfortunately, the miracle was only one of perception. The FMLN rode around in jeeps, met with ambassadors, and worked on CONPAZ — but initially had no office, few funds, and almost no infrastructure. They needed everything, down to the money to buy desks. In these conditions, the FMLN had to negotiate with a government which had all the resources of the State at its disposal. The peace process ended the organised armed conflict. There was some success in restructuring the military. But the power of the tiny minority

remained intact, while the reconstruction plan was used to implement a neo-liberal strategy. Access to power by the poor majority was not radically improved, the economic institutions were not transformed, and the causes of conflict were neither addressed nor resolved. The government still controlled the media and the institutions of justice. And, although they moved freely about the country, several FMLN leaders were killed in 1992–93. The greater the threat they were perceived to pose to the right wing, the more danger they were in.

It took some time to gauge the real importance of symbolic change, in part because we were still measuring the achievements of peace with the yardstick of war. Then, the three-hour drive to a town in the conflict-ridden north of the country meant running a gauntlet of military checkpoints. This made the distance more psychological than physical. After the Accords, we just drove through. It felt extremely disorienting, as if we had magically compressed a journey of ten hours into three. Living in a prolonged war makes one forget that it is an extraordinary situation. One forgets that peace, at best, brings one back to the norm. Making that step back to the ordinary does not necessarily mean a major step towards structural change. It is no more than a step towards the former definition of equilibrium. Hence the yardstick used to measure reality in war was an obstacle to understanding the complexity of peace.

The stress on electoral politics

The Peace Accords provided the framework for the FMLN to enter electoral politics, and emphasised that winning power through elections was a means to reconcile the enormous divisions between different groups in the country. This overlooked the fact that the route to real power in El Salvador was not traditionally through the ballot box, but through the oligarchy's control of the country's economic resources, and through them the legal and judicial institutions, the banks, the media, and the military. Msgr Urioste put it well when he said, 'Democracy is a symphony, of which the elections are just one note'. The FMLN leadership decided to try for that one note, and to win the Presidency in the national elections to be held one year after the peace negotiations. They concentrated all their post-war efforts on mobilising support for this goal, rather than on building up a participatory political party.

The popular movement was drawn into that effort, in the belief that the FMLN could bring about widespread change by gaining control of the government in this way. Their work and resources became increasingly focused on this campaign, which had a grave impact on their ability to define their own new role in peace-time, just at the time when they, as well as the churches and NGOs that supported them, needed to embark on a process of reflection, assess what advantages the Accords offered, what still had to be fought for, and then re-define how to pursue that struggle during the peace process. At that crucial moment, the only alternative that they saw or accepted was that the best way forward was to work for the election of the FMLN.

The FMLN itself faced the enormous task of trying to change a politico-military institution into a political party, identify allies, and build widespread support in a country where only very recently to support them was to risk one's life. Building a political party under those conditions was difficult, and was compounded by the fact that people's political experience at the grassroots had been forged in the fires of war and repression. People in the popular movement had learned to analyse the *status quo* and to understand their exclusion. They had learned to count the cost of mobilising against repression and to find creative ways to express opposition to an intolerant government. If a popular organisation ever made public its criticism of the government, that brought it into immediate and violent conflict with the authorities, and all its members' energies had to be put into resistance and survival. This school did not teach people to develop and defend political proposals, build alliances, and work through the political system.

For the popular movement to make the transition from such harsh political experience to building a party in peace-time, and learning the advantages and limitations of electoral democracy, was the work of years, not months. The FMLN felt an urgent need to move into electoral politics; but, with so little experience in that arena, they carried over much of their military methodology into their political work. This further delayed the process of political change that the popular movement needed to experience in order to re-define their own role.

Reconciliation without justice

Two years after the Accords, the popular movement and NGOs began to see that peace had not brought justice. The Truth Commission had recorded violations of human rights, but its members were so threatened by right-wing forces that its report had to be written abroad. All conflicting parties had agreed that the report would not mention names, so the guilty would not be tried. The concept of reconciliation in the peace process was thus very shallow. It did not provide for the need for public recognition of the human-rights abuses, and acknowledgement by those responsible — far less any legal process to bring them to justice.

This was very painful for the victims of such abuses. Many felt that those responsible for the killings and disappearances had wanted to wipe their victims off the map. Remembering them was a way to fight against amnesia. Forgetting them was to complete the work of the murder, and be an accomplice in erasing their memory. During the war, they had hoped that peace would bring justice. People who had lost loved ones wanted public and official acknow-ledgement of what had happened, so that this would form part of a collective memory and national history. Organised groups who struggled through the war, people who were tortured, or had lost friends and relations, were not asking for vengeance or for compensation. They were asking for acknowledgment as a step towards reconciliation. Only with that could the past be put to rest and reconciliation begin.

However, there were diametrically opposed versions of the reality of the war. The elite would not acknowledge the extent of the human-rights abuses; the military and para-military would not acknowledge that their actions were crimes; and the FMLN did not have to acknowledge any guilt. The fact that neither side in the negotiations recognised the need for a common version of events created a huge obstacle to reconciliation: people just positioned themselves around their private truth of the war. If a society refuses collective responsibility and does not undertake some form of justice for the victims of large-scale human-rights violations, it cannot build a reconciliation process. Rather, it fosters fragmentation.

91

The transition trap

'Transition' was the buzzword in El Salvador right after the Peace Accords. It was as if transition was a train that was leaving the station, and the government and the United Nations had said, 'This is the only transition train. Jump on or you will miss it, and be left out of the process.' Once the NGOs, the popular movement, and even the various international agencies jumped on, they began to see that there were not many seats for them, and that perhaps this particular train wasn't going in the direction they wanted to go in. But they continued nevertheless to believe for a long time that it was the only train.

Transition happens at many different levels and with many different rhythms. It is not one linear process, but a complex series of processes, whose timing can both conflict and coincide with each other. Transition must happen within people's hearts and minds, within the practice of institutions, within the move from military considerations to political ones, and within the larger political system. Why should NGOs let funders and the UN decide which part of this enormous, complex, and dynamic process is to be defined as *the* transition? Why should donors think that they can sit at their desks and decide how many months or years they will allot to transition, and what they will recognise it to be? Why do NGOs accept the thinking that transition can be measured in dollars and cents, and can be purchased as a formula to be applied with minor local adjustments?

As soon as the Accords were signed, everything accelerated; everything had to be done by the next day. If the NGOs wanted to be part of the transition, they had to get a proposal in right away. Sometimes it seemed as though while one was attending a meeting in one part of the city, there was an even more urgent one starting somewhere else. There was not time to consult with the grassroots: it had to be done now or you would miss out on *the transition*. The implication was that if NGOs did not have a proposal at any given negotiating table, they would not get a share of resources, and the process would pass them by. Many of us missed the basic truth that transition does not happen because the international community, the FMLN, and the government decide on and fund a programme for it.

After the Accords, NGOs and popular organisations needed to reflect on how they had functioned in the past and what had to change in the post-war era. They needed to re-define their relationship with the FMLN, the government, and the international community. They also needed to look at popular forms of social organisation and reflect together on the best way to deal with the new situation. But no one felt there was time to do that. Looking back, I feel that the most basic fact about transition from conflict to a negotiated peace appears so obvious that it is easy to miss it: peace is completely different from war. This was hugely significant for those organisations which were formed out of the needs and exigencies of war; and it was far from apparent how immediate and total the change really was.

Rules change: but who has the new rulebook?

An NGO colleague said to me in June 1992, 'You know, I am very clear-headed under fire. That was important when we were working in the conflict zones during the war, but now it's completely irrelevant.' No one in the Salvadoran or international NGO community suspected that signing the Accords would thrust us so quickly on to a new playing board where our skills and tools were of so little use, and the unfamiliar new ones were of paramount importance.

The Salvadoran NGOs had experience in responding to emergencies, and administering projects in the conflict zones, even where the necessary infrastructure was largely destroyed. They developed flexibility and ingenuity in working in areas to which the military blockaded the entry of supplies and consistently harassed beneficiary communities and the NGOs working with them. The repression in 1988–1990 was so intense that over a five-week period some 40 people connected with humanitarian work had been detained by the military, half of them tortured. Political trust and a common analysis were as essential as the security strategies that ensured survival. For those who had lost loved ones or had suffered injustice, their work was a way to resist, to remember and keep faith with the dead, to change a system which they saw as wrong. It gave a transcendence to everyday work.

The world in which these NGOs and popular organisations moved during the war was one in which the structures were rigid but clearly understood, making for great cohesion. The shared analysis provided a map which was easily recognised by others doing the same kind of thing. Sharing beliefs and risks gave people an invisible bond that was a source of strength. Survival and resistance shaped the tools and strategies developed in response to the war.

After January 1992, NGOs needed different tools and strategies from one day to the next. Technical skills became much more important. NGOs were supposed to move from emergency responses into comprehensive development work, almost overnight. Funders wanted complex project proposals based on economic growth and a neo-liberal model, different in both conception and philosophy from the communal, economic survival projects that had been developed in the conflict zones during the war. NGOs had been accustomed to operating in a very polarised world, never dealing with the government, but supporting people's parallel education and health services. Now they had to learn how to deal with the government, and how to construct tactical and strategic alliances for their goals. They had to deal with a range of people, including major new donors, with whom they did not share a common analysis or philosophy.

No role for NGOs in the reconstruction process

In El Salvador, physical reconstruction was an important part of the peace process. After the scorched-earth campaigns, the bombing, and the economic sabotage, people needed houses, roads, bridges, electricity, and infrastructure. Control over the reconstruction plan was crucial. In the weeks following the Accords, both the government and the FMLN were roughing out such plans. The government's plans focused on economic viability and sustainable development, distributing reconstruction funds through municipalities (one year before national elections), and repairing economic sabotage. The NGOs they consulted had worked closely with government programmes and civic–military programmes for the displaced; many were conservative church groups, many were funded by USAID. The FMLN worked with the popular movement and NGOs who had worked in the conflict zones, and its ideas were based on the kind of work carried out during the war. The different aims of these reconstruction plans were yet another reflection of how polarised society still was.

The donors pressed for one reconstruction plan under one national secretariat, but did not make their support conditional on these being bi-partisan. Negotiations took place between the government and the FMLN, with no NGO participation. The FMLN agreed to let the government control both the plan and the secretariat, in exchange for a promise that the NGOs working in the conflict zones would have access to some of the funds, most of which would be distributed through the municipalities. This decision effectively lost the NGOs any real role in either framing or implementing the reconstruction plan. In part, it was a problem of protagonism: the FMLN negotiating with the government. The FMLN was convinced that if it won the elections in 1993, all would be put right. So the reconstruction plan went ahead with no challenge from the NGO community or the FMLN, neither of whom sufficiently appreciated the implications.

Since reconstruction funds were channelled through the municipalities, the potential to use them for political gain was enormous. In the war zones, people had built their own service structures, funded by NGOs and aid agencies. These came into direct conflict with government service-providers, who saw them as former guerrilla supporters. The FMLN, the popular movement, and the NGOs never formed a common policy on how to deal with the question of government services versus those of the popular structures; how to give the latter resources and recognition, but without allowing the government to abdicate its responsibilities or de facto to privatise basic services. In many former conflict areas, where fledgling economic structures had been built on the basis of communal provision of services, prosperous townspeople who before the war had monopolised resources and trade began to return, challenging the communities, undercutting their economic structures, and trying to install old patterns of domination under the rubric of reconstruction. What this all added up to was a crisis of vision on the part of the NGOs and the popular movement.

Violence: the personal cost

The failure of the peace process to deal with the legacy of human-rights abuses had a direct effect on the people who had worked in the NGOs and the popular organisations. Those people had lost family and friends, some had been tortured, they had endured years of tension and harassment, seen terrible things, heard of many atrocities. These people had been, and were still, wounded by the war. Many had long had to suppress their own grief and fear. Their work had been a way of reaffirming their beliefs and their dignity as human beings.

After the war, they had no access to help in dealing with what they had survived, or with their own damaged selves. There was little acknowledgement of what happened. But if people and organisations don't deal with it, they get stuck. The surge of hope, energy, and creativity after the war was palpable. But people failed to deal with the underlying issues. They did not say, 'OK, the power reality is unchanged, so we must re-define our struggle.' Instead, they said, 'The terms of the game have changed, and we need to learn new rules and a new analysis.' Many now feel that injustice has been the price of peace. We all know that peace built on injustice is unsustainable. To change this, we need new ways and strategies of working. Reconciliation too must be based on a very frank look at ourselves, our roles, where we are, and where we need to be.

Notes

1 For an account of the background to the war, and of the effects of living and working in a situation of chronic political violence, see my two-part article 'Empowerment and survival: humanitarian work in civil conflict', *Development in Practice* 6/4 and 7/1.

The author

Martha Thompson worked in Central America for various international and local NGOs from 1981 to 1995. She is currently the Oxfam Canada Programme Development Officer for Cuba and the Eastern Caribbean, based in Havana.

Rwanda: beyond 'ethnic conflict'

Anne Mackintosh

A shared vision, a global cause

Let me begin with a personal reminiscence. Like many others, I vividly recall the day of Nelson Mandela's release from prison in February 1990. It was the eve of my departure to Rwanda for a three-month assignment for Oxfam. I was at home watching television. I still recall the excited anticipation of Mandela's walk to freedom, the overwhelming sense of achievement (utterly insignificant though my own part in the South African struggle had been), the tears of jubilation when he finally appeared. 'He did it! He did it!' I cried, punching the air. I well know that my feelings were heightened by apprehension of the challenges I anticipated facing in Rwanda, though these were as nothing compared with what I was actually to experience. Nevertheless, I was conscious of sharing an extraordinary moment with millions of sympathisers around the world.

With hindsight, I wonder whether this was the last time the world community united effectively behind a just cause (though one should not overrate or idealise the role of external actors in bringing about the end of apartheid). However, it is no exaggeration to say that the Anti-Apartheid Movement, and the campaign to release Nelson Mandela from prison, inspired a generation. There was almost a sense of loss when the goal was achieved: what would replace the rallying cry of 'Free Nelson Mandela!'? While this sentiment could rightly be regarded as self-indulgent (and as demonstrating the failure to understand that solidarity was needed as never before — after all, the hard part was just beginning), it also reflected something not so trivial: the loss of a shared vision, a universal aspiration uniting people across national and continental boundaries. I shall return to this later.

The following day, I departed for Rwanda. I had no idea that this would eventually lead to my being drawn into one of the greatest cataclysms of the twentieth century. It was partly as a consequence of this assignment that I later became Oxfam's Regional Representative in Kigali. I took up this post in June 1991, just over six months after the outbreak of fighting between the Rwandan government army and the Rwandan Patriotic Front (RPF). The war had by then reached a semi-quiescent phase. However, over the next three years, violence gradually escalated until, on 6 April 1994, President Habyarimana's plane was shot down, triggering the genocide with which we are now so dreadfully familiar.

Paradoxically, while my experience in Rwanda inflicted terrible wounds — even for one who escaped so lightly — it was a tremendous learning experience. Through the crisis, I was exposed to people, ideas, and challenges I would never otherwise have encountered, and I have undoubtedly grown as a result. It also brought me a certain minor prominence, such as appearing on CNN and publishing papers such as this one! I have mixed feelings about this: the Rwanda crisis has provided career opportunities for many, and generated material for Master's degrees, doctorates, and academic conferences for decades to come. It has led to a proliferation of relief NGOs, electronic information networks, and conflict-resolution initiatives — a bandwagon of which I am now a small part. Billions of dollars continue to be spent on the relief effort, yet the international community completely failed to act before the genocide. Why?

In this paper, I shall explore some of the reasons for the failure to act, which are rooted both in long-distant history and in the dynamics of international politics in the contemporary world. I shall also look critically at the widely accepted explanations of the genocide and its aftermath as 'simply tribal fighting'. I conclude with some reflections on the nature of our international responsibilities in the modern world, and on the complex challenges posed by 'reconciliation' in the wake of such an extreme experience as genocide.

A failure to act: indifference, indecision, and incomprehension

The short answer to the question why the international community failed to take decisive and timely action is that Rwanda did not matter. A tiny, landlocked country with few natural resources, it was considered strategically and materially unimportant. Unlike Kuwait, it does not produce oil and was of no consequence to the influential members of the UN Security Council, with the exception of France.

The French government played a baffling role in relation to the former Rwandan regime, attributable in part to its preoccupation with retaining its influence on the world stage by fostering the community of French-speaking nations known as *la francophonie*. Hence the previous French-speaking régime in Rwanda received unwavering support, despite mounting evidence of human-rights abuses instigated largely by Habyarimana's inner circle; and hence the hostility and suspicion with which the current government — mainly English-speaking — is regarded by the French. However, as I write, even the French government is announcing its intention no longer to intervene politically or militarily in the affairs of its former colonies in Africa, preferring to support 'African solutions to African problems' — the euphemism for disengagement now current in international circles.

Another reason for the international community's failure to respond to danger signals in Rwanda was the 'Somalia factor'. The UN's intervention in Somalia had been so disastrous, and the humiliation of US troops in particular so profound, that the Security Council hesitated to repeat any such exercise.

Coupled with this reticence was the increasingly prevalent analysis — epitomised by Robert Kaplan's paper 'The Coming Anarchy' — of conflicts in Africa as controlled by dark, unpredictable forces, impenetrable to out-siders, and impossible to influence. Kaplan's paper was circulated to all US embassies early in 1994, as required reading for US diplomats. The following quotation illustrates Kaplan's drift:

Sierra Leone is a microcosm of what is occurring ... throughout West Africa and much of the underdeveloped world: the withering away of central governments, the rise of tribal and regional domains, the unchecked spread of disease, and the growing pervasiveness of war. (Kaplan, 1994).

The belief that several African countries were threatened by 'an anarchic implosion of criminal violence' reinforced the tendency of powerful Northern nations, since the end of the Cold War, to pull back from meaningful engagement with Africa. Detachment can more easily be justified if African States are perceived to be disintegrating along internal fault-lines. The impact of external factors, such as structural adjustment policies and international terms of trade, appears to have been conveniently forgotten.

Yet, nearly two years before the genocide, Oxfam UK and Ireland commissioned a report on the question of Rwandese refugees and migrants in the Great Lakes region. The author had warned that 'the ... region remains potentially extremely unstable, and ... unless serious work is done on all fronts to tackle the economic, social and political problems of the region ... [t]he potential for further explosive conflict is considerable' (Wiles, 1992). He made a series of recommendations, emphasising the need for a concerted approach, arguing that regional co-operation and development offered the only long-term solutions.

One year later, Oxfam's former Representative in Kigali wrote:

Rwandan society is now more violently divided against itself than at any time since Independence. The war has done incalculable damage to the economy and environment, and much needs to be done to encourage people to work together to heal the wounds of sectarian hatred ... Rwanda stands on the brink of an uncharted abyss of anarchy and violence, and there are all too many historical, ethnic, economic, and political pressures that are likely to push it over the edge. (Waller, 1993)

However, despite the unequivocal nature of such warnings and the urgency of their tone, it seemed impossible to push Rwanda higher up anyone's agenda even within the aid-agency world — whether in terms of programme funding or as a focus for lobbying and communications work. One reason for Rwanda's marginalisation was that, as a former Belgian colony and part of *la francophonie*, it was virtually unknown in the English-speaking world. Many agency staff were simply unable to read reports about or emerging from the region.

Then, in February 1994, just as the situation was becoming more grave, the 'South Africa factor' supervened. Elections were forthcoming; given South Africa's place in the British consciousness, there was real potential to interest Members of Parliament and the general public. In addition, Oxfam (like many other aid agencies) had a long-term commitment to advocacy on South Africa. When the genocide began, many of the sympathetic parliamentarians whom we would have lobbied, or serious journalists who might otherwise have reported on Rwanda, were in South Africa. As a result, the crisis was not covered until the genocide was virtually over, by which time it had been overshadowed by a refugee crisis as the RPF gained control of the country, prompting the mass exodus of mainly Hutu refugees (including the former army and militias) into Tanzania, Burundi, and eastern Zaïre. Coming in at this late stage helped to create a distorted view of what the crisis was about. Genocide and the refugee crisis became conflated. Refugees were *not*, as some journalists and aid agencies stated, 'fleeing the genocide': they fled with those who had perpetrated it, fearing revenge.

Long-term neglect, instant expertise

Suddenly, everyone was there: a plethora of aid agencies, some of them newly created, and over 500 journalists were operating out of Goma (the principal city of North-Kivu in eastern Zaïre) at one point. Yet, only a year before, Oxfam had even had to pay journalists to visit Rwanda and Kivu, and help them place their stories, simply to ensure some serious coverage in the British media of the region and its latent conflicts.

It appeared that, having failed to act on the political front, governments were anxious to raise their profile in the relief effort. 'In effect, humanitarian action substituted for political action' (Joint Evaluation, 1996). In lieu of meaningful involvement at an earlier stage,

donors were now running after a piece of the action, eager to fund high-profile but relatively short-term interventions, in order to conceal a 'policy vacuum'.

Describing and shaping events

As I have already mentioned, there was so little interest in the Great Lakes region before the events of 1994 that Oxfam had facilitated visits by selected journalists, in order to raise the profile of the area, and to generate international concern about what was taking place. However, 'foreign news' stories in the major national media are strictly rationed; even the BBC World Service will rarely feature more than one African story during a half-hour news programme. When a foreign news story *is* featured on domestic radio or television, it is generally because there is a crisis of some kind. But there is seldom much exploration of the background, even in a situation given as much exposure as the war in former Yugoslavia. For parts of the world considered to be of less importance, all too often there is just a one-off report which is never followed up.

In the wake of the Goma experience, NGOs have been criticised for competing for favourable media exposure (for months, one agency or another featured on every news bulletin), and unduly influencing reporters by facilitating and even financing their visits. With a plethora of new organisations now in the lists, profile is all, and accentuating the positive becomes a 'must'. This is particularly important for those agencies that depend heavily on official funding, since governments want to support organisations that are doing highly visible work. Even an agency like Oxfam, which draws most of its long-term funding from the British general public, is far from immune to such pressures.

Jostling for media coverage seems to go hand-in-hand with the development of a 'contract culture' in the aid world — where NGOs compete to be contracted by donors, UN agencies, and local government bodies to carry out relief and long-term welfare work. This may be a way of identifying those who are efficient or, rather, those who best meet the criteria of funders as regards reporting and accounting, for example. The disturbing corollary, however, is that NGOs' accountability is perceived more in relation to their donors than to the supposed beneficiaries of their aid programmes.

The Goma experience was in many ways a watershed for relief agencies which will have implications for their work elsewhere in future. The proliferation in the number of relief NGOs, their sudden prominence (not only in the media, but in terms of access to decision-makers), their increasing dependence on money channelled through UN agencies and competition for funds in general have all resulted in pressure for efforts to regulate NGOs. There is still little such regulation beyond a voluntary code of conduct that was drawn up in the wake of the Rwanda crisis. Nevertheless, the code is being developed into a set of minimum standards which are expected to be widely adopted, and the likelihood is that NGOs will have to demonstrate greater 'professionalism', and enjoy less individual autonomy, in future.

I am referring here to *international* NGOs, local NGOs having been almost completely marginalised during the crisis. The reasons for this are not only that few of the international actors who became involved in the emergency response had any prior experience in the region, still less knowledge of, or contact with, local organisations. Despite their reputation within the region as a substantive force in civil society, and notwithstanding the courage of individual staff in attempting to combat ethnic hatred, Rwandan NGOs as a body — along with every other institution in the country, including the Churches — completely failed to provide any moral leadership or counterforce to the violence, prior to or during the genocide. Following the epic exodus of refugees into neighbouring countries, a situation arose where the staff of Rwandan NGOs who had ended up on the Zaïrean side of the border fought for legitimacy — and control of their organisations' resources — with other (often more junior) staff who remained inside the country. The NGO staff in exile were regarded by many as apologists for the perpetrators of genocide and inadmissible as 'partners', while, on the other hand, some international organisations made the egregious mistake of employing known killers.

A critical assessment of the performance of aid agencies and NGOs is necessary, especially in light of some of the more shameful spectacles witnessed during the Rwanda crisis. However, to focus primarily on the 'humanitarians' is, in my opinion, to pick the wrong target. It isn't the firefighters who should be receiving most of the attention, but those who allowed the fire to ignite, or, worse, fanned the flames.

The relief–development 'continuum'

It has become very obvious to those working in situations of conflict, though not always to donor agencies, that conflicts do not follow a linear pattern: from crisis through rehabilitation and back to 'normal'. Conflicts fluctuate in intensity or may become chronic: aid agencies and donors need, therefore, to think more in terms of permanent emergency. In many situations (as in Liberia), perpetuating war is how the fighters and their entourage sustain themselves; it is not in their interests to win. It becomes increasingly implausible to see emergencies as temporary interruptions to a smooth process of linear development. More positively, it is crucial to recognise that development can take place, and sometimes be precipitated, in the midst of crisis.

However, even agencies who recognise the inappropriateness of regarding 'relief' and 'development' as separate phenomena perpetuate this false dichotomy, through resourcing long-term and emergency programmes in different ways and having them managed by different departments and staff. This often leads to unhelpful tensions and rivalry. Linked with this is a widespread rejection of 'developmentalism'. Given the evident failure of development programmes to realise the aim of convergence, i.e. an ideal world where everyone is on the same material level, the cry goes up that 'development is dead'. This is equated in some quarters with rejection of everything that long-term programmes have ever aimed to do. In my view, this is a false argument. Recognition of the need to reassert the 'redistributive function of aid' (Macrae, 1997) does not in any way imply that we should disregard the value of long-term process work.

The legacy of the past: can lessons be learned?

The case of Burundi is being handled rather differently by the international community, thanks to greater awareness of the dangerous nature of the situation. No-one wants 'another Rwanda', and some investment in preempting it has been made by the UN and EU, as well as by what Jenny Pearce calls the 'peaceologists' — through, for instance, facilitating visits to South Africa by Burundian politicians. Journalists have tended to blow hot and cold on Burundi: they are waiting for the country to explode, and it hasn't — or so they seem to think. Only the handful of those who covered Burundi before 1994 retain any interest.

However, the current concern over Burundi in important and influential circles hardly constitutes conflict-*prevention*: the explosion has already happened, but few international actors took any notice at the time. It was back in October 1993 that Burundi's first democratically elected leader, President Ndadaye, was assassinated by the army, after barely four months in power. Many saw in this the end of hopes for peace in the region. Up to 100,000 Burundians, both Hutu and Tutsi, are believed to have died in the violence that followed, and 700,000 refugees fled into Tanzania, Zaïre, and Rwanda. Humanitarian agencies, already struggling to respond to the needs of people displaced by civil conflict in Rwanda and Kivu, opened up operations on yet another front. Meanwhile, intransigents in the Rwandan political establishment used the crisis to justify further retreat from the peace accords signed with the RPF a few months before: after all, how could anyone trust the Tutsis now?

Yet the international community scarcely blinked, despite the elections having been hailed as a 'model of democratisation' for Africa — which they were not. The elections were too rushed, and they were not preceded, or followed, by anything like the kind of process South Africa has been through. President Ndadaye was no Nelson Mandela, but he was nevertheless a sincere moderate. When an earlier coup attempt failed, it seemed as if accommodation could work. The assassination brought a crushing sense of betrayal, a destruction of hope not only for Burundians but for all those working towards non-violent resolution of conflict in the region.

The impact of events in Burundi on the Rwanda peace process was significant. The former régime could argue that Tutsis were not to be trusted, while the feebleness of the international community's response served to reinforce the 'culture of impunity' in both Rwanda and Burundi — where, for decades,

massacres and atrocities have gone unacknowledged with no-one held to account, thus beginning the next cycle of violence. As a result, the International Tribunal investigating the Rwandan genocide commands little respect: the international community failed to prevent the genocide but is now, it seems, setting itself up to try the perpetrators. Is this mere hypocrisy? In my view, while the UN is flawed, it remains the best mechanism we have. But it requires the whole-hearted commitment of its member States: the Tribunal has been further hampered by delays in setting it up, difficulty in obtaining funding and, more recently, accusations of mismanagement.

In any event, the Tribunal cannot deal with every case, but only the main architects of the genocide. Of these, only six suspects have been detained so far, and none has yet been prosecuted. Meanwhile, the new Rwandan administration is attempting to bring to justice the huge number of minor players, as well as some of the more significant actors. Some 100,000 Rwandans suspected of having participated in the genocide are being held in prisons with the capacity for barely one quarter as many, and thousands have already died of disease. The Rwandan judicial system was effectively destroyed in the genocide, but appeals for international assistance to rebuild it are being met only after considerable delay. The enormity of the task of dealing with so many suspects, while simultaneously trying to rebuild the entire system, presents the relatively inexperienced new administration with an unprecedented challenge.

Ironically, while the death sentence is ruled out for those being tried by the international Tribunal, it is admissible under Rwandan law — so that those who masterminded the genocide are likely to receive lighter punishment than lesser suspects. Nevertheless, however unsatisfactory this dual process, until there has been some form of *public* recognition of what happened, and punishment for those principally responsible, there can be no 'reconciliation' in either country.

Ethnicity, poverty, and political power-games

In both Rwanda and Burundi, ethnic division has long been fostered by the 'culture of impunity' referred to above, along with the politics of 'winner-takes-all'. With the formation of a transitional government in Rwanda in early 1992, and in anticipation of negotiations with the RPF, political activity intensified. A pattern began to emerge in which, whenever negotiations with the RPF became particularly strained or delicate, 'spontaneous' inter-ethnic violence would suddenly break out somewhere in the country.

The killings in north-west Rwanda which provoked the RPF advance early in 1993 erupted within hours of the departure of an international commission investigating abuses of human rights. The commission's report provided evidence that government authorities were involved in the systematic killings of Tutsi and political opponents; their findings were supported by the UN Special Rapporteur on extrajudicial executions, who visited the country a few months later. However, neither the UN human-rights bodies nor the donor countries with most influence on the Rwandan government responded to these reports in any meaningful way.

Scarcely had the renewed fighting in Rwanda abated when conflict erupted in the North Kivu province of neighbouring Zaïre, chiefly between the Hunde people and the Banyarwanda: ethnic Rwandans who are a mixture of refugees, economic migrants, descendants of people resettled by the Belgian colonialists, and those who affirm that their ancestors have always lived in Kivu and that only colonial manipulation of national boundaries has separated them from their fellow countrymen. Around 250,000 people were displaced and up to 10,000 killed during the violence, in which hundreds of villages were burned down, one after the other, in tit-for-tat sabotage attacks. At issue was the entitlement of the Banyarwanda to Zaïrean citizenship, strongly contested by the Hunde, who dominate the traditional authority structures but are outnumbered by the Banyarwanda in many areas of the province.

A few months later, a peace agreement was signed in Arusha between the government of Rwanda and the RPF, after which it was hoped that there would be relative stability. The agreement was a compromise, ungraciously reached, but a start. However, it rapidly became clear that at least one of the signatories (President Habyarimana) had no intention of implementing the accords. Every conceivable pretext was used to delay the installation of a new, broad-based transitional government, which had been expanded to include the RPF. One reason adduced was the failure of UNAMIR (the UN force tasked with overseeing implementation of the accords) to materialise within 35 days of the agreement being signed, which everyone knew to be impossible. (UN troops eventually began to arrive in November 1993.)

In January 1994, General Roméo Dallaire, the Canadian commander of UNAMIR, faxed the UN Security Council with detailed evidence of preparations for the large-scale, organised massacre of Tutsis. Although the fax was seen by senior UN officials, it was not circulated to members of the Security Council. Later, he requested permission to search for arms caches (which was beyond the existing mandate of the UN force) and appealed for reinforcements to bring UNAMIR up to its agreed strength. It appears that UN officials judged these requests so unlikely to succeed that they omitted to convey them to the Security Council.

The following month, there was what with hindsight could be seen as a 'dress rehearsal' for the massacres to come: politicians from two rival parties were murdered amid mutual accusations, and hundreds of Tutsi were killed in revenge attacks in Kigali. The killings ceased after barely 48 hours — an indication that they were far from spontaneous, and that the violence could be switched on and off at will by those in control. I was away at this time, and returned to Kigali at the end of February feeling sick with apprehension. Before doing so, I had told senior managers in Oxfam that the war was certain to start again soon and that the consequences would be very serious. I did not imagine what would precipitate the resumption of fighting between the two armies, nor how monstrous this would be.

Nevertheless, it is critical to counter the conventional notions of 'tribal fighting' so prevalent in the initial reporting of the Rwanda crisis. To explain away the genocide in terms of atavistic, irrational hatreds — typical of conflict on the 'dark continent' of Africa — is to avoid looking at some of the root causes, to distance ourselves from the conflict, and to justify our impotence in the face of it. At the same time, it is now clear that, whether or not it was truly so before, 'ethnicity' has *become* a key factor. However specious the arguments on which it is based, playing the ethnic card has succeeded: the reality is that divisions between Hutu and

Tutsi have now been dug deeper, and wounds have been inflicted which will take decades to heal.

'Ethnic conflict' remains, however, a profoundly inadequate description of what happened in Rwanda in 1994. Regional, economic, and party-political divisions were also part of the dynamic. And there does not in any case seem to be a consensus as to what exactly is meant by 'ethnicity'. Is 'ethnic group' just another word for 'tribe', but one which is deemed more politically correct?

In fact, many anthropologists contest the notion that Hutu and Tutsi can be considered distinct groups. They share a common language and traditions; there has never been segregation of territory between them (though the north-west region is Hutu-dominated); and they have inter-married for centuries. The distinction, it is argued, is more one of class or caste, but has been fossilised largely as a result of colonial influence. Moreover, unlike many African countries where the re-drawing of national boundaries by the European colonial powers brought together very disparate groups within the same nation-State (such as Sudan), Rwanda is no such artificial creation.

On the other hand, according to a widely accepted version of history, what is now Rwandan territory was originally inhabited by pygmoid, forest-dwelling hunter-gatherers known as the Twa, who now form a minute proportion of the population. Between the tenth and fifteenth centuries, the Twa were increasingly displaced by Bantu-speaking peoples migrating northwards; these were predominantly settled agriculturalists, supposedly the ancestors of the Hutu. The Tutsi, by contrast, are said to have originated in the Horn of Africa: a Nilotic people, tall and fine-featured, who migrated south with their large cattle herds, from the fifteenth century onwards. Through a mixture of conquest and control of access to land and cattle-wealth, they gradually achieved dominance over the other two groups.

Whichever theory you pick, it is clear that by the late nineteenth century the Tutsi were at the top of the social hierarchy, with Hutu and Twa at the bottom, though there was considerable mobility between Hutu and Tutsi at middle-ranking levels.

Both the Germans, who controlled the territory as part of German East Africa before the First World War, and the Belgians, who were subsequently mandated to administer it (first by the League of Nations, then by the UN), elected to govern indirectly through the indigenous (Tutsi) monarchy. This was partly because of the so-called Hamitic thesis, according to which 'everything of value in Africa had been introduced by the Hamites, supposedly a branch of the Caucasian race' (Joint Evaluation, referring to Sanders 1969). In Rwanda, it was the Tutsi who were identified with the Hamites, and with whom the colonialists felt a greater sense of affinity. As 'natural leaders', they were given favoured access to education, and a virtual monopoly of political and administrative power. When the Belgians introduced identity cards in 1933, all Rwandans were classified according to how many cattle they had: if you owned more than ten cows, you were counted as Tutsi; with fewer than ten cows, you must be Hutu; and if you were a mere potter, you were Twa. Thereafter, it was the father's ethnic group that determined his children's group identity: the stratification was complete and irreversible. Thus, a complex web of socio-economic relations and mutual obligations was transformed into something far more rigid and divisive.

By the late 1980s, however, many Rwandans asserted that ethnic divisions were a thing of the past; after nearly 30 years of Independence, the use of ethnic quotas in government appointments and the allocation of secondary-school places had ensured that unfair historical advantages were overcome and the *mention ethnique* might as well be abolished. Far more contentious was evidence of discrimination in favour of those from the President's home area (particularly in the allocation of secondary-school places, which were universally regarded as the passport to escape from poverty). However, with the outbreak of the civil war in 1990, ethnic divisions were once again sharpened. Ethnicity was used as a tool to foster mistrust of the minority, and to conceal divisions within the majority — in order that a tiny élite might retain its power and privileges. When the *interahamwe* road-barriers went up in April 1994, the very identity cards which the liberals had fondly imagined to be an anachronism served to facilitate the task of genocide, enabling the killers to determine who could live and who must die.

Do we share a common humanity?

I recently heard two women from Northern Ireland, one Protestant, one Catholic, speak about the vital contribution of community groups to the peace process there. Not for the first time, I was struck by the many parallels with Rwanda and Burundi: there, too, the cycle of violence has obscured a history of injustice in the control of economic resources and political power, and ensured that successive generations on both sides of the sectarian divide have reason to be imbued with hatred for the 'other' group. It is also noteworthy that, in both cases, the perpetrators of violence (though not the planners) have often been disaffected, poorly educated young men with little hope of a better future.

In 1995, Europe celebrated the fiftieth anniversary of the end of the Second World War, and re-examined the dreadful history of the holocaust. In countless radio and television broadcasts, those involved — combatants and non-combatants alike — recalled their experiences and reflected on how they now regard their former enemies. For many, despite the fact that the warring parties have become political and economic allies, it is still impossible to forgive; their distress and bitterness is as acute today as it was 50 years ago. Rwanda cannot even expect the palliative of an 'economic miracle', yet some in the international community appear to expect the Rwandese already to 'forgive and forget', to resume cohabitation as if nothing had happened — and allow them to turn their attention elsewhere.

If we accept a shared humanity, then we must also accept greater responsibility for the consequences of poverty and injustice. In the case of Burundi and Rwanda, for instance, international responsibility should not have been confined to picking up the pieces afterwards, but should have ensured a more effective response to the *poverty* afflicting those two countries before. There is a need to reassert notions of collective responsibility in the world community, what Mark Duffield (1994) calls 'a new political consensus [which would] re-establish a sense of collective international responsibility for poverty and violence ... Never before has there been such a need for sustained public action and an unflinching support for international mandates.'

However, the fact is that the notion of eventual convergence between Northern and Southern economies has been quietly abandoned. Even within strong Northern economies, there is now a tacit acceptance of increasing polarisation and disparity between rich and poor. The economist Will Hutton (1996) has written of the '30/30/40' society in Britain: 40 per cent of the population are in prosperous, secure employment and are pulling away from the rest; 30 per cent are in insecure, often low-paid employment; while the bottom 30 per cent are either unemployed or working for poverty wages. To project economic decline and the risk of social chaos on to the South, without recognising what is going on within the North, is therefore mistaken.

The serious media have begun to look more critically at the rôle of NGOs, particularly in complex emergencies such as the Rwanda crisis. It is right that NGOs' performance be scrutinised more closely, and that they be challenged to face with greater openness the dilemmas posed by humanitarian work. The honeymoon period for NGOs is over at last, and that is healthy. However, I would argue that the focus is wrong: NGOs, and the UN's humanitarian agencies, have gained such prominence only because of the effective *disengagement* by powerful governments from parts of the world which no longer interest them. Equal attention should be paid to what the academic Fred Halliday has called the 'retreat from universalism',[2] and to the effects of the new international economic order in terms of the enormous and growing disparity in standards of living between and within North and South: *poverty*, in other words.

Similarly, legitimate criticism of the performance of UN agencies, and cynicism regarding the effectiveness of the UN generally could easily slide into a retreat from commitment to international moral and legal obligations, and diminished respect for the *principles* on which the UN was founded. An example is the 'Fortress Europe' mentality with regard to admitting refugees and immigrants, as typified by the 1995 Asylum and Immigration Act passed under the former Conservative government in the UK. Wealthy governments are far more ready to contribute to emergency relief than to long-term measures to promote post-conflict recovery, still less comprehensive programmes aimed at combating the poverty and inequality which do so much to fuel conflict.

102

If only the enormous sums expended on the Rwandan refugee crisis had been invested earlier to help to create the conditions for peace and stability in Rwanda, and to ensure viable livelihoods for more of its citizens, it is just possible that the genocide would not have happened.

Reconciliation: justice and acknowledgement

There can be little hope of reconciliation in Rwanda without justice; however, as discussed above, there is no simple means of achieving this. Many look to South Africa, with its Truth and Reconciliation Commission, to provide a model which might be applied in Rwanda and Burundi. But there are significant differences between these countries. In Rwanda, for example, there was a complete takeover by one side in the battle, with no political settlement, no critical mass of political awareness among the general population, nor the will to move forward together in peace. The current government is criticised for being drawn almost exclusively from the ranks of the victors in the civil war — but most of the moderate opponents of the former genocidal regime were also killed.

Moreover, one cannot look at the peace-making process in isolation from other factors. Rwanda has very few resources and little potential for development. The desperate shortage of land remains a problem, along with an increasingly youthful population with little prospect of serious employment or other means of earning a living. Attempts to apply a regional approach to developing the various national economies are undermined by recurrent conflict. Both Rwanda and Burundi were on a knife-edge before the fighting began: it is hard now to see how they could return even to that precarious position.

At the human level, how does a society deal with so many killings and so many killers — in particular, the 'victim-killers', those who were indoctrinated, and those who faced the choice between killing or being killed? How does a society respond to the thousands of bereaved, mutilated, and disabled people, and victims of rape? Traditional community-support mechanisms have been completely swamped by the scale and nature of the bereavement. Moreover, many of those to whom it would have been normal to turn for support — teachers, church leaders, local administrators, members of the extended family — themselves participated in the genocide. As people look through their photograph albums, they point to the individuals whose faces appear, and recount: 'He's dead, she's dead, these two disappeared, this one killed'.

Many of the killers stayed in Rwanda throughout the crisis; many more re-entered the country in the massive wave of returning refugees late last year. The fact that killers and victims are mixing in the same society means that redress and reconciliation must happen at many different levels. In addition to the main orchestrators of the genocide, and those at the forefront of the killing, there are those who were complicit, others who tacitly consented to participate, those who feared they would be killed if they did not, and those who stood by. And there are those who feel that because a member of their family killed, they too are guilty by association. NGOs and the Churches were completely divided by the crisis, and are in no position to provide leadership in any reconciliation process until they have honestly examined their own role in the genocide.

'Reconciliation' in Rwanda has been used to mean many, quite different, things: the return of the refugees, peaceful cohabitation between killers and survivors, public naming and punishment of the main offenders, forgiving and forgetting, atonement. Within the international community, it too often appears to signify 'getting back to normal' — and ceasing to be a drain on its political and financial resources. As a team, we in Oxfam came to regard 'reconciliation' as a dirty word and agreed not to use it.

The key issue is that of acknowledgement. In the words of a friend and colleague who lost 31 members of her family in the genocide, 'I'm ready to forgive, but no-one has said they're sorry'. In an attempt to honour those killed in 1994, there have been ceremonies of remembrance and symbolic re-burials of some of those whose bodies had simply been dumped in pit latrines and ditches, or left in the schools, health centres, and churches in which they sought refuge. However, many feel that the failure to deal with the thousands of detainees, along with abuses by the present government and its allies, amount to a *dishonouring* of the dead.

Survivors also have to contend with the poisonous process of denial. Many of the refugees are simply not prepared to accept that genocide took place: they claim that those who died were the victims of war. In addition, they point to abuses committed by the present government and those associated with them, notably the alliance which recently brought Laurent Kabila to power in the Democratic Republic of Congo (formerly Zaïre). There is little doubt that many refugees have suffered greatly, thousands have died in appalling conditions, and it is feared that many others have been killed. As I write, a team of UN human-rights and forensic experts is attempting to investigate the fate of around 200,000 refugees 'missing' in the DRC, and is, it would seem, being hindered by the new régime at every turn.

International observers have also equated the atrocities of 1994 with the abuses perpetrated by the present government and its allies. Indeed, the former UN Secretary-General referred to the refusal by Laurent Kabila's forces to allow access to civilians trapped between the warring parties as 'genocide by hunger', while others spoke of a 'hidden holocaust'. But abuses committed in the wake of the genocide must not be allowed to obscure the enormity of what happened during it. Memories are already becoming blurred; if they are allowed to disappear, and Rwanda fades into the background once more, we will all be diminished.

References

Joint Evaluation of Emergency Assistance to Rwanda (1996) *The International Response to Conflict and Genocide: Lessons from Rwanda*, Volume 2, Copenhagen: Joint Evaluation.

Duffield, Mark (1994) 'Complex emergencies and the crisis of developmentalism', *IDS Bulletin* Vol. 25, No. 4.

Fédération Internationale des Droits de l'Homme et al (1993), *Report of the International Commission of Investigation of Human Rights Violations in Rwanda since October 1 1990*, Paris and Washington, March 1993.

Hutton, Will (1996) *The State We're In*, London: Jonathan Cape.

Kaplan, Robert D. (1994) 'The coming anarchy', *Atlantic Monthly* March 1994.

Mackintosh, Anne (1996) 'International aid and the media', *Contemporary Politics* Vol. 2, No. 1, South Bank University, Spring 1996.

Macrae, Joanna (1997), 'Aiding An Unstable World', unpublished paper prepared for a seminar on conflict organised by Oxfam UK and Ireland in January 1997.

Sanders, E. R. (1969) 'The Hamitic hypothesis: its origin and function in time perspective', *Journal of African History*, pp. 521-32.

Waller, David (1993, revised 1997), *Rwanda: Which Way Now?*, Oxford: Oxfam UK and Ireland.

Wiles, Peter (1992) 'Rwandese Refugees and Migrants in the Great Lakes Region of Central Africa', unpublished report, Oxford: Oxfam UK and Ireland, December 1992.

Notes

1 Parts of this paper appear in an earlier article (Mackintosh 1996), in which I focus in more detail on my personal experience of the genocide and the media's role in reporting on Rwanda.

2 Speaking in the World Tonight debate on conflict in the twenty-first century, BBC Radio 4, 17 March 1997.

The author

Anne Mackintosh began working on Oxfam's Central Africa Desk in 1985, and was Oxfam's Regional Representative for Rwanda, Burundi and Kivu (Zaïre) from 1991 to 1994. In 1995 she was awarded an MBE for humanitarian work in Rwanda.

Reconstruction and reconciliation: emerging from transition

Graeme Simpson

Transition: result or process?

I wish first to address some of the simplistic myths about solutions to social conflict, and then reflect on problems that I have experienced with aid efforts organised by the international community, through the UN. In this, I shall focus on Bosnia rather than on Africa. Bosnia, as part of Europe, did not suffer the apathy that characterised international responses to events in Rwanda and Burundi before 1994. The second part of my presentation will address what I see as the flawed assumptions that often underlie the emphasis on economic reconstruction in the wake of war and conflict.

My first and obvious point is that war, or intense and violent conflict, affects a society: it causes massive social dislocation, and taints or destroys social relations — from national political relationships to very basic human interactions — whether through racism, violence against women, or the destruction of families. And it also destroys economic infrastructure. But so much international aid for the recovery or reconstruction process seems almost blind to this social dislocation and to the vital and basic need to rebuild social relationships. It appears obsessed with the assumption that if we can reconstruct economies, and create wealth and jobs, the problem of social conflict will go away. This is very clear in South Africa, where human-rights organisations in particular now contend with the perception that after the 1994 elections, and the establishment of a formal consitution and many 'paper rights', the process of transition has been sealed. In fact, it has only just begun. This misperception has resulted in international donors (and particularly bilateral agencies) moving rapidly towards the 'normalisation' of government-to-government relations, and

setting the conventional aid machine in motion. Now they want to talk about development, and to stop talking about human rights, the building of a culture of human rights, or the restoring of a social fabric. This shift in funding priorities towards 'hard' development, economic reconstruction, the delivery of basic social services — critical though these be — is in danger of masking the need for comprehensive social reconstruction.

Integration and change

To answer the question of *how* we reconstruct societies that have been seriously damaged by conflict, two basic things need to be acknowledged from the outset. The first is that we must adopt an integrated approach, which is premised on a recognition of the fact that economic reconstruction, or redress for past economic inequities, is inextricably linked with social development: with political and human empowerment. To understand social conflict, whether we label it political, ethnic, or class-based, we must understand the dynamic and intimate relationship between social, political, and economic interests. To start looking at conflict-resolution in a way that detaches these inter-linked interests from each other is to create a recipe for sustained conflict and violence. We can rebuild economic infrastructure, but political upheaval will destroy it again overnight. We can rebuild the social fabric and negotiate political settlements; but unless we meet people's economic needs, those agreements are worth very little.

The second thing to recognise is that conflict is not static. The sources of social conflict shift over time, taking on new forms and manifestations. In this sense, there is no such thing as 'post-conflict'. The question is how we manage conflict, and whether we can ensure that it does not translate into violent confrontation. But if we fail to recognise that conflict changes in shape and in form — as evidenced by the slide between political and criminal violence in societies that are undergoing dramatic political change — then our approach to conflict-management is likely to amount to little more than window-dressing.

The UN in Bosnia

The UN's role in Bosnia gives us a striking illustration of how *not* to reconstruct a society. The following anecdote will illustrate my point. A man with a broken watch eventually found a shop with a window display full of watches. He went in, and asked the white-coated assistant whether he could have his watch repaired. The reply was, 'I'm sorry, we don't fix watches'. 'Oh', said the would-be customer. 'Well what do you do?' 'We neuter cats', was the response. 'Pardon me', said the man, 'but why then do you have watches in your window?'. The assistant smiled and said, 'If your job was to neuter cats, what would you put in the window?' The art of window-dressing, in this case, is to display one thing, while actually doing something else.

The UN's involvement in Central Bosnia is ostensibly about putting up a military shield to keep warring factions apart. There is an irony here, in that the ultimate objective is to bring these people together. But it is also a shield behind which much is supposed to be happening — though most of it is simply not taking place. This dividing wall is quite effective, though not always in the ways intended. In one village that had previously depended on the timber trade, the local authorities explained to me that the 'shield' had separated the saw-mill from the woods: the result was that both sides were unemployed. Since the second aim of UN involvement is to ensure a decent level of welfare on all sides, this means that people are forced to survive on hand-outs, rather than on their own productive labour.

The most troublesome aspect of this, in my view, is the vacuum between military 'peace-keeping' (not peace-making) intervention, on the one hand, and a huge humanitarian assistance programme, on the other. Hardly anywhere to be seen was any assistance in the process of rebuilding social relations, bringing people together, breaking down the barriers and prejudice which had played such a part in generating social conflict in the first place. There were 'civil affairs officers', who were supposed to be facilitating a process of discussion between local government officials on both sides. But they all wore UNPROFOR uniforms, which linked them directly to the widely discredited military effort. A number of international NGOs were actively involved, mainly in relief work, but also in modest (and largely unsupported) local reconciliation efforts.

The substitute for direct intervention at the local level to take full account of the consequences of war and its impact on social relationships and human development has been an internationally brokered peace agreement: a diplomatic initiative based on the idea that peace can be made by getting government leaders to talk with each other. The irony here is that the peace agreements have effectively consolidated the gains made through war. Worse, it was peace-brokering which masqueraded as constitutional negotiation. It generated not a federal constitution — as has been claimed, for instance, by Washington — but a constitutional arrangement which did more to entrench ethnicity as the organising principle of politics in the Balkans than even the war itself had done. What it did was to create a vehicle for compromise in the federal constitution, but one which also lent itself to competing interpretations. For one side, federalism meant integration; for the other, it meant the consolidation of regional power bases and was potentially a route to ethnic segregation.

While this is clearly not the entire picture of international involvement in Bosnia, there are some lessons that might be taken into account in considering the role of NGOs in Southern Africa, and how we shape our views and our relationships to external intervention and facilitation. This is an issue that absolutely must be addressed in trying to deal with transition in any society. Further, the way in which the peace agreements are internationally brokered, and the content of such accords, may play a fundamental role in shaping the nature of present and future conflict.

Economic reconstruction and social conflict

The idea, described earlier, that economic reconstruction and growth will bring about an end to social conflict is flawed for several reasons. The first is that it fails to deal with the residual issues of identity, which have often been intrinsic to the history of social conflict. Once mobilised, ethnic or religious identity, for example, is nearly impossible to demobilise. To substitute economic growth and economic development, or to insert it on the assumption that it will automatically overcome those social fissures, is to base such efforts on a myth.

The second reason is that economic development generates its own forms of social conflict. Since much social conflict has concerned access to scarce resources, especially for impoverished communities, it is very obvious that if resources are injected into such a context, they will in all likelihood *fuel* any existing conflicts, rather than the reverse.

There is a good example of this from CSVR's work in Alexandra township, just north of Johannesburg. Through a process of warfare, there had been a cycle of displacement in that community. Migrant labourers from the single-sex hostel invaded an area of the township and drove people out of their homes and into the overgrown and under-resourced informal settlements. Meanwhile, rural poverty was driving more people into the hostels, thus perpetuating the cycle. The government then came up with a very creative response, within the framework of the priority now given to housing. A building project was designed for the township. But who would get the houses? The first thing the developers had to do was to fence off the area in which houses were to be built, to ensure that the building materials were secure. Even assuming that the houses were successfully built, how could 'invasions' be prevented without the threat or use of force? What was actually needed was a social compact: some kind of agreement on the criteria to be applied in allocating the new houses. This is a process that must be properly managed. The assumption, therefore, that economic development will not *generate* such conflicts is very dangerous.

The third reason to challenge the primacy of economic development is that conflict may change its shape, but it will not go away. In South Africa, for example, there has been a tendency to blur the dividing lines between political and criminal violence. A serious warning sign is the prevalence of well-organised criminal activity, very often associated with high levels of violence, in societies going through

major transition. Some of the processes associated with transition may themselves encourage this. Demobilisation does not equal demilitarisation. Unless alternative incentives are offered to members of a society in order to demobilise them and remove them from formal or politically oriented military activity, then they are not going to discontinue their militarised interventions. And people are creative. The systematic marginalisation of black youth from South African society was met by them with immense creative energy. These are people who were economically dis-empowered by apartheid, they were politically voiceless, they were under-educated, they were totally rejected by the dominant culture in society. They therefore found an alternative 'home' within the political organisations, which provided a new identity for them. It gave young, black South Africans a stake, and allowed them a central role as the 'shock troops' of liberation. The irony about the shift from the struggle in the streets to the negotiating table is that it compounded the marginalisation of those people. The Party had given people a new uniform, a new language, new songs of liberation, but now the criminal gangs offered ready-made alternatives. Membership of these gangs provides an identity, social clothing, a language of its own, and the added advantage of providing some alternative forms of wealth-creation. We need to recognise the subtle shifts in the ways that social conflict manifests itself, for, if we fail to do so, the social deficits that generate it will be left intact.

The fourth problem with economic reconstruction alone is that it does not inherently redress past inequity. It does not necessarily deal with war crimes, nor with the history of human-rights abuse, and the lasting impact which this has on people. It does not necessarily deal with gender inequality, or with the dispossession of land. Indeed, very often economic growth and wealth-generation are built upon inequity in society, and cannot then address poverty in and of themselves. If such inequity is the root of social conflict, then economic growth may serve to reinforce rather than to overcome it.

Lastly, we need to recognise that recon-struction in a society that is undergoing profound transition is as much about building democracy and democratic institutions as anything else. And economic reconstruction offers no guarantees for transforming State institutions, nor the potential to render them accountable, transparent, and empowering. In a sense, what I am saying is that these concerns should define our agenda.

As NGOs in Southern Africa, we should feel proud to advocate a 'bottom-up' approach to reconstruction: an approach that is not about humanitarian aid alone, is not about diplomatic intervention alone, and is certainly not about military intervention at all. What it *is* about is a recognition of the simple thing that was said to me in Central Bosnia when we were interviewing teachers, religious leaders, police chiefs, judges, and women's organisations. Their voices were not being heard. They were saying, 'This divide is not of our making. We want one education system. We want one system of policing in this society. This arrangement is simply not functional for any of us.' And it is to these concerns that we should be relating when we talk about social reconstruction, about filling the gap, about rebuilding the social fabric.

To conclude, I am not suggesting that economic reconstruction is not vital to the social reconstruction process, nor that we can afford to ignore the phenomenal capacity of global forces to derail local-level initiatives: to do so would be naive. What I am saying, however, is that NGOs and other components of civil society need to be far clearer about the nature of the contribution that economic reconstruction may make, and more assertive in staking out the space for social, political, and human empowerment.

The author

Graeme Simpson is Director of the Centre for the Study of Violence and Reconciliation (CSVR), and has a particular interest in the links between violence and development, and in issues concerning criminality, policing, and prisons reform.

Collective memory and the process of reconciliation and reconstruction

Wiseman Chirwa

Over the last five years, several African and Latin American countries have experienced major political changes. Civil wars have come to an end, autocratic and oppressive regimes have crumbled and have been replaced by democratic ones. A new political dispensation has been ushered in. As this process unfolds, and the culture of openness deepens, a number of questions come to mind. A special issue of the *Index on Censorship* (Volume 5, 1996) raised several such questions concerning the relationship between truth, reconciliation, and the process of national healing: can people divided by civil war, torn apart by hatred and mutually inflicted atrocities, made sick by terror and oppression, heal themselves? Can nations, like individuals, be reconciled to their past and be cured of their ills by working through traumatic events, by telling and hearing the truth? Whose truth is it? Can nations cleanse their past and start again? More important, perhaps, can they ensure 'never again'?

These and similar questions were at the centre of the discussions at the Symposium on conflict-related issues, sponsored by Oxfam (UK and Ireland) and the Centre for the Study of Violence and Reconciliation, held in Johannesburg in June 1996. Of particular interest to the participants were the various ways adopted by communities and States in Africa and Latin America to achieve some form of reconciliation, healing, and reconstruction.

State-backed strategies for uncovering the truth

On the legal and political fronts, countries like South Africa and Rwanda have set up Truth Commissions to investigate the past and 'to facilitate a truth recovery process' so as to establish 'as complete a picture as possible of the causes, nature, and extent of past abuses' (Hamber, 1995). In Chile and Argentina, truth commissions 'arose in the context of new governments making a transition from dictatorship to civilian rule', while in El Salvador and Guatemala they emerged as part of the negotiations for transition from civil war to peace (Edelstein, 1994; see also Hayner, 1994 and 1996).

The understanding is that the process of truth-recovery will result in some kind of psychological healing. If victims of violence and other forms of rights-abuse are left without knowing the truth, or the opportunity to recount their experiences, they will remain traumatised and shattered. They will feel vulnerable and helpless and will have 'a distorted picture of society and humanity' (Hamber, 1995). Without truth there is no justice; and there is the danger of repeating the old mistakes. Thus, despite the differences in their mandate, scope, and approach, truth commissions are generally viewed as a starting point for national reconciliation and reparative measures (Edelstein, 1994: 5).

Truth commissions are not the only way of dealing with the past. Compensation tribunals and other mechanisms of reparation have been set up, for example in Malawi, to requite victims of abuse and as part of the process of promoting national reconciliation. A war-crimes tribunal has been set up in Rwanda, and some perpetrators of injustice during the apartheid regime in South Africa have appeared in court. These processes are among the ways of providing legal redress to victims, recognising the responsibility of the State, acknowledging the rights and interests of the victims, and raising public consciousness (ibid: 3). The last is an aspect of collective memory.

The participants at the Symposium felt the need to distinguish between the local communities and the State in this process. Truth commissions, compensation tribunals, and war-crimes tribunals are usually, though not always exclusively, State strategies for creating collective memories. They require a legal framework for their operation and a State bureaucracy for implementation. How then do local communities in the countries that do not have legal provisions for the setting up of truth commissions deal with their past? The available evidence suggests that they have devised their own ways. Sometimes supported by non-State agencies, and operating outside the State structures, they have embarked on the process of creating their collective memories to facilitate the process of healing, reconciliation, and reconstruction.

Alternative strategies

A good example here is the case of the Recovering the Historic Record Project (*Recuperación de la Memoria Histórica*, REMHI) in Guatemala, started by the Catholic Church (see Linsmeier, 1995; Hayner, 1994). This was designed to document testimonies from those who, in various ways, witnessed or were victims of the violence in the country from the 1960s. The testimonies would be submitted to the Truth Commission set up by the government. They would also be 'given back to the people in the form of pastoral statements to study and discuss. Thus begins what will be a long process of reconciliation' (Linsmeier, 1995:5). Several rural communities also embarked on the exhumation of the mass graves of the 'scorched earth' massacres of the 1970s and 1980s. The exercise was aimed at recognising the lives of those who were brutally murdered, giving them a proper burial and the reverence they deserve; to 'clarify the truth of what had happened', and to let 'the government, the military and the world realise that there is a law in Guatemala, and that justice must be served' (ibid). The new graves will serve as a reminder both to the government and the local communities of the atrocities of the past, so that any repetition of those events is avoided.

The Guatemalan exhumation exercise and the documentation of memories through interviews serve as good examples of how societies, independent of the State, deal with the past and the problems of reconciliation and healing.

Another illustration of a local group that has taken the initiative on its own to create a collective memory is that of the *Madres de la Plaza de Mayo* (Mothers of May Square) in Argentina. Ingo Malcher (1996:132) reports that 'every day the mothers [members of the group] meet here to continue their 20-year struggle, begun during the military dictatorship (1976-1983), to establish exactly what happened to their disappeared sons and daughters and to demand retribution against those who imprisoned, tortured and killed their children'. Documents, oral accounts and various other forms of evidence are examined and put together to establish a comprehensive account that can provide clues to what happened. It is worth noting that the 'mothers' refused to accept monetary reparation, because 'they felt that the state was buying their silence rather than social and historical recognition' (Hamber, 1995; see also Malcher, 1996). They want 'truth and justice', and an end to impunity, not money.

The case of Malawi

Similar exercises are planned, and some are indeed being undertaken, in Malawi. Victims of State murder have been given proper burial and memorial services, and a history project to document and publicise past abuses has been proposed by a group of scholars at Chancellor College, the country's main university campus. It aims to collect testimonies from both victims and perpetrators in various parts of the country; and publish popular works on these for use in schools, religious organisations, and other institutions. The dissemination of the results will also be undertaken through newspaper articles and radio and video documentaries.

On their own, communities in some parts of Malawi are making home videos and documentaries of their experiences under the dictatorial regime of Dr Hastings Kamuzu Banda. Lists of detainees and those who 'disappeared' have been drawn, showing the dates when they were picked up by the police (where the information is available), where they were detained, when they died or came out of prison, what happened to their family members, and other details of that nature. These have been submitted to the History Project proposed by the scholars at the university. The country's Compensation Tribunal has also collected voluminous accounts from victims of abuse. Members of the History Project are now requesting the Tribunal to allow them to document and preserve these accounts properly and professionally, so that they become an authentic record of the past for use by the present and future generations.

The Project is also proposing the establishment of local museums where artefacts of victims — personal belongings, pictures, and works — and those of the perpetrators of abuse would be preserved and displayed to the public. The weapons used by the perpetrators, and other tokens of State oppression, would also be housed in these museums, to provide symbols of the local communities' pride and identity, and to raise public consciousness. The museums would also become historical sites, an attraction to tourists, and thus give greater publicity and recognition to the victim communities. Lack of funding has delayed the implementation of this Project.

The case of South Africa

In South Africa, Christian organisations and non-government organisations (NGOs) are also actively involved in creating, documenting, and preserving collective memories. A good example is the Practical Ministries of the Christian Development Agency for Social Action. Some issues of its publication, *Practical Ministries*, have carried accounts of past abuses and the personal experiences of the victims (see, for example, *Practical Ministries* Volume 1, No. 1, Jan-March 1996). The organisation has also provided material support to those who suffered. Homes that were destroyed by politically motivated violence have been re-built, and relief supplies and facilities such as safe water have been provided to the victims of forced removals and those of post-apartheid political violence. According to Cosmas Desmond (1996), 'practical ministries are setting out to show that, given appropriate assistance, even the most devastated community can rebuild itself'.

The *khulumani* (speak out) groups in South Africa are another practical example of how collective memory is created, documented, and preserved. These are groups of the victims and/or relatives of victims and sympathisers who regularly meet to discuss their experiences. They also map out the strategies to follow in engaging the government in detailed consultations on issues of justice, reparation, and physical protection. The emotional support provided by the members of these groups to each another serves as psychological therapy in the process of reconciliation.

Collective memory: some questions

It should be noted that collective memories have some shortcomings. To begin with, how collective are 'collective memories'? Whose memories are they? There is always the danger that the memories of the victims will take precedence over those of the perpetrators. Individuals are also good at suppressing some of their memories and highlighting and emphasising those that might be attractive to their sympathisers. As Michael Ignatieff (1996) has rightly observed, 'peoples who believe themselves to be victims of aggression have an understandable incapacity to believe that they also committed atrocities. Myths of innocence and victimhood are powerful obstacles in the way of confronting unwelcome facts.'

The memory becomes collective when it goes beyond an individual account, subscribed to and shared by a group. It must have historical and emotional relevance, connecting seemingly discrete events in a cause-and-effect manner. An account of a simple event that has no historical and emotional relevance is not collective memory. It becomes so when it invokes shared emotions and consciousness. It is for this reason that collective memory becomes part of the process of healing, reconciliation, and reconstruction at both the individual and communal levels.

However, the connection between collective memory and national reconciliation is rather unclear. Ignatieff (ibid) has further observed that we vest our nations 'with consciences, identities and memories as if they were individuals'. 'But', he asks,

... do nations, like individuals, have psyches? Can a nation's past make people ill as we know that repressed memories sometimes make individuals ill? Conversely, can a nation or contending part of it be reconciled to its past, as individuals can, by replacing myth with fact and lies with truth? Can we speak of nations 'working through' a civil war or an atrocity as we speak of

individuals working through a traumatic memory or event? ... If it is problematic to vest an individual with a single identity, it is even more so in the case of a nation (ibid).

The participants at the Symposium considered that collective memory can be an effective tool for reconciliation and healing for individuals and local communities. The examples cited above are ample evidence for this. It may not be fully effective for the nation as a whole. But these examples also show how local communities, on their own, acting independently of the State, deal with their past; and how they work towards the declaration: *nunca mais* — never again!

References

Desmond, Cosmas (1996) 'Rebuilding homes, restoring hope', in *Practical Ministries*, vol. 1, no. 1, pp. 4–5.

Edelstein, Jayni (1994) 'Rights, Reparations and Reconstruction: Some Comparative Notes', Seminar Paper no. 6. Centre for the Study of Violence and Reconciliation, Blaamfontein, South Africa.

Hamber, Brandon (1995) 'Dealing with the Past and the Psychology of Reconciliation: The Truth and Reconciliation Commission, A Psychological Perspective', Public Address Presented at the Fourth International Symposium on The Contributions of Psychology to Peace, Cape Town, 27 June 1995.

Hayner, Priscilla (1994) 'Fifteen Truth Commissions — 1974 to 1994: A Comparative Study', in *Human Rights Quarterly*, vol. 16, no. 4, pp. 597–655.

Hayner, Priscilla (1996) 'Commissioning the truth: further research questions', in *Third World Quarterly*, vol. 17, no. 1, pp. 19–29.

Ignatieff, Michael (1996) 'Articles of faith', in *Index on Censorship*, vol. 5, pp. 110–122.

Linsmeier, Alice (1995) 'Documenting memories: the Church helps reconciliation in Guatemala', in *The Mustard Seed*, Fall, pp. 1–8.

Malcher, Ingo (1996) 'No truth, no justice', in *Index on Censorship*, vol. 5, pp. 132–6.

The author

Wiseman Chirwa teaches at the University of Malawi, and is involved both in training activists and parliamentarians in human-rights issues, and in documenting the experience of State repression in Malawi.

Reconciliation: the role of truth commissions and alternative ways of healing

Noel Muchenga Chicuecue

This paper discusses the issues of reconciliation, truth commissions, and alternative ways of healing, focusing on the following questions:

- Does reconciliation mean the same to all people and cultures?
- How does reconciliation work in practice?
- What is the role of truth commissions in the reconciliation process?
- What alternative ways of healing have been used in Mozambique?

I should clarify from the outset that my thinking is not based on established theories about reconciliation, but rather on my understanding of how people become reconciled with each other in practice. However, this does not exclude the need for a conceptual framework in which to make sense of the learning and results of practical experience drawn from the day-to-day problems of reconciliation, reconstruction, and conflict-resolution in war-torn societies.

Reconciliation: restoration of relationship

The term 'reconciliation' is generally used to mean the restoration of friendship in order to reach an agreement and make peace with an enemy or adversary. Reconciliation has different meanings for different people, depending on the specific cultural setting. People's beliefs and values determine their understanding about the way the world is, about self and the other, and about how both should be. In some societies, conflict is considered inevitable, positive, and necessary. Other societies and cultures consider harmony as the best way of living together. In such contexts, conflict is not seen as normal: when a relationship is broken, there is a need to restore harmony. For practical reasons, I shall here use the term 'reconciliation' as defined by Dr Paul Lederach during a workshop on conflict-resolution held in 1994 in Mombasa, Kenya:

Reconciliation, in essence, represents a place, the point of encounter where concerns about both the past and the future can meet. Reconciliation as encounter suggests that space for acknowledging of the past and envisioning the future are necessary ingredients for reframing the present.

From this, it seems to me that reconciliation poses a contradiction related to dealing with the past and envisioning the future. The past has been characterised by negative emotions resulting from dehumanisation, division, hatred, misunderstanding, humiliation, destruction, anger, despair, fear, injustice, and demoralisation. Addressing the past implies acknowledging the earlier wrongs done, as a first step towards restoring the person and the relationship. On the one hand, the truth about the past may lead to amnesty or forgiveness; on the other, it may lead instead to the re-opening of wounds, or to demands for peace with justice which may jeopardise the future relationship of the parties to the conflict. In practice, addressing the past involves emotions which may lead each side to demand justice, which may in turn impose unbearable costs on the party found guilty. The practical solution to the contradiction differs from case to case. Although the ideal solution would be to embrace truth and amnesty, as two sides of the same coin, in practice it is difficult to strike the balance. We have, for example, cases where there are truth commissions on one side, coupled with the push for 'amnesty' on the other, as in El Salvador and South Africa. At times, in a spirit of 'forgive and forget', emphasis is placed on the future relationship. Examples of this can be drawn from both Nicaragua and Mozambique.

In the case of Mozambique, a document drawn up in 1995 by the UNRISD War-torn Societies Project study group explains that

the conversations that led to the Rome Peace Agreements were considered Reconciliation (per se) — it meant the encounter of compatriots, over-passing the causes of the war and making a compromise to walk together towards the reconstruction of the country. At that moment, the two parties to the conflict agreed tacitly that there was no need to get locked on the analysis of the causes of the war and find who was to blame.

To make this reconciliation sustainable, it is necessary to build confidence among the various parties to the conflict, through working together towards interdependence by reconstructing the social, economic and cultural life of the community, as well as by building a shared common future. Confidence will help to open channels for dialogue about the past, without obstruction from negative emotions. Embracing the past and the future is important in shaping the present.

The role of truth commissions

In Mozambique, no formal truth commission was created, but the issue is sometimes raised by educated members of the community. A good example of how the debate on the role of truth commissions elicits different opinions can be drawn from the discussion between parliamentarians during a study visit to South Africa and Malawi, in which I participated on behalf of the Maputo office of the UNESCO Culture of Peace Programme.

The topic came up during this visit, in which 12 Mozambican parliamentarians participated from across the political-party spectrum. In both Malawi and South Africa, the Mozambican parliamentarians were exposed to the ways in which the two countries are endeavouring to deal with the past. The South Africans briefed their Mozambican counterparts on the Truth Commission, in which people who had abused human rights during the apartheid era will be granted amnesty in exchange for confessing the truth. Some form of compensation, to be decided once all cases have been heard, is to be offered to the victims.

In Malawi, the former President and some of his close officials were on trial on charges of murder. A national compensation tribunal had been set up to analyse cases of human-rights abuses perpetrated by the previous government, and to compensate the victims. Interestingly, some of those in the government, as well as parliamentarians who had served in the previous government, were also on the list of the victims to be compensated.

The Mozambicans had mixed views on whether redressing past wrongs by offering compensation would be desirable and practicable in the national context. Speaking in support of the concept of truth commissions, one Mozambican parliamentarian stressed that forgiving does not mean forgetting. Others felt that the processes being undertaken in South Africa and Malawi would not be feasible in Mozambique, because they would jeopardise the reconciliation process by re-opening healing wounds. They also argued that the sheer costs implied would be difficult to meet, given the fragile state of the Mozambican economy.

With regard to compensation, one might also ask who will be the judge, in a situation where some of the alleged participants in human-rights abuses are in government and may well be in a position to influence the outcome of the judgement? Since justice implies costs, who will pay the bill? The situation could arise where tax-payers are essentially paying for something they did not do: the victim ends up paying the bill. It is important to stress here that concepts of justice differ from one culture to another. For example, justice seen as balancing the scales would not lead to rebuilding relationships in a war-torn society. And justice may mean different things to the parties in conflict.

At the institutional level, truth commissions, peace agreements, constitutions, and other peace structures do have an important role to play, but it depends on the historical, social, and cultural contexts in which they are applied, as well as on the nature of the conflict. At the non-institutional level, the change from a culture of war to a culture of peace depends crucially on formal, informal, and non-formal education for peace, human rights, and democracy that is aimed at conveying the knowledge, skills, attitudes, and values of peace. This culture of peace is characterised by participation in shaping a common future, respect for human rights, solidarity, cooperation, mutual understanding, equality, and justice.

The last part of this paper will try to explain how 'alternative' ways of healing have contributed to re-weaving the social fabric in post-war Mozambique. People have wondered how the Mozambicans have managed to recover from the traumas of war in a country with a great shortage of experts and professionals. In response, it is important to stress that all societies and cultures, the world over, develop their own ways of keeping and restoring a damaged social order, through religious practices and traditional beliefs and values. In Mozambique, many of these practices have been used in the process of healing post-war trauma. Some of these alternative ways of healing have had great impact in Mozambique.

Traditional purification rituals

Community institutions, religions (whether Christian, Islamic, or syncretic), traditional healers, community leaders, and extended family structures have developed procedures to assist in healing those who have been damaged by war. People in Mozambique hold firmly to the belief that purification rituals — often involving some days of separation, treatment with herbs and potions, and communication with the spirits of the ancestors — can heal people from the effects of bad spirits and war traumas. Ex-soldiers, returning refugees, child-soldiers, sexually abused women, and internally displaced people have all passed through cleansing rituals upon returning to their communities and families.

UNICEF and the Red Cross have encouraged those working with traumatised children and child-soldiers to respect traditional culture and collaborate with communities in their re-integration. The results of traditional ways of healing have been widely reported by UNICEF.

Traditional cleansing rituals are part of a cultural practice that dates from the pre-colonial era. Warriors underwent purification rituals in order to free them from revenge by the spirits of their victims. It is a common belief that, without these healing rituals, the spirit of the victim will bring bad luck or death, not only to the killer but also to members of his extended family or community.

Returning refugees and internally displaced people have organised traditional ceremonies to ask for forgiveness from dead relatives to whom they did not give a decent burial, so that they can be reconciled with their spirits and be protected. A good relationship with the spirits of the dead is important within traditional culture in Mozambique, with its links between the dead, the living, and the natural world.

A good example of how the traditional methods of reconciliation work in daily life has been given by a study group from Karibu, a local NGO working in Nampula Province. According to their findings, all the conflicts that arise in the Makuwa society (constituting about one quarter of the Mozambican population) are given due attention, irrespective of whether the offending party deserves forgiveness or punishment. A Makuwa who has offended a person (dead or alive), or a sacred place or object, is expected to become reconciled with the person concerned, or with the spirits. This reconciliation is seen as a sign of good education as well as preventing bad luck, problems, and troubles in future. It is believed that offenders, if they do not acknowledge their wrong-doing, may fall victim to depression or stress, lose their job or their money, lead a very difficult life, and, in extreme cases, die.

To be healed, or freed from bad spirits, an offender must go to his relatives or community elders, or to a traditional healer, and confess and acknowledge his wrongful deeds in order to be forgiven or freed from punishment. The traditional healers and chiefs play a vital role in the reconciliation process. The chief is the adviser, judge, and supreme authority of the group (*n'loko*). He is assisted by a woman adviser (*Apiyamwene*), the most important woman in the extended family. These also act as mediators between the living and the dead, and are responsible for conflict-resolution and reconciliation among the living.

If anyone who is suspected of wrong-doing does not confess voluntarily, the suspect may be subjected to various methods of pressure and persuasion to confess and acknowledge this wrongful behaviour, whether past or present.

In some cases, people who have committed serious offences are led to take an oath: they may be seated on the ground, on a reed mat, or on the grave of a close dead relative (father, mother, brother, grandmother, or grandfather). The offender will confess his wrongdoing and promise not to do it again. Sometimes, this oath is made with the offender placing one hand on the Koran. If an individual does not comply with what he swore, then he will suffer the consequences of his behaviour in the future.

It is also common practice to resolve past grievances by paying a fine to the offended. This follows a resolution of the dispute through mediated dialogue, in which the offender and the offended bring together their family elders or chiefs to resolve their conflict.

Traditional healers are sometimes called to mediate conflicts that involve the spirit of the dead. One report from 'the media fax' (a local newsletter sent by fax in Maputo) tells of a case that occurred in the northern part of Inhambane Province, in which the Mozambican association of traditional healers was called to intervene. In this case, the spirit of a traditional chief who had been killed during the war was demanding 'an eye for an eye' as a means to resolve a dispute that involved an ex-combatant who had ordered the chief's killing.

To conclude, I would emphasise that reconciliation focuses on building a relationship between the parties in conflict. Relationships are the basis of both the conflict and the long-term solution to it. All societies have their own ways of understanding conflict and reconciliation. Focusing on the outcomes and impact of the traditional healing process, rather than on any scientific explanation of the processes, shows that they can be as effective as any other means. Traditional rituals have had a tremendous impact in healing former child-soldiers, refugees, the displaced, and many others affected by the civil war in Mozambique.

The author

Noel Muchenga Chicuecue works with the UNESCO Culture of Peace Programme in Maputo.

Reconciliation in Zimbabwe: reality or illusion?

Val Ingham-Thorpe

Reconciliation without change

After Zimbabwe became independent, the then Prime Minister Robert Mugabe announced a policy of reconciliation. This was hailed at the time as taking a very mature and statesman-like approach. However, with hindsight, we can see that this policy caused several problems, having left intact many of the structures of oppression — such as various laws that were left on the books, including the notorious Law and Order Maintenance Act, and a repressive and brutalised police service, central intelligence agency, prison service, and army. Similarly, many structural inequities remained: indeed, whites often used the reconciliation policy to entrench still further their advantageous social and economic positions. They were not, and did not feel, obliged to integrate themselves into the new Zimbabwe.

Both the 'imposed' peace settlement and the well-meant policy of reconciliation left unresolved the major problems of land distribution, economic inequity, and racism, which were the burning issues for which most freedom fighters took up arms. Racism and ethnicity, instead of being dealt with, are now often used as a way to make scapegoats of certain individuals or groups, and also to create a smokescreen that conceals the failure to deal with the underlying issues such as land reform, or the transfer of economic power. It is far easier for politicians to blame any difficulties on racial conflicts than to tackle such issues in a genuinely problem-solving and just manner.

Further, some of the events that have taken place since the end of the liberation war have demonstrated not reconciliation but rather silence, denial, and amnesia. This is linked in part to unrest over issues related to land, demobilisation, and power-sharing. For instance, the so-called 'dissident problem' in Matabeleland during 1983–85 was repressed with considerable brutality. However, the victims have received no form of reparation; and those whose loved ones 'disappeared' have never been able to bury their dead. Since the scale and impact of what took place have never been fully acknowledged, many wounds are still unhealed; ethnicity is now glossed over, but it has the potential to become a more divisive issue than it had been before.

Unhealed wounds

The existence of unhealed wounds also prevails in a wider and more spiritual sense throughout Zimbabwe. As people's hopes and expectations of independence were increasingly disappointed, so they struggled to give some form of meaning to what the war had actually been about. Today, for example, we see a tension concerning many of those 'traditional' values that had been a source of unity during the war, but which are now perceived as divisive. The land-reform issue also remains largely unresolved, but tends to be seen solely in racial terms rather than as a conflict between large farmers and the peasant sector. This distracts attention from the emergence of a new elite of landowners, and plays down the lack of economic planning and infrastructure for the agricultural sector.

Further, while most Zimbabwean farmers are women, their rights remain ambiguous, since their access to land is through men. The situation of widows and single mothers is becoming increasingly difficult in rural areas. In 1995, there were a number of what became known as 'Grain Marketing Board suicides' among women: women who had done and been paid for all the work, only to have their income taken from them by their husbands and who felt that the only way out was to take their own lives. There is, then, a major gender dimension to the land question. The voice for change is, however, weak. A series of droughts and dependence on food distribution through Party channels (ZANU PF)

117

have deepened the silence and acquiescence perceived necessary for survival.

In society more generally, women had great hopes of what independence would bring, having played an important role in the liberation war. However, they have since lost some of the position and status they had gained. The women in decision-making public office are still often hamstrung by owing their position to male patronage.

Displaced violence

There has also been a displacement of violence following demobilisation. Many war veterans are unemployed, and in some parts of the country up to 92 per cent have not worked for more than three months since the war. Some were resettled on the land or in cooperatives without adequate backing or training, and are still marginalised and poverty-stricken. Youth unemployment is also very high. There has been a rise in armed criminality (associated with the easy availability of arms from neighbouring countries), and also an increase in domestic violence. There are many reasons for this: stress, poverty, economic migration, overcrowding, the breakdown of extended families, as well as unhealed war trauma and the resort to self-help 'remedies' of alcoholism and drug abuse. Many women ex-combatants returned home to be shunned by their families and 'war husbands', and they and their children became vulnerable to poverty and abuse, as did disabled people, especially women and children.

There is a widespread sense of hopelessness. Even within the university sector, rather than being allowed to contribute creativity and new ideas, students are stifled. The riot police regularly enter the university and use tear-gas. The reasons are different each time, but the event has become an annual routine. Feelings of hopelessness and helplessness contrast dramatically with the way people felt at the end of the war, when there was a feeling that we were now masters of our own destiny. The socialist State offered hope but also — in fostering the belief that the State will provide — increased dependency. The withdrawal of the State, and the breakdown in health and educational services, have generated widespread suffering. The switch to a market economy and its myth of a 'trickle-down' effect have made the elite (black and white) rich, while the majority have fallen further into abysmal poverty.

The changing face of society

In response, there has been a growth in the number of right-wing fundamentalist churches which, instead of looking at issues of social justice, preach the gospels of prosperity in this world, and faith in the next. Indigenous churches, with their emphasis on conservative, patriarchal (usually polygamous) values, have weakened the advancement of women.

Numerous cases of HIV/AIDS have brought multiple bereavement. Nobody was prepared for this. HIV/AIDS now affect about 25 per cent of Zimbabweans aged between 16 and 50 years. Every day, at least one of my colleagues is away from work, attending a funeral. By the year 2000, there may be as many as 600,000 orphans whose parents have died of AIDS. Women, on top of their 16-hour working days, are being expected to become the care-takers. Excellent work that has been done by Zimbabwean women's organisations, literacy groups, and NGOs is being eroded. Many development agencies and NGOs are still, however, carrying on as if nothing was happening. We should already be focusing our work on children and grandmothers. In many families, it is grandmothers who are bearing the burden.

Since a poor and helpless population is easily manipulated, a culture of fear and patronage further reduces the opportunity to engage in debate and consider mechanisms for peaceful change. Zimbabwe never had a vibrant civil society under British colonial rule; nor has the State apparatus allowed it to develop since Independence. For instance, though the Zimbabwe Human Rights Association is relatively weak, its actions having been described like 'the flapping of a butterfly's wings', the government has been anxious to clamp down on it.

The hope is that the ordinary people of Zimbabwe are starting to demand a re-thinking of a policy of reconciliation that was only skin-deep, a re-writing of our constitution, respect for human rights, a challenge to a *de facto* one-party State, and, above all, a more equitable distribution of wealth. The road is not easy, especially when meeting obstacles of entrenched power, corruption, and bureaucratic sloth, but Zimbabweans of courage have started the journey.

The author

Val Ingham-Thorpe works with the human-rights NGO ZimRights, and is also a member of the Africa Network for Treatment and Prevention of Torture.

Physical, psychological, and political displacement in Angola and Mozambique

Francisco Tunga Alberto

Introduction

The impact of displacement affects many areas of a person's life. It may imply separation from the nuclear family and/or the disappearance of the extended family, with the consequent loss of sources of affection, protection, and support. It certainly means an uprooting from an individual's familiar surroundings and cultural environment, along with a loss of social safety-nets and close personal contacts. It may also mean a change in the functioning of the family: for the displaced child, parents are no longer so powerful. It may mean the start of a strange adventure, and (probably) a farewell to school.

Discovering a new community (urban or rural) is also a struggle for integration within it. For children, it may mean a continuing search for their parents, difficulties in returning to school, problems in cultural reintegration, and in making new friends. It may also be associated with difficulties in finding food and clothing, and with having to lead a new way of life geared to survival (such as becoming a street-child, or begging). The family may assume new forms, while the child may have to take responsibility for helping her or his parents. The possibility of a return to the place of origin may even be distressing.

The consequences of war may have long-term effects on those who are displaced by it. A socio-cultural study that analysed the causes, duration, and the effects of psycho-social development showed that young children and women were most profoundly affected.

This paper is not the result of formal research, but comes from my lifetime of contact with communities within Angola and abroad, in refugee camps, in urban and peri-urban areas, and in the countryside.

The impact of displacement on children

There is no doubt that, among a whole range of effects, displaced children experience a kind of cultural transformation, a spiritual and mental stagnation that affects their entire psycho-social and cultural development.

These children's spirits and minds tend to dwell on their emotions: on the images and dreams of witnessed events; the death of close friends, the destruction of property; physical and mental torture; the long distances walked; the sudden loss of familiar surroundings. All such experiences may generate behaviour which may be aggressive, or intolerant of others who attempt to intervene in their lives. Such children may feel that their ideal is to get on with adapting their lives in line with how they perceive their world. Thus, life for them becomes merely a case of adapting to the environment that adults have provided. For displaced children in Angola, where there has been no real infrastructure to help people to recover, there has been only one solution: to migrate to a place where their role or educational background does not make them feel rejected, such as the street.

Even children who have been cared for by an adult, but who have endured the effects of war, may experience learning and educational difficulties. If our country's leaders do not plan to create special educational structures for these children, their future will continue to be without hope.

The consequences of displacement for women

No matter how their displacement occurs, women bear the main burden and subsequent repercussions, since they continue to be responsible for their families while their husbands are away, perhaps looking for work. Women often take on the tasks of helping their husbands, their own parents as well as their husband's parents, and the sons, nephews, and cousins of both sides of the family. They face the daily problems of finding food and water, and providing care and education for the children.

A major obstacle confronting them is the need to adapt to the local culture, and at the same time to take on new challenges when their partners are absent for prolonged periods — whether because of abandonment, divorce, death, or travel. They may no longer be able to rely on friends and companions for any form of support. The many effects of such constraints include psycho-social crises which, coupled with material shortages, can affect women's physical development and well-being, for example through problems with blood pressure, irregular menstruation, and inadequate vitamin intake. They may also have unwanted and high-risk pregnancies, or give birth prematurely, since they have no access to any antenatal care.

Such women may, therefore, have only anxiety and fear, desperation and spiritual instability to guide them in their day-to-day life. Thus, in the towns, many women turn to drink or to prostitution, a precarious way of life which also affects their children. By the time things reach this stage, these women no longer observe their traditional roles: society has already cast them out as disruptive elements within the community, as women who may also have a bad influence on their neighbours' husbands. There have been cases in which illegitimate children who have been born in such circumstances have been abandoned on rubbish heaps or in garbage drums.

Displaced youths and the effects of war

Since adolescents and young men will tend to fall into whatever role seems most relevant to them at the time, they are often the most disoriented: they urgently need to find solutions for the sake of their own well-being, as well as for society as a whole. The worst thing is the feeling of being a misfit and not belonging, as a result of their desperate socio-economic circumstances and the breakdown of their social environment. No matter how well they might have been able to been able to cope before, socio-economic insecurity is the first obstacle they have to face.

The most common situations are disintegration of the family unit, unemployment, involuntary divorce, and loss — of cultural values, of dignity, and of legitimacy. There is also the issue of their questionable legal status, for both in civilian and military life young men invariably end up acting as guards or sentries. Since their erstwhile political leaders are no longer in power, these young men always find that this acts as an obstacle to their resuming a normal life within society. A typical example of what displaced Angolan youths find is that their communities, and sometimes even their families, no longer trust them, since they are still connected to the political tendencies that controlled the areas in which they took refuge, or they maintain contact with the socio-cultural circle of that time. If the social breakdown and displacement took place outside the areas of government control, these young men are viewed as being allied with the opposition, even if they are now reintegrated back into their own family, community, village, neighbourhood, commune, municipality, province, and country. Thus, if they ever express a different opinion from those around them, or are slow to adapt to the local political and social context, then someone only has to accuse them of being with the opposition, and these young Angolans may be slaughtered like animals, very often without even being given a hearing.

As for those returning from other countries, they are always considered as foreigners within their own land. They are denied privileges and never treated fairly, especially if they do not speak perfect Portuguese. Anyone with a French accent is called Zairian, while those with an English accent are referred to as Zambians. Just having sought refuge outside Angola is enough on their return to limit their access to many types of better-paid employment. Even in the field of sport, those who fail to meet local socio-political qualifications have no chance of being selected for the national team. These young men suffer more than anyone from oppression, torture, and threats from public security agents, and are the most likely to face arbitrary arrest.

As a solution, many emigrate. There are three main categories of migrant: professionals, 'commercial travellers' (or *candongueiros*), and those with a technical training. Socio-cultural disintegration leads them to imagine that exile is the best place for them, or at least somewhere where they are unknown and can relax.

As far as the young men displaced within Angola are concerned, the frustration is the same: they avoid talking about the past, they do not circulate freely, and they have real problems in obtaining new identity documents. Those who were away for a long time from their places of origin return to find that the women are married to men who are sympathetic to whoever is in power, and they can say nothing about it.

Whenever suspicions are raised, these men are the first to be arrested. As an alternative to constant harassment, they often become drug addicts — taking drugs so they can forget about everything. They are not involved in violence or criminality, since they are under constant surveillance. The best way out is for them to move elsewhere, although the authorities seldom lose track of their movements. Even those who have never indicated support for the opposition may be observed by secret agents who will monitor their political behaviour.

The other group of displaced young men who return home or seek help are those who were mutilated or have a physical defect. Their needs are scarcely recognised at all, and the only option for them is to beg.

General conclusion

A family which is displaced loses all the support systems it enjoyed in the place that was home. It abandons everything: land, house, extended family, possessions, social security, psycho-social equilibrium, social relations, and so on. The family's political leanings or allegiances also become an issue. Thus, for their own physical security, a family's political affiliations may have to be abandoned or concealed temporarily, if not for ever.

Displacement also implies a complete break from any status the family had acquired, and from everything that is related to this. A displaced person is an 'outsider', a neutral person who may be open to many new experiences and relations. Such people seek to enrich themselves in every way (socially, economically, politically, spiritually, and culturally) in their new community or *terroir*.

During the war for national liberation, civilians as well as fighters were armed. Following independence, the people remained divided and were often armed by the warring political parties. For decades, the people of Angola and Mozambique have become accustomed to bearing arms. Even criminals can get hold of weapons: in Angola, the toy which most children can draw best is the gun. A major long-term campaign of sensitisation and education is required, which would enable the people of Angola and Mozambique to free themselves from the bad habits acquired as a result of the possession and use of arms.

The fact that the people remain both armed and partisan does not imply that the parties in conflict should continue to be armed. Yet popular armed factions are often just an extension of the parties' own militia. Disarmament of the civilian population would be a critical step on the path to lasting peace. A substantial education campaign should be run through the churches, schools, social communication networks, youth associations and so on, linked with rigorous efforts to fight criminal activity by the Ministry of Justice and the Forces of Internal Order. One should not overlook the educational and corrective campaign of the political parties themselves, which used to be armed, and who should now persuade their members to hand over their weapons so as to bring about a real change in people's mentality.

More emphasis should be given to persuading every citizen to regard his or her compatriots not as enemies but as brothers, sisters, friends, all with the right to think differently, and to hold and to defend different ideas. The example should come from above, from the politicians at the top. Implementation of real democracy will be a decisive step in shaping this change in mentality, since the opposition sympathisers will see that responsible politicians have also changed their stance, and no longer consider themselves to possess the one and only truth. If this came from those at the top, desirable change would be brought about more decisively and more rapidly.

Arms were also used by people who took justice into their own hands: whoever had and used arms was in power and could impose their wishes on others. The political authorities appeared to tolerate this behaviour, despite some statements to the contrary made by the

121

government — statements that appear to have been largely for international consumption.

Large sectors of the population have suffered as a result. It is sad that the urgent need for disarmament in Angola has not been given top priority, for this has allowed the continued use of illegal arms which is claiming innocent lives every day, either for political motives, the settling of personal accounts, or purely for criminal reasons.

If one political faction remains armed, then the others will find it difficult to believe in its desire for peace. This will generate not only a lack of confidence, but, more importantly, the continuation of an 'army in disguise' with the clear (but unacknowledged) objective of one day retaliating against the other, an attitude which does not represent a real, sincere, and total commitment to peace — and which cannot lead to the change in mentality we need.

The author

Francisco Tunga Alberto is the Secretary-General of FONGA, the Forum of Angolan NGOs.

Child soldiers: the experience of the Mozambican Association for Public Health (AMOSAPU)

Viriato Castelo-Branco

Mozambique was devastated during 15 years of civil war which left the country in extreme poverty and economically destabilised. Although the situation now seems to be changing gradually, with good prospects for the future, much work still has to be done to reconstruct the social fabric of the nation.

The main victims of the civil war were the children living in rural communities: an estimated 250,000 children have been separated from their families in Mozambique since 1980. Many were kidnapped and forced to serve as porters and soldiers, making them both victims and perpetrators of violence. As victims/survivors of the armed conflict, these children have experienced immense torment from the sense of fear, loss, and trauma, in addition to the deprivation already imposed by the hunger, disease, and poverty that resulted from the disruption or destruction of social, economic, or health services. As perpetrators, they were forced to undergo military training, to be programmed to commit atrocities, to steal, and to kill. In many cases, they were made to murder even their own parents or people very close to them, in order to prove their courage and capacity to be good soldiers.

The bandits gave me a knife and forced me to kill my father by cutting his throat. They threatened me with being killed in the same way if I did not do it. Then they gave me a heavy bag to carry and took me to the base. (Carlos, 17 years old)

The families of the children were also subjected to many distressing events. Their incapacity to protect their children from the atrocities and to fulfil the role of 'good parents' makes them feel guilty for what happened to their children.

While children used to learn to regard authority as something necessary and appropriate, many came to know the arbitrary use of authority and force during the war. They did not have their parents to help and direct them, to give them the love that they needed, and to contribute to the development of self-esteem, appropriate behaviours, and personality in general. Normal family structures and community life were severely affected, and now they must support the education and social-isation of their children without the necessary resources to help them.

The process of demobilisation and social reintegration

A major step towards 'peace' in Mozambique is the demobilisation of soldiers. However, the process has dealt mainly with adult soldiers and ex-soldiers. Child soldiers were excluded from the military demobilisation process. Their existence was strongly denied, until the weight of evidence forced a change of response. Even so, they were simply sent back to their places of origin, or transferred from the bases to transit centres, from where most have subsequently been taken to their district of origin.

Community resources

As a means of coping, communities have used their own skills to recover and protect themselves and their values against the risk of military actions.

The role of traditional healers and religious leaders was very important in encouraging people, by promoting belief in the protection of their ancestors. In some communities in the south of Mozambique, children were reported as being sent back to their village after being kidnapped at the school, because of the retaliation of 'Mungoi's spirit', a very famous folk healer who died long ago. The people believe that his spirit is still alive and that during the war he protected the village against attack.

Religious leaders have likewise been instrumental in re-integrating child soldiers into their communities. They perform 'purification rituals', during which a person is bathed in specially prepared liquids. Through such rituals, the children are cleansed from the bad spirits associated with the violence of the war.

One of the methods used by the traditional healers is *khufemba*. Through this, a former child soldier who wants to return to a community where he committed wartime offences can speak with the spirits of those whom he killed, and seek counsel on how to atone for his sins. The healer enters into a trance and acts as a medium for the spirits of the dead. In this way, the child can be integrated back to the community by performing tasks requested by the spirits.

Effects on personality and individual coping

Symptoms experienced by war-traumatised children include the following:

- loss of confidence in themselves and in others
- poor capacity to project their future
- isolation, depression, resignation, aggression
- loss of sensitivity
- regression
- introversion
- phobias
- loss of adequate mechanisms for resolving conflicts and problems
- poor tolerance of frustration
- various neurotic and psychotic symptoms
- poor intellectual flexibility
- poor memory capacity, concentration, and imagination
- constant fatigue
- headaches, vertigo, and disturbed sleep
- gastric pains
- flashbacks
- disrupted socialisation mechanisms, especially in accepting social norms and values
- a range of other symptoms that are difficult to classify and interpret with the classical psycho-diagnostic tools, but which reflect the psycho-cultural mechanisms developed in response to trauma.

Although it is difficult to tell which aspects constitute the child's basic personality and which do not, it is important to take into account that some forms of behaviour may not be symptoms of trauma, but are characteristic of a particular child. For example, introversion may not be a problem if it is the case that the child is by nature quiet, or prefers to be alone.

Child soldiers who survived the war and coped with their experiences are now coping with the long-term effects of their involvement in violence. However, their coping mechanisms may not always be appropriate to their present context, while their behaviours are, naturally, carry-overs from the past. They may, therefore, experience difficulties, psychological and practical, in adjusting to new conditions, to their change in function from guerrilla fighters to regular civilians and citizens.

The AMOSAPU programme

Since many of these children have been destabilised, both psychologically and in economic terms, the assistance programme of the Mozambican Association for Public Health is directed towards helping them to re-establish themselves. Efforts have been made to re-unite them with their families where possible, and if they want to go back. Therapy is offered, individually and in groups, not only to the children themselves but to the family as a whole. The huge number of these children makes it necessary to work with activists or volunteers who monitor the families on a regular basis.

Therapy includes play, art, dance, and counselling. Occupational therapy is included, as a response to the children's economic needs. Self-help groups are encouraged with material support and training. For example, bullocks have been provided for those who want to engage in agriculture, and a group of fisherfolk were provided with a boat. Carpentry training workshops are planned.

The approach here is community-oriented. Maximum use is made of those community structures which were previously damaged. Basically, AMOSAPU works through and with schools. It supports those victims of violence who are unable to attend school to understand their situation. Sometimes AMOSAPU arranges special classes, so that later the children can enter the State educational system.

The author

Viriato Castelo-Branco is a teacher who works for the Mozambican Public Health Association in Maputo.

Training for peace

Glenda Caine

After 300 years of colonialism, South Africa began its transition to democracy in April 1994. Among the legacies of the past are fractured communities that are out of touch with their cultures and traditions, shattered family structures, and a deep-rooted history of division. On top of this, South Africa also has been left with a culture in which violence is commonly used as an acceptable method of problem-solving.

It is within the constraints of this environment that the Independent Projects Trust (IPT), an NGO, offers training in conflict-resolution skills. This training is delivered throughout the region of KwaZulu Natal and focuses on structures such as the following:

- South African Police Services and Community Police Forums
- School Boards, including Management Committees, principals, teachers, and pupils
- women's groups
- political parties
- traditional structures and grassroots leadership in rural areas

In this paper, we focus on our work with traditional structures in rural areas.

Background

The province of KwaZulu Natal is situated on the eastern seaboard of South Africa, and is bordered by Mozambique in the north and the former Transkei in the south. It occupies approximately one-tenth of South Africa's land mass and has a population of about 9.4 million. The region is characterised by hilly terrain, and the northern-most reaches are remote and often inaccessible by road. A large portion of the province is rural, and the IPT has three offices in these areas: Port Shepstone in the south,

Ulundi in the far north, and Empangeni in the north. The organisation's head office is in Durban, which is the urban centre of KwaZulu Natal.

Most people in the region are Zulu speakers, and it is the second most densely populated region after Gauteng. Although there is significant economic development, this is largely concentrated round the port of Durban and the Richards Bay and Empangeni area. Important crops are sugar and citrus, but the associated activities do not generate enough employment, and it is estimated that the unemployment rate in rural KwaZulu is as high as 70 per cent. Some 46 per cent of all households depend on remittances from male family members who work as contract labourers on the mines and in the industries of Gauteng. The continuation of this system of migrant labour exacerbates the spread of HIV/AIDS: the region has the highest rate of infection in South Africa, as high as 40 per cent in some rural areas.

Infrastructure is — at best — rudimentary, with little or no provision of running water, or access to electric power outside the urban areas. The average monthly per capita income is R210, while the household subsistence income is estimated at R900 per month. Approximately one million children do not attend school.

KwaZulu Natal has a history of political violence which dates back to the 1980s and frequently threatens to undermine the stability of the new dispensation. At risk of over-simplifying things, it can be said to have arisen from the mid-1980s, when the Inkatha Freedom Party (IFP) sought to consolidate its influence in the province, against the growing support for Congress of South African Trade Unions (COSATU) and the United Democratic Front (UDF), both aligned with the African National Congress (ANC). The IFP also threw its weight behind the effort of the National Party to crush the Mass Democratic Movements, a factor which had a long-term negative effect on relationships in the region.

The rural areas of KwaZulu Natal are dominated by traditional structures. This is a system of chiefs (*amakhosi*) and headmen (*indunas*) who exert a major influence over rural life. The rural areas are generally controlled by the IFP, and the urban areas by the ANC. There is continuing tension between the political parties in the province, which is likely to increase as the second general election approaches in 1999.

It is against this backdrop that the IPT trains in rural areas and gives community workers the skills to help their own communities to handle disputes in an effective and peaceful manner.

Definition of community-based peace-workers

Rural areas in KwaZulu Natal have been scarred by years of deprivation, and then further damaged by internecine violence. It is critical that we begin to build peace mechanisms into community structures. Little development takes place where there is war and, left unchecked, communities then enter a downward spiral from which there is little hope of return.

The successful peace structures in this region have generally had spontaneous origins, and have often comprised two-person teams, one from each of the combatant groups — for instance the ANC and IFP. These are the types of structure which have the most chance of success in terms of a sustainable peace.

A spokesperson for one of the longest-surviving peace structures in this region gave the following qualities as essential for aspiring peace-workers and a successful process:

- fear of God
- honesty
- 'knowing the opposition', understanding and accepting them
- a willingness to 'take it slowly' and handle setbacks
- both parties must be fearless and committed enough to appear in public together
- neutral zones must be identified for joint meetings
- hard-liners may be elected into office, and should be kept in the process and visible at all times

- peace must have a high value for both parties
- small peace cells must be active throughout the community and able to react to crises.

Peace-workers at the grassroots level face unique problems. They will be beset by daily challenges, and their constituency — which is usually at the bottom of the pile in the struggle for food, water, and shelter — is often sustained by the violence. This violence may also serve the needs of middle leadership, because it draws the focus from them and any failure on their part to deliver services. Thus peace-workers battle continually against adversity. They need to be brave and have a deep commitment which will sustain them through the failures which characterise this type of work.

Training community-based workers and strengthening existing social structures

The type of training and skills transfer in which we are involved is long-term, tedious, and difficult to measure. Both the training and funding agencies must have a realistic picture of these difficulties.

We have had some success in training for changing attitudes. For this we concentrate on the following modules:

- Communication: effective skills, including active listening skills
- Assertiveness: in a country where confrontation is the norm, assertiveness is a vital component for changing attitudes
- Problem-solving skills
- Cooperative behaviour and consensus-building.

There are certain steps which it is helpful to follow. Firstly, it is essential to work with both sets of combatants, in order to give each group an equal opportunity to provide community trainers. Secondly, the training organisation must be accepted as impartial and trusted by all the groups involved. Openness and integrity on the part of the training agency are imperative.

Our strategy at IPT is to meet with each party to conflict and share our plan, which is to provide training services which will foster skills and assist the parties to manage a changing and stressful environment. Having done that, we work with as many key players at grassroots level as possible, and draw these from all interest groups in the community, such as women's groups, youth, development committees, and so on. The provision of this skills-training serves a two-fold purpose, since it also strengthens community ties for people to begin to work together, to realise that they share a common vision and purpose, and start to interact with each other on issues of concern to the community.

What does and does not work?

Where a community has some structures of its own, and has not been too depleted by violence and poverty, it is often possible to enable and support structures which will contribute to peace-making in the area. It is, however, impossible to do so without some of the following:

- a spontaneous desire for peace among the people at grassroots level
- strong leadership from both sides of the conflict to carry the process forward

- some external support
- hope of real change and transformation in the community, through the provision of jobs and infrastructure, which will assist in creating new psychological attitudes
- grassroots and middle leadership who support the process
- media which are prepared to play a constructive role.

In conclusion, our experience is that this type of work is never easy and there are no 'quick fixes'. Long-term commitment and dedication are needed. No 'outsider', such as a training organisation, can bring peace: this has to start in the hearts and minds of the affected community.

The author

Glenda Caine is Director of the Independent Projects Trust, and has a special interest in peace education and training in conflict-resolution.

Change and continuity: the challenge of transition

Deborah Eade

It is critical during the transition to be able to talk frankly with the international aid agencies — that is, with trusted individuals within them — on how we should define our role in peace-building. (Guatemalan NGO worker)

International NGOs seldom offer clear career paths to their staff. While the aid-agency scene does sometimes resemble musical chairs — the same people keep cropping up, but in different places, and wearing different hats — there is also a strong tendency to limit how long any one person will stay in a given 'front-line' post. However prized, NGO 'field' jobs are usually offered only for fixed periods. Individuals may renew the initial contract, but there is a built-in expectation that they will 'move on' after a couple of stints. Constant staff turnover is thus positively encouraged.

The conventional rationale for this has been twofold. Firstly, that the NGO concerned wants to remain flexible, especially given the increasing uncertainty of funds. It is also frequently implied that if you stay 'too long' in a given country, you will lose your 'objectivity' by getting 'too involved' with what is going on there, or too locked into a particular set of relationships, commitments, and ways of doing things. In other words, 'going native' implies losing the critical capacity and independent judgement that are seen to be what the head office values — and, presumably, what it believes that it epitomises.

The second major concern among international NGOs has been to avoid 'burn-out' among its programme staff. So-called field jobs (which are often concerned as much with servicing the NGO's bureaucracy as with anything resembling fieldwork) are taxing: they tend to involve a lot of hectic travel, large and complex workloads (from negotiating with government ministries to arguing with the head office about whether a can of beer is a permissible meal expense), and high levels of stress resulting from the perception (often the reality!) that they are on 24-hour duty — at the beck and call of the head office, and available at all times to respond to any local crisis. Any dividing line between one's private and professional lives is erased. Here, the sub-text amounts to the following: we know that working around the clock is not good for you or your family, but it's the only way to do the job — so do it just for a couple of years, then we'll get someone else to take over. That the job could be done differently is seldom considered, not least because it is how the NGO asserts its *own* importance: to be at the centre of things means being there all the time, while being there all the time proves that one is at the centre of things.[1]

Some of these habits of thought and practice have their roots in the way the diplomatic service traditionally operates: an officer is 'posted' for a tour of duty, after which he (it usually is a 'he') returns to base or is 'posted' elsewhere. Many multilateral agencies also expect considerable flexibility on the part of their employees: UNHCR, for instance, now has a policy of rotating its programme staff, and maintaining only a core of administrative and policy-making staff at the centre. Not an approach that can easily accommodate staff with children or other dependants!

However, NGOs may be changing. For instance, among those NGOs that are committed to multiculturalism, there is a greater willingness to recruit senior programme staff from the countries or regions in which they will work.[2] Unlike foreigners, their social, political, and cultural status does not depend on the NGO. On the contrary, their own experience and identity enhance the NGO's work and status. Concerns about 'going native' or 'burning out' take on a different character in such a setting!

However, the focus of this paper is on the discrepancy between the formal policy of promoting staff turnover and what seems to happen in situations of prolonged armed conflict. For, in the 1980s and early 1990s, instead of leaving after a couple of years, many international NGO staff in 'tough' situations stayed on ... and on. For instance, in Central America, a situation in which burn-out was inevitable,[3] it was not unusual for foreign aid workers to stay for 10 years or more. Their commitment to working for peace and justice was beyond any doubt. So the interesting thing is that within 18 months after the Salvadoran Peace Accords were signed, most of these long-timers had left or were packing up to go.

Why leave when peace breaks out?

An individual's reasons for leaving a war-ravaged region once peace has broken out are many and complex. More often than not, they are deeply personal rather than professional: many dedicated and experienced NGO staff left Central America with no job to move on to, nor any clear plans for the future. They were, quite simply, exhausted. But after such prolonged stress, in a context where to admit (much less attend to) your own needs seemed self-indulgent, there were many pent-up emotions. For me, the changes taking place in the region made me feel both that I had lost something of my adopted identity; and that I needed to re-affirm my own culture, society, and language. After several years of being a key to access resources, I was longing to be myself: however sincere my friendships, there were times when I had felt like a walking cheque-book! And yet, without this role, I feared finding that I meant nothing to anyone.

What does leaving mean?

Departure itself stirred up more ambivalence: there could be no way to say goodbye to the people whose struggles I had in some way shared. Yet I was also a foreigner in my own country, indifferent to much of what was going on, and sometimes unable even to understand what people were talking about — or to share my own feelings. Whole political and cultural eras had passed me by: I had not listened to the same music, seen the same (any!) films, watched the same television programmes, participated in the same political campaigns. My experience and preoccupations did not translate easily into this setting. It took time to get used to not having to speak in code when using the phone. Once the pressure was off, many friends and colleagues also found that either that their personal relationships had become dependent on the adrenalin-charged atmosphere of war, or that they had forgotten how to live a life of their own.

But why stay?

Within the professional sphere too, rapid changes within the NGO ethos and structure as peace becomes a reality can also make it hard for an 'old-timer' to stay on. Rather like veteran cars, people are made to feel that, although they performed good service in their day, new skills and analyses are needed now. A new context needs new blood, not someone whose batteries need re-charging, and who is 'mired in the past'. Harping on about popular education or social transformation or land reform is seen to be out of keeping with today's development agenda: production, entrepreneurship, efficiency, Logical Framework Analysis (or, for the milder types, PRA), and monitoring indicators. The 'old guard' may still talk about Freirean conscientisation processes, or class conflict; but what today's hard-headed NGOs demand are skills in Project Management and Strategic Planning, and fluency in the language of input, throughput, and output. Accountability and appraisal replace 'accompaniment'; counter-parts become clients. Overnight, those who worked throughout the war years are the romantics; the new guys on the block are the true realists!

Does it matter?

Does it matter? The short answer is, 'Yes it does'. In Central America alone, one international NGO lost some 60 years of experience between 1991 and 1993 as most of its long-serving staff walked through the door. When we realise that this trend was replicated across the entire NGO scene, the accumulated loss in the region is staggering. Their expatriate replacements often had little or no prior experience of working in the region (how could they have gained it, if all the jobs were taken?) and were often just as new to the NGO itself.

It is beyond question that there is a need in a post-war period for new energy and fresh insights. The problem is one of scale and balance, on the one hand; and timing and phasing, on the other. With the pressures of transition already a reality, there is little time for new staff really to get to know the background, or to acquire the trust of local people. Almost inevitably, then, the first loyalty of a new NGO worker must be to his or her employer; commitment to counterparts and processes must fit around this.

Yet precisely because the processes of transition and reconstruction are complex and multi-layered, knowledge, experience, and trust are paramount. After the fighting is over, most locals have nowhere else to go: they must come to terms with the various levels of transition as these occur in their daily lives. With no chance to take a metaphorical deep breath, they just have to get on with it. Their experience of the war necessarily shapes their response to the challenges of transition, for there is no clear and absolute break between them. It is then that it becomes so important to call on trusted friends, with whom experiences have been shared over the years.

A Guatemalan friend and colleague, with some 25 years' experience in international NGOs, has been looking into how Central Americans regard the various negotiation processes and transitions towards peace and reconciliation.[4] Her informants' perceptions of what has happened among the international NGOs are telling:

Individuals within the international NGOs are very important. In Guatemala, we feel that many new people have arrived without having any real experience or knowledge of the country's recent history. This has meant that we've had to 're-invent the wheel' with them. (Guatemalan NGO)

After the Peace Accords, even one of the 'friendly' international NGOs got us into an intense dynamic of Strategic Planning. It didn't work, because of the design that was imposed ... but it went on for about two years, and cost a huge amount of money. (Leader of Salvadoran popular organisation)

If they want to talk about being our 'partners', they too need to get involved in the whole process. They must be flexible in order to make real progress, take on board that there will be some failures, and have a long-term

vision. To support processes, as opposed to projects, means being committed at least into the medium term. (Guatemalan NGO).

What is most worrying is that the lessons that were learned through the harsh experience of war — the need to develop a shared analysis of the causes of the conflict, the knowledge that trust must be earned and cannot be assumed, the immense value of inter-agency co-ordination, the life-and-death importance of not acting unilaterally — become dissipated or lost. The risk is that the values and principles that informed the work of NGOs during the armed conflict may be absent from the support they offer during the transition to peace.

If these criticisms matter to international NGOs, the challenge is how to minimise such abrupt and negative personnel changes. How can NGOs prevent their staff from burning-out? How can they work more co-operatively together? And how can the experience and trust that have been earned by individuals be passed on to others? How can people who are deeply committed be *enabled* to leave, without having to 'abandon ship' altogether?

Addressing these issues implies a mix of practical measures, both to enable staff to vary the pace at which they work, and to reassure them that others are being trained up to take their place. These might include:

• Building 'time out' into the staff member's contract, by insisting on several periods of paid leave in the course of the year, and ensuring adequate cover to make this possible.

• Pacing the staff turnover by bringing in new staff as assistants or deputies, or for in-service training, well in advance of the previous incumbents' leaving; not imagining that a real handover can be achieved in a couple of weeks, and not waiting until they are on the runway before placing a job advert!

• Actively identifying local people to be trained for senior programme roles, in order to minimise the dependence on foreign aid workers — and also helping to ensure that management styles and policies both incorporate a range of cultural approaches and are culturally appropriate in each setting.

• Seeking opportunities for staff members to be seconded to local NGOs or other organisations for a period of time within their contract period: a change is as good as a rest, and this would also promote mutual understanding among agencies.

- Enabling staff to take sabbaticals or spend time with another programme in order to 'systematise' or reflect on their experience *during* their contract, rather than after they have already left; a written report is not the only way to do this.

- Enabling staff to return to the region for a brief period may, paradoxically, make it easier for them to leave definitively. In addition, many have found that it is only when they have 'stood back' that they can begin to work through the difficult emotions and feelings to which they have been clinging.

Finally, the notion that the best way to ensure staff turnover is to offer fixed-term contracts is, at best, questionable. My own experience is that these encourage individuals to work at an artificially accelerated pace, while also acting as a disincentive to those with families (and, hence, other healthy demands on their time!) to apply for such posts.

The cessation of armed conflicts in Central America and in Southern Africa coincided with a time of major international upheaval. People emerged from many years of war to find that the entire political map had changed, the old signposts pointed nowhere, and the milestones were overgrown. International NGOs may simply add to the disorientation if they too make abrupt shifts in their staffing and policy direction, rather than seeing this, more than ever, as a time to accompany their counterparts in shaping the process of change.

Notes

1 It is not uncommon to find a discrepancy between an NGO's domestic and 'foreign' employment policies. Commonly, the programme staff in the head office have tenure, while their colleagues overseas face the insecurity of fixed-term contracts. This insecurity is often (not always) materially compensated. However, what is remarkable is that 'burn-out' and rigidity are *not* perceived to be a problem facing staff 'at home'!

2 As we can test an NGO's commitment to gender analysis by looking at the pattern of female employment, so we should not to assume that declarations about multiculturalism translate into affirmative action. In one international NGO, for instance, the proportion of senior non-expatriate staff in one continental area has *dropped* from three-quarters to one-quarter since the mid-1980s.

3 See Martha Thompson, 'Empowerment and survival: humanitarian work in civil conflict', (Part 2), *Development in Practice*, Volume 7, Number 1.

4 Patricia Ardón's study is entitled 'Los Conflictos en Centroamérica'. This is as yet an internal report, but an edited version is due to be published in Spanish in 1998. It is hoped that an English translation will also be published by Oxfam GB in the course of the same year.

The author

Deborah Eade worked in Mexico and Central America from 1982 to 1991, much of that time as Oxfam's Deputy Regional Representative. Since then she has been Editor of *Development in Practice*.

Conflict, reconstruction, and reconciliation: reciprocal lessons for NGOs in Southern Africa and Central America

Martha Thompson

The Johannesburg Symposium illustrated the value of sharing experiences across continental divides on the common thematic and programmatic challenges facing NGOs involved in post-conflict work. This brief reflection identifies some of the areas in which there is potential for NGOs in both regions to learn from each other's experiences.

As Jenny Pearce has observed, peace is becoming an industry. The multilateral agencies such as the United Nations Development Programme (UNDP) are increasingly seen as having a blueprint for reconstruction. Other organisations, particularly USAID and the European Union, can have substantial influence on both the processes and programmes involved in reconstruction. There is a growing body of literature about reconstruction and reconciliation in post-conflict contexts.

In both Central America and Southern Africa, the way in which NGOs and grassroots organisations respond to armed conflict and the post-conflict context differs significantly from that the response of donors, governments, and UN organisations. This engagement leads to a unique vision and understanding of the situation. It is crucial that NGOs and grassroots organisations should have a voice in the post-conflict stages of reconstruction and reconciliation. It is vital that the whole range of NGOs which worked with civilian structures in situations of armed conflict, as well as the popular and community organisations themselves, begin to create a space within which to exchange experiences and learn from one another about how to deal with the different international actors who appear on the stage once the formal hostilities are over. Only then can NGOs be equipped to apply much-needed critical thinking to reconstruction and reconciliation work.

This reflection aims to stimulate discussion on possible exchanges between NGOs and others in Southern Africa and Central America who are currently working in post-conflict reconstruction and reconciliation. There are several areas in which there is considerable overlap of interest, concern, and experience.

Reconstruction plans

While each armed conflict is quite distinct from all the others, certain packages for reconstruction and reconciliation, particularly those designed by the multilateral agencies such as UNDP, tend to be applied irrespective of the context. For example, a reconstruction package similar to the one that UNDP and USAID promoted in El Salvador in 1992 is now being proposed for Angola (despite the fact that it was heavily criticised for the problems which arose in the implementation phase).

In both El Salvador and Nicaragua, there is already a wealth of experience of such funding programmes for reconstruction. For instance, in El Salvador donors promised US$800,000 for a reconstruction plan which was designed to promote integrated development in areas affected by the war; meet the immediate needs of civilians and ex-combatants, both FMLN and government forces; and repair damaged infrastructure. Although they had prepared an alternative plan, the FMLN agreed not to present it and to let the government put forward its reconstruction plan as *the* concerted plan. This plan did not, however, reflect the needs or experience of the people living in the conflict zones, nor of the NGOs that had worked with them. Further, to the post of Director of the National Secretariat for Reconstruction the government appointed a person who had previously headed a government agency that was deeply involved in the counter-insurgency effort in the mid-1980s.

The aid was supposed to be administered through the municipalities. The mayors were to hold open meetings to gather opinions on how the reconstruction funds were to be used, although they had the power to make the final decision. This was particularly problematic in the former conflict zones where the people's own self-governing structures were not recognised by the government. Mayors who had been elected by displaced populations while they were living outside the war zones then moved back to the towns whence they had fled, and in their capacity as local government authorities began to disburse reconstruction funds. Municipal structures had become weak and polarised as a result of the long civil war. In the few areas where local mayors agreed to invite NGOs and others to discuss projects and coordinate work, the mayors were reprimanded by their parties and denied access to funds. Most importantly, there were no accountability mechanisms. The mayors were not accountable to the populations, and the National Secretariat was not accountable to the donors for the use to which the reconstruction funds were put.

Now UNDP wants to implement a similar structure in Angola, with a national reconstruction body and implementation through the municipalities. Exchange between NGOs in El Salvador and Angola could be particularly useful, and could draw on published critiques of peace and reconstruction in El Salvador.[1] In particular, some of the people who played leading roles in the Salvadoran NGO movement during the war and the transition period were deeply involved in the discussions concerning an alternative reconstruction plan, and have also experienced the difficulty of getting access to reconstruction funds through the national plan. Some Salvadoran NGOs have also analysed the problems posed when an economic structural adjustment programme is implemented at the same time as a national reconstruction programme. In effect, in El Salvador (and perhaps in Guatemala) the government intends to use the reconstruction funds to soften the impact of structural adjustment.

Access to — and redistribution of — land has also proved a thorny aspect of reconstruction and reconciliation in Central America, as it is likely to be in southern Africa. In El Salvador,

access to fairly apportioned plots of land was crucial to the chances of a sustained peace; and, despite enormous difficulty, four years after the war ended, all ex-combatants had received some land. For many, however, this is just the beginning of the problem, and land disputes continue. There are many lessons to be learned from the experience, including the huge financial support needed by the FMLN in order to develop their technical and operational capacity to carry out their part of the land agreement.

Post-conflict tensions for NGOs

After a time of armed conflict, NGOs often have a harder time responding to needs, articulating new ways of working, and coping with the peace than they had when working together in adversity. Divisions and differences tend to increase — which is upsetting to the NGOs themselves, and also weakens their ability to respond quickly to transition. It may be useful to compare experiences in El Salvador, Nicaragua, and Guatemala with those of the post-conflict NGO world in Southern Africa.

Reconciliation

In Southern Africa, a considerable amount of work has been done to promote community-level reconciliation and recovery from violence. Neither response has been comprehensively developed in Central America, apart from Nicaragua, where the focus has been on the ex-combatants. In El Salvador, little has yet been done. Four Christian Base Communities around the capital city have just published their own history of the deaths and violence they suffered during the war. A Committee to Find the Children has formed, to seek children who were kidnapped by the armed forces during military raids in the rural areas. The FMLN formed its own NGO to work with its own ex-combatants, and this did have a mental-health programme. However, it remained largely unused, because the former fighters did not want to be tainted with the tag of 'mental illness'. In Guatemala, there is a great need for local-level reconciliation, especially given the violence carried out by the civil patrols on their own communities.

What *is* clear from Central America is that the Peace Accords do not offer solutions to the deeply rooted societal conflict which was the cause of the wars. People have returned to their communities after the armed conflict only to find that many aspects of the reconstruction plan have intensified existing tensions. For instance, structural adjustment policies in El Salvador have worsened the economic situation of the rural poor and further deprived them of scarce government-funded services. Since neither the Peace Accords nor the reconstruction plan really promoted any kind of local reconciliation, NGOs need to address it. However, in Central America, there has been far more emphasis on reconstruction than on reconciliation.

The other important work that is going on in Southern Africa at the grassroots level is addressing the trauma experienced by those who lived through the years of violence and repression. The need to address this is hard to articulate in many rural communities; either it is ignored in favour of economic programmes, or it is assumed that the time for it has passed. Unfortunately, the fact that these problems have not been addressed does not mean they disappear with time. Rather, they persist, as people end up expressing their feelings through other kinds of negative behaviour.

Guatemalan NGOs who are working with returned refugees and communities might learn useful insights from the experience of their counterparts in Southern Africa working on local-level reconciliation. The Catholic Church in Guatemala has been trying to gather documentation from the grass-roots on the history of the repression and violence, but compared with the support offered by the Centre for the Study of Violence and Reconciliation in South Africa, virtually nothing is being done to address the trauma and loss experienced by victims of the conflict in Guatemala, or to support those who are giving testimony. Likewise the Centre's experience of the workings of the Truth Commission might be a basis for useful exchange with Central American NGOs and human-rights groups.

Demobilisation and re-integration of ex-combatants

Demobilisation is proving problematic in the cases of Mozambique, Angola, and Namibia, and has also been difficult in Nicaragua and El Salvador. Again, the type of 're-integration' package that is being offered to the African countries — involving training for ex-combatants in micro-enterprise management — has already proved unsuccessful in El Salvador and Nicaragua in terms of providing any real economic security. This is a critical area for exchange and mutual learning, particularly since — if re-integration programmes fail — the potential for social conflict is so enormous. In Nicaragua, for example, where the Peace Accords are several years old, ex-combatants from both sides have frequently taken up arms, sometimes together, sometimes in separate bands, in order to make the point that they are not happy with the results of the Accords, the re-integration package, or the way in which the political process is being managed. In El Salvador, the ex-combatants received help in a land-distribution programme that was far more successful than that of Nicaragua, but combatants on both sides complain that the economic re-integration package has not helped them significantly. The increase in armed crime in both El Salvador and Nicaragua after the end of the wars suggests that ex-combatants are still armed and by no means re-integrated into society. In Guatemala, the issue of demobilisation remains to be defined.

NGOs in Southern Africa and Central America would have a great deal to contribute to discussion on these matters. Two major issues are the failure of the economic reintegration programmes which depend on turning ex-combatants into small entrepreneurs, and the problems encountered in the course of implementing the expensive training programmes funded in the Salvadoran re-integration programme. The Salvadorans now realise the importance of asking questions, such as who should do the training, who selects the trainers, who defines the content, and what is the methodology? What happened in practice was that USAID and other donors would approve or even hire NGOs to do the training, although none of them had any prior experience of working in the conflict zones, or even much understanding of the issues over which the war was fought.

Other aspects of demobilisation which require careful consideration are the particular problems confronting women, the fate of child-soldiers, and support for psychological recovery. In El Salvador, the high proportion of women combatants within the FMLN, especially among the mid-level commanders, would provide useful leads on gender-specific issues to be addressed in economic re-integration processes. The work in Mozambique with former boy-soldiers appears to be unique, and could yield useful lessons for El Salvador, where the issue of child-soldiers was simply never addressed. Valuable experience has also been developed in Mozambique in the psychological aspects of re-integrating ex-combatants into their rural communities — work that might be useful in both El Salvador and Nicaragua.

The participation of civil society in the Peace Accords and beyond

In both Southern Africa and Central America, NGOs are directly affected by many aspects of the peace negotiations, especially questions of human rights and economic, social, and institutional reform — particularly reform of the judiciary and the security forces. Experience in Central America continues to show the importance of involving civil society in the peace negotiations, although this has never been given formal recognition. The National Debate in El Salvador and the Assembly of Civil Sectors in Guatemala are both examples of civil society's attempts to participate in negotiations. Both provide insights into NGOs' attempts to contribute to national debate about reconciliation. In each case, the sectors and institutions which were represented developed their own proposals for many of the problems that had been identified in the peace negotiations, and would be a rich source of information and inspiration. A further example is the attempt in El Salvador to create a civilian police force from ex-combatants from both

sides, a process being supported by UNDP.

On the basis of my own experience in Central America, and what I observed and heard in South Africa, I have tried here to identify the themes and issues where contact would be most useful. If I were to select priority areas within which to foster exchange, they would be:

- Exchanges between NGO workers with experience of the Salvadoran reconstruction plan and Angolan NGOs who are concerned about the reconstruction plan proposed for Angola.
- Systematisation and exchange of experience on demobilisation, economic and social re-integration, and work with ex-combatants among groups in El Salvador, Nicaragua, Angola, and Mozambique.
- Local-level reconciliation and work on post-violence trauma.
- Contact between NGOs in Guatemala, Nicaragua, and El Salvador and the Centre for the Study of Violence and Reconciliation.

Notes

1 See, for example, a report by Jack Spence and George Vickers: *A Negotiated Revolution? A Two Year Progress Report on the Salvadoran Peace Accords*, Hemisphere Initiatives, March 1994; and a report by Kevin Murray with Ellen Colleti and Jack Spence: *Rescuing Reconstruction: the Debate on Post-War Economic Recovery in El Salvador*, Hemisphere Initiatives, May 1994. They are available from Hemisphere Initiatives, 110 Maryland Avenue, N.E., Washington, D.C. 20002, USA; and Washington Office on Latin America, 130 Prospect Street, Cambridge MA 02139, USA.

Annotated bibliography

This is a selective listing of recent English-language works on the relationship between development and crisis, with particular reference to complex emergencies. We have focused here on major works and material that is readily accessible; most of them also have bibliographies to which readers can refer. Details of major international research projects are included; most of them publish studies in their own right, and hold specialised databases or documentation centres. The Bibliography was compiled and annotated by Deborah Eade and Caroline Knowles, Editor and Reviews Editor respectively of Development in Practice, *with Stephen Commins and Chris Jackson.*

African Rights: *Humanitarianism Unbound? Current Dilemmas facing Multi-mandate Relief Operations in Political Emergencies*, Discussion Paper No 5, London: African Rights, 1994
A study of the moral and practical dilemmas posed by the unbridled involvement of humanitarian NGOs in post-Cold War complex emergencies, and a fierce critique of their role in making influential (and often naive or opportunist) political judgements that are 'apparently unimpeded by limits on their mandate and expertise, or by accountability'. Examining the performance of NGOs and the specialised UN agencies in Ethiopia, Sudan, Angola, Somalia, Bosnia, and Rwanda, the authors call for NGOs to clarify their ethical mandate and operational principles and apply these in a clear and consistent manner.

Mary B Anderson and P J Woodrow: *Rising from the Ashes: Development Strategies in Times of Disaster*, Paris: UNESCO, and Boulder: Westview Press, 1989
Drawing on several case-studies, the authors show that relief programmes are never neutral in their impact on development. They present a simple framework for understanding the dynamic relationship between different people's needs, vulnerabilities, and capacities,

known as Capacities and Vulnerabilities Analysis (CVA). Offering a critique of current emergency-relief practice, the authors show various practical ways in which it might be improved.

Jon Bennett: *Meeting Needs: NGO Co-ordination in Practice*, London: Earthscan, 1995
A compilation of eight case-studies documenting examples of NGO co-ordination in emergencies in the Middle East, the Horn of Africa, Cambodia, and Central America. An overview examines the dangers of NGO expansion in emergencies, especially where this allows bilateral and multilateral aid to be channelled through the non-government sector at the expense of Southern governments and public-service structures. The author asks why NGOs co-ordinate best in crisis, and what their true impact is if they undermine government structures.

Ilene Cohn and Guy S Goodwin-Gill: *Child Soldiers: The Role of Children in Armed Conflict*, Oxford: Oxford University Press, 1994
War has caused the deaths of two million children, and left six times as many without homes, since the mid-1980s. Related to this is 'the increased participation of children in hostilities, in terms both of numbers and the ... nature of their involvement'. Written for the Henry Dunant Institute of the Red Cross, this book considers child soldiers in the context of International Humanitarian Law (IHL) and the 1989 Convention on the Rights of the Child. Drawing on data from Africa, Asia, and Latin America, the authors explore the motivations of child soldiers, as well as those of the adults who recruit and exploit them.

Michael Cranna (ed): *The True Cost of Conflict*, London: Earthscan with Saferworld, 1994
Since 1945, some 22 million people have died in wars, and many of the 42 million displaced persons world-wide are victims of conflict. This

136

book assesses the true costs, using case-studies from the Gulf War, East Timor, Mozambique, Peru, Kashmir, Sudan, and former Yugoslavia. It examines the human casualties, as well as the consequences in social, developmental, and environmental terms. It also attempts to calculate the wider costs both to the countries involved and to their economic partners, and asks who ultimately benefits from conflict.

Mark Cutts and A Dingle: *Safety First: Protecting NGO Employees who Work in Areas of Conflict*, London: Save the Children Fund, 1995
Humanitarian organisations which work in war zones must weigh their responsibility to the affected populations against their obligation to protect their own employees. This book advises NGOs on how they can better protect their staff, and so improve their chances of continuing their humanitarian work. Based on SCF's experience, it examines safety in terms of basic principles such as risk-management and non-partisanship; safety-conscious management practices; and practical security measures. It also offers advice on the evacuation of employees, and explaining actions to the media.

Mark Duffield: 'Complex emergencies and the crisis of developmentalism', *IDS Bulletin*, 25/4: 37-45, October 1994
In this influential paper, the author demonstrates a direct link between political instability and the rise of internal wars and complex political emergencies, which threaten to destroy the entire cultural, civil, political, and economic integrity of a society. Ethnic factors are common to these emergencies. Relief agencies and NGOs often fail to recognise the distinction between natural disasters and complex emergencies, and so adopt 'linear' analyses and responses based on inappropriate assumptions about the possibility of 'a return to normal'. Instead, they should design their programmes around the fact that complex emergencies are the norm in the post-Cold War era. However, in shaping their appeals (and hence their accountability) to their donors rather than to those affected by political violence, NGOs may implicitly further Western disengagement from a commitment to equitable development.

Deborah Eade and Suzanne Williams: *The Oxfam Handbook of Development and Relief*, Oxford: Oxfam Publications, 1995
This 3-volume reference book offers an authoritative guide to thinking, policy, and practice in every area of development and emergency relief work in which Oxfam is involved. Chapter Two, 'Focusing on people', explores those aspects of social identity that should inform all development and emergency relief work, such as gender, ethnic and cultural identity, childhood, old age, and disability. Chapter Six, 'Emergencies and development', focuses largely on complex emergencies involving war and armed conflict. Oxfam's accent is on building sustainable local capacities, both to identify needs and deliver assistance and also to reduce vulnerability in the longer term. Detailed sections address practical issues concerning NGO co-ordination, needs assessment, nutrition, environmental health (including water, sanitation, and housing), and food security. Each section includes Key Questions and Further Resources.

Susan Forbes Martin: *Refugee Women*, London: Zed Books, 1992
Despite growing awareness of the disproportionate vulnerability of women in situations of conflict, and the so-called 'gender violence' of rape and sexual abuse, aid agencies still show a weak understanding of how to design relief interventions in a gender-sensitive way. Even agencies with gender policies may suggest that gender analysis is an unaffordable luxury in a crisis. The book examines five areas which are central to refugees' well-being: protection, access to social and material services, economic activity, repatriation and reconstruction, and resettlement in a third country. Simple and gender-sensitive alternatives of policy and practice are presented for each area.

Ted Robert Gurr: *Minorities at Risk: A Global View of Ethnopolitical Conflicts*, Washington: United States Institute of Peace Press, 1993
Communal identity may be based on shared historical experiences or myths, religious beliefs, language, ethnicity, region of residence, and, in caste-like systems, customary occupations. Often referred to as ethnic groups or minorities, their identification depends not on the presence of particular traits, but on the shared perception that these set the group apart. Surveying over 200 politically active groups, the author asks: what communal identities and interests are most at odds with the structures and policies of existing states, and why? Strategies to reduce ethnic conflict, such as autonomy, pluralism, and formal power-sharing, are discussed.

International Committee of the Red Cross:
Basic Rules of the Geneva Conventions and their Additional Protocols, Geneva: ICRC, 1983
A booklet summarising the basic rules of International Humanitarian Law (IHL), this lays out agreements concerning the protection of the victims of armed conflicts, for which there are some 600 provisions in the Geneva Conventions and their Additional Protocols. Further information about IHL and details of other publications are available from ICRC.

Michael T Klare and Daniel C Thomas (eds):
World Security: Challenges for a New Century, New York: St Martin's Press (second edition), 1994
A collection of essays on the post-Cold War world, reflecting on the implications of recent global changes for future world security. The first four focus on the broad political and social contours of the emerging international system. Others cover nuclear proliferation, arms trafficking, ethnic and regional conflict, Third World militarism, international human rights, violence against women, environmental degradation, demographic change, under-development, and hunger.

Mary Ann Larkin, Frederick C Cuny, Barry N Stein (eds): *Repatriation Under Conflict in Central America*, Georgetown: CIPRA and Intertect, 1991
World-wide, most displaced persons either do not qualify for, or do not have access to, international aid; and most refugees return home with little or no international assistance. In analysing specific cases of spontaneous and/or unassisted voluntary repatriation, the essays in this book (which include several by Latin American writers) illustrate the wider policy and practice dilemmas the phenomenon poses for humanitarian agencies.

A companion volume, *Repatriating During Conflict in Africa and Asia* (1992), also edited by Cuny *et al*, is published by the Center for the Study of Societies in Crisis. For a summary of the main issues, see B N. Stein and F K Cuny, 'Refugee repatriation during conflict: protection and post-return assistance', *Development in Practice*, 4/3: 173-87.

Joanna Macrae and Anthony Zwi (eds): *War and Hunger: Rethinking International Responses to Complex Emergencies*, London and New Jersey: Zed Books, 1994
A compilation (with papers by David Keen, Alex de Waal, Mark Duffield, and Hugo Slim) examining the relationships between poverty, armed conflict, nutritional insecurity, and the dilemmas of providing humanitarian relief in times of war. Complex emergencies are inherently political, whether they take the form of genocide (or 'ethnic cleansing') or other forms of human-rights violations (such as the denial of food to certain population groups). Donors and NGOs often fail to comprehend the underlying political causes; and the failures of international aid efforts are partly due to this. Drawing largely on case-studies from Africa, authors call for greater clarity and accountability in the international relief system, arguing that transitional (post-conflict) issues must be addressed by local organisational structures.

David Millwood (ed): *The International Response to Conflict and Genocide: Lessons from the Rwanda Experience*, Steering Committee of the Joint Evaluation of Emergency Assistance to Rwanda (5 volumes), available from Overseas Development Institute, UK, 1996
The Joint Evaluation of Emergency Assistance to Rwanda takes as its starting point the fact that the massive humanitarian operation engendered by the Rwandan crisis ought never to have been necessary in the first place. Had appropriate political and diplomatic action been taken at an earlier stage, much of the devastation resulting from the genocide might have been prevented. The report, which comprises four separate studies and a synthesis document, examines the background of the 1994 crisis, the role of key international players, and the performance of the myriad organisations involved in humanitarian assistance and post-war reconstruction efforts. Few of those involved escape criticism: the report poses serious challenges for the UN General Secretariat, the Security Council, influential regional and OECD governments, the UN's humanitarian agencies and human-rights machinery, NGOs, and the media. Important recommendations are made concerning the future management of such interventions, and the report is likely to influence debate on 'complex emergencies' for some time to come.

Larry Minear and Thomas G Weiss:
Humanitarian Action in Times of War, Boulder: Lynne Rienner Publishers, 1993
A handbook synthesising lessons and setting out humanitarian principles and policy guidelines for civilian actors involved in providing

humanitarian assistance and protection in wars and other armed conflicts. Despite differences among them, UN organisations, donor governments, NGOs, ICRC, and institutions working in conflict areas all share a basic commitment to these principles. Agencies which are clear and consistent in the way in which they articulate and observe certain humanitarian principles are thought to function most successfully in situations of conflict. But when agencies rely on improvisation, unconstrained by fidelity to stated principles of action, they perform less adequately. A range of practical considerations is offered for improving performance and accountability, as well as a proposed practitioners' code of conduct for humanitarian organisations, both individually and as a community.

Larry Minear and Thomas G Weiss: *Mercy Under Fire*, Boulder: Westview Press, 1995
Describing the experience of the international community in responding to the increase in violent conflict in the early post-Cold War period, the authors review its efforts to provide assistance and protection to civilian populations. Writing for the concerned international public, the authors draw on many interviews with relief workers, and provide non-specialists with an insight into the challenges faced by aid professionals.

Terence Loone Mooney (ed): *The Challenge of Development within Conflict Zones*, Paris: OECD, 1995
Three papers from a 1994 OECD Colloquium, with an overview and conclusion. Larry Minear sets out a conceptual framework for discussing development in conflict. He analyses the responsibilities of, constraints on, and opportunities for donors, UN peace-support operations, and NGOs. Mary B Anderson looks at how the international community might provide political and moral help to societies emerging from conflict, in order to reduce tensions, support development, and build the wider conditions for sustainable peace. Kumar Rupesinghe discusses the relationship between conflict and development and calls for a 'strategic umbrella' approach to conflict-prevention, under which country-specific consortia of concerned government bodies and NGOs, co-operating with inter-governmental groups, would focus on addressing situations of emerging conflict.

Oxfam Working Papers include *Development in Conflict: The Gender Dimension* (1994), *Conflict and Development: Organisation Adaptation in Conflict Situations* (1995) *The Somali Conflict: Prospects for Peace* (1994), *Famine, Needs Assessment, and Survival Strategies in Africa* (1993), and *War and Famine in Africa* (1991).

Rosemarie Rogers and Emily Copeland:
Forced Migration: Policy Issues in the Post-Cold War World, Medford, Massachusetts: Tufts University, 1993
This book highlights the lack of international protection and assistance for internally displaced persons who have 'fled conditions of generalised violence in which their own government is involved or which it cannot control'. It questions the conventional separation between internal and external affairs where national sovereignty acts as a shield behind which a government allows sectors of its population to be forcibly displaced. The obligation to protect and promote human rights resides with States, and hence with the international community. Policies to assist refugees and displaced persons require that forced migration be addressed primarily as a major violation of human rights.

Shawn Roberts and Jody Williams: *After the Guns Fall Silent: The Enduring Legacy of Landmines*, Washington: Vietnam Veterans of America Foundation, 1995
Describing the effect of landmines on people, their communities, their lives and livelihoods, this book examines the consequences of landmine use in terms of refugee movement and resettlement, and the environment. It also covers issues such as mine-clearance and mine-awareness, and medical, rehabilitative, and psychological costs.

Robert I Rotberg and Thomas G Weiss (eds):
From Massacres to Genocide: the Media, Public Policy and Humanitarian Crises, Cambridge, MA: Brookings Institute/The World Peace Foundation, 1996
Discussion of the influence of media coverage of international crises on policy-making. Contributors all agree on the importance of well-informed and well-developed media attention and the formulation of sensible policies regarding the resolution of ethnic and religious conflict and complex humanitarian crises. The issue is examined from many angles: how the media covers emergency situations, and the influence of the media (particularly

television) on both government decision-making and NGO actions; the views of humanitarian groups on the limitations of media coverage, especially how they can help the media to maintain high standards when issues are reduced to sound-bites; the current state of policy-making in the United States; and the disputed effects of media coverage and public opinion on policy formulation.

Kumar Rupesinghe (ed): *Ethnic Conflict and Human Rights*, Tokyo: UN University Press, 1994

Based on a 1986 seminar (sponsored by the UN University, International Alert, the Norwegian Human Rights Institute, and the International Peace Research Institute). Contributors explore ethnic conflicts and their relationship to human rights, reviewing theories of ethnic conflict resolution, and various historical, social, political, and legal factors. The collection includes case-studies from Northern Ireland, South Africa, Nicaragua, and Sri Lanka.

Hugo Slim: 'The continuing metamorphosis of the humanitarian professional: some new colours for an endangered chameleon', *Disasters*, 19/2: 110-126, June 1995

Relief workers now work in operational situations — complex emergencies — that call for re-training (or re-skilling). This requires a fundamental reappraisal of what constitutes humanitarian work, which now includes political analysis, negotiation skills, conflict pre-diction and management, and information-gathering capacity. For NGOs, new demands include working with armed guards and/or military forces, specific country information (not relief generalities), involvement in com-munity peace-building, and a better under-standing of physical and mental health issues.

Rodolfo Stavenhagen: *The Ethnic Question: Conflicts, Development, and Human Rights*, Tokyo: UN University Press, 1990

A comprehensive picture of contemporary ethnic issues as manifested in most of the world's major regions. After discussing such issues in relation to the theories of nation, State, modernisation, and class, the case of Latin America is analysed in depth. The author examines the extent of ethnic-rights protection in the UN and other international systems, the problems of indigenous and tribal peoples, racism in Western Europe, and government cultural and education policies in relation to ethnic minorities.

Geoff Tansey et al.: *A World Divided*, London: Earthscan, 1994

Global militarism — the legacy of the Cold War — is, together with deepening economic polarisation between North and South, and environmental constraints on economic growth and development, seen as a central factor in contributing to insecurity. Using illustrations from both North and South to diagnose the problems caused by increasing militarism, the authors analyse the links between conflict, poverty, development, and environmental degradation; and ask why Northern governments pursue policies that exacerbate North-South tensions. They propose alternative policy measures for demilitarisation, sustainable development, and environmental management.

UN Centre for Human Rights: *The Human Rights Fact Sheet series* (available in English and in French), Geneva

The series of booklets (over 20 titles) offers a good account of basic human rights, what the UN is doing to promote and protect them, and the international machinery available to help to realise those rights. Relevant titles include *The International Bill of Human Rights, Advisory Services and Technical Assistance in the Field of Human Rights, Methods of Combating Torture, Enforced or Involuntary Disappearances, Summary or Arbitrary Executions, International Humanitarian Law and Human Rights, The Committee against Torture*, and *Human Rights and Refugees*.

UNESCO: *Non-military Aspects of International Security*, Paris: UNESCO, 1995

With the end of the Cold War, genuine security and stability cannot be ensured without addressing problems of a non-military character, in particular those related to environmental protection, economic and social development, the prevention of discrimination and violations of human rights, and extreme poverty and exclusion. The book considers new forms of international, regional, and national security which would be compatible with aspirations for a world in which the ideals of democracy, human rights, and development can be realised.

UNHCR: *The State of the World's Refugees*

Annual report examining the plight of displaced people and analysing the world's changing response to forced migration. Contains current statistics, together with appendices giving details of UNHCR's work, international instruments and their significance, and a bibliography.

UNRISD: *States of Disarray: The Social Effects of Globalisation*, Geneva: UNRISD (available in English, French, and Spanish), 1995
A comprehensive examination of contemporary problems that often underlie violent conflict and which thus form a context for complex emergencies and post-war reconstruction. These include poverty, unemployment, inequality, and organised crime; as well as the declining responsibility of public institutions. Part I discusses the impact of globalisation on impoverishment, inequalities, work insecurity, weakening of institutions and social support systems, and the erosion of identities and values. Part II explores these developments in relation to crime, drugs, ethnic conflicts, and post-war reconstruction. Part III looks at the policy environment and the impact of the principal forces shaping contemporary societies on various institutions, stressing the links between misery and insecurity, and social conflicts, including the rise of extremist movements.

UNRISD: *Ethnic Violence, Conflict Resolution and Cultural Pluralism*, UNRISD: Geneva, 1995
This reports on a 1994 seminar on ethnicity and ethnic conflict. Since ethnicity tends to become most destructive when under threat, reducing tension depends on protecting people's rights to form ethnic loyalties, not on repressing them. This does not imply support for policies to entrench ethnicity in social and political structures. Ethnicity evolves, and some ethnic markers lose significance, while new ones emerge.

Given the limitations of third-party intervention in ethnic conflicts, the report discusses policy approaches to facilitate accommodation in ethnically diverse societies. To promote peaceful relations, all groups need a shared interest in society as a whole. This sense of civic identity cannot be forced on people, but is one which they must freely adopt. They are most likely to do so when their society respects and meets everyone's needs, including that of a sense of ethnic identity.

Thomas G Weiss and Larry Minear (eds): *Humanitarianism Across Borders: Sustaining Civilians in Times of War*, Lynne Rienner Publishers: Boulder and London, 1993
This, the second of three books from the Humanitarianism and War Project (qv), is aimed at both humanitarian agencies and the concerned public. It comprises essays by nine authors who examine values, the use of military force, and the future shape of humanitarian institutions.

Aristide R Zolberg, Astri Suhrke and Sergio Aguayo: *Escape from Violence: Conflict and the Refugee Crisis in the Developing World*, Oxford and New York: Oxford University Press, 1989
Offering a theoretical framework for understanding the refugee phenomenon, this book also provides a survey of refugee movements in Asia, Africa and Central America. Refugees, defined as people with a 'well-founded fear of violence', are classified in three categories: activists, targets, and victims. While the first two are generally able to claim refugee status, the 'mere' victims are often denied international protection. The widespread violation of fundamental human rights *by governments* is the main cause of forced migration, and so must be addressed as such by the international community.

Journals

DHA News ISSN: 1020-2609 (published 5 times p.a. by the UN Department of Humanitarian Affairs)
This addresses issues concerning the provision of humanitarian assistance, particularly in conflict. For example, the May-June 1995 issue, 'Focus: Aid Under Fire', shows how distinctions between relief and development are increasingly blurred in practice, and NGO workers need negotiation and assessment skills as they face situations of violence and predation. As NGOs are often in the forefront in complex emergencies, they face a crisis of professionalism and the maintenance of integrity (credibility) in the growing humanitarian market.

Disasters: The Journal of Disaster Studies and Management ISSN: 0361-3666, Overseas Development Institute, UK
A journal for research on disasters, vulnerability, and relief and emergency management. The scope of the journal extends from disasters associated with natural hazards such as earthquakes and drought through to complex, conflict-related emergencies.

Journal of Humanitarian Affairs ISSN: 1360-0222, electronic journal published at the University of Cambridge: http://www-jha.sps.cam.ac.uk/ (no print version available) The journal brings together academics, policy-makers, and practitioners in the field of humanitarian assistance and aims to provide a means for policy debate, the sharing of lessons learned, and the fostering of co-operation within and between the different professions concerned with the many aspects of this work. The journal encompasses all aspects of humanitarian assistance, from early warning and emergency provision to post-conflict peace building and the transition to development. This includes law, politics, the military, logistics, and the work of national and international organisations.

Journal of Peace Research ISSN: 0022-3433 (published quarterly by Sage on behalf of the International Peace Research Institute, Oslo) With a global focus on conflict and peace-making, this journal concentrates on the causes of violence, and on practical approaches to conflict-resolution.

Journal of Refugee Studies ISSN: 0951-6328 (published quarterly by Oxford University Press) A multidisciplinary journal dedicated to academic exploration of the problems of forced migration, and national and international responses to these. It promotes the theoretical development of refugee studies, new perspectives on refugee populations, and the reappraisal of current concepts, policies, and practice.

Research projects and relevant organisations

African Rights: Works on issues of human-rights abuses, conflict, famine, and civil reconstruction in Africa. It believes that the solutions to these problems — emergency humanitarian needs, political reconstruction, and accountability — must be sought primarily among Africans; and that the role of international organisations should be chiefly to support Africans' own attempts to address these.

Hemispheric Migration Project (HMP): Sponsored by the Centre for Immigration Policy and Refugee Assistance (CIPRA) at Georgetown University, the HMP supports research on refugees and labour migrants in the Americas. and seeks to bring the findings to the attention of policy-makers of both sending and receiving countries. Publications include: Aguayo(1991), *From the Shadows to Center Stage: NGOs and Central American Refugee Assistance*; AVANSCO (1990), *Assistance and Control: Policies Toward Internally Displaced Populations in Guatemala*; Ramirez (1989), *Refugee Policy Challenges: The Case of Nicaraguans in Costa Rica*; O'Dogherty (1989), *Central Americans in Mexico City: Uprooted and Silenced*.

Humanitarianism and War: Learning the Lessons from Recent Armed Conflicts: A major project assessing how international and multilateral agencies and NGOs might improve the response to the devastation resulting from war. Launched in 1991, it is sponsored by Brown University's Thomas J Watson Jr Institute for International Studies, and supported by many governments, UN organisations and NGOs. Focusing on 'the interface between theory and practice', the project has published a prodigious range of material, from field manuals to high-level policy documents, from newspaper articles to scholarly papers.

Human Rights Watch (HRW): Holding governments accountable if they transgress the rights of their people, HRW conducts thorough investigations of human-rights abuses in some 70 countries, irrespective of political ideologies and alignments, or of ethnic and religious persuasions. HRW documents and denounces murders, disappearances, torture, arbitrary imprisonment, discrimination, and other abuses of internationally recognised human rights. Its timely and reliable reports make it an essential source of information.

International Alert: An NGO engaged in research on the causes of violent conflict, training in mediation and negotiating skills, advocacy to persuade decision-makers to be devoted to conflict-resolution and prevention. International Alert has regional and country programmes in East and West Africa, and South Asia.

International Committee of the Red Cross (ICRC): ICRC's role is to protect and assist the victims of international and civil wars and conflicts. It is recognised as a neutral humanitarian agency in the Geneva Conventions and their Additional Protocols, which accord ICRC's delegates the authority to visit protected persons, such as prisoners of war, or civil internees. Its operations are conducted confidentially, and any alleged human rights abuses are raised privately with the controlling authorities. The ICRC takes a prime role in developing International Humanitarian Law, and has a wide range of publications, in English and in French.

Mennonite Central Committee: The relief service and development agency of the churches of the North American Mennonite and Brethren in Christ works in long-term development in over 50 countries, and considers peace education and peacemaking to be central to all aspects of its work. The MCC Peace Office, based in the USA, serves as a resource for MCC workers world-wide, and as a connection to the United Nations.

Minority Rights Group (MRG): Publishes authoritative reports on minority groups all over the world, and on many issues relevant to emergency and crisis, for example *Minorities and Human Rights Law*; *International Action against Genocide*; *The Social Psychology of Minorities*.

Quaker Peace and Service: QPS supports long-term programmes by sending experienced workers who contribute to reconciliation at all levels, sometimes working with the victims of wars or violence. QPS works with the UN in the areas of disarmament, human rights, refugees, and economic development through its staff in Geneva. It also works with decision makers, whether diplomats, politicians, or funders in non-official ways as intermediaries to encourage the peaceful resolution of conflict. In special circumstances QPS carries out non-official political reconciliation and communication work between different sides in war.

Refugee Policy Group (RPG): An independent centre for policy research and analysis on refugee and related humanitarian issues which publishes detailed reports and policy briefings, and houses an extensive documentation centre, on matters concerning refugees and displaced persons. Of particular note is *Strengthening International Protection for Internally Displaced Persons* (1993).

Refugee Studies Programme: The Refugee Studies Programme is part of the University of Oxford's International Development Centre. RSP's aim is to increase understanding of the causes, consequences, and experiences of forced migration through multidisciplinary research, teaching, publications, seminars, and conferences. Independent of governments and assistance agencies, RSP provides a forum for discussion between refugees, researchers, practitioners, and policy makers.

Relief and Rehabilitation Network: Part of the Relief and Disasters Policy Programme of the Overseas Development Institute (ODI). The Programme combines research, evaluation, and communications activities in collaboration with a range of bilateral, multilateral, NGO, and academic partners. The Network serves some 300 members in over 50 countries, mostly field-based. Mailings are in English and French, and members can obtain advice on technical and operational problems from within the ODI or via the Network itself.

Saferworld: An independent foreign-affairs think-tank and public-education group, formed to alert governments to the need for new approaches to dealing with armed conflicts. Saferworld focuses on identifying key issues on which movement is possible, and harnessing the diverse contributions of a wide range of people, from political leaders to concerned members of the public, in order to generate creative solutions.

War-torn Societies Project, UNRISD and Programme for Strategic and International Security Studies (PSIS): Analyses experience and practice in transforming a fragile cease-fire into a lasting political settlement, to provide the basis for sustainable development. Much research is conducted by in-country teams, co-ordinated via Geneva. The project seeks policy options for international donors, multilateral organisations, NGOs, and local authorities and organisations who are tackling these problems; and to seeks to contribute to integrating international assistance — economic, humanitarian, political, and military — within a coherent policy framework. It produces various publications, including *After the Conflict: A review of selected sources on rebuilding war-torn societies* (1995), compiled by Patricia Weiss Fagen.

Addresses of publishers and other organisations listed

African Rights, 11 Marshalsea Road, London SE1 1EP, UK

Centre for Immigration Policy and Refugee Assistance (CIPRA), Georgetown University, PO Box 2298-Hoya Station, Washington DC 20057-1001, USA

Collaborative for Development Action Inc, 26 Walker Street, Cambridge MA 02138, USA

Department of Humanitarian Affairs, Palais des Nations, 1211 Geneva, Switzerland

Humanitarianism and War Project, Thomas J Watson Jr Institute for International Studies, Brown University, Box 1970, 2 Stimson Avenue, Providence, RI 02912, USA

Human Rights Watch, 485 Fifth Avenue, New York NY 10017-6014, USA

International Alert, 1 Glyn Street, London SE11 5HT, UK

International Committee of the Red Cross, 19 avenue de la Paix, 1202 Geneva, Switzerland

International Peace Research Institute, Fuglehauggata 11, 0260 Oslo, Norway

Mennonite Central Committee, 21 South 12th Street, PO Box 500, Akron PA 17501-0500, USA

Minority Rights Group, 379 Brixton Road, London SW9 7DE, UK

OECD, 2 rue André Pascal, 75775 Paris, Cedex 16, France

Overseas Development Institute, Regent's College, Inner Circle, Regent's Park, London NW1 4NS, UK

Oxfam Publishing, 274 Banbury Road, Oxford OX2 7DZ, UK

Oxford University Press, Walton Street, Oxford OX2 6DP, UK

Quaker Peace and Service, Friends House, Euston Road, London NW1 2BJ, UK

Refugee Policy Group, 1424 16th Street NW, Suite 401, Washington DC 20036, USA

Refugee Studies Programme, Queen Elizabeth House, 21 St Giles, Oxford OX1 3LA, UK

Lynne Rienner Publishers, 1800 30th St, Boulder, Colorado 80301, USA

St Martin's Press, 175 5th Avenue, New York NY 10010, USA

Saferworld, 33 Alfred Place, London WC1E 7DP, UK

Sage Publications Limited, 6 Bonhill Street, London EC2A 4PU, UK

Save the Children Fund, 17 Grove Lane, London SE5 8RD, UK

The Fletcher School of Law and International Diplomacy, Program in International and US Refugee Policy, Tufts University, Medford, Massachusetts 02155, USA

UN Centre for Human Rights, UN Office at Geneva, 8–14 avenue de la Paix, 1211 Geneva 10, Switzerland

UNESCO, 7 Place de Fontenoy, 75372 Paris 07 SP, France

UNHCR, Centre William Rappard, 154 rue de Lausanne, 1202 Geneva, Switzerland

UNRISD, Palais des Nations, 1211 Geneva, Switzerland

UN University Press, Toho Shimei Building, 15–1 Shibuya 2-chome, Shibuya-ku, Tokyo 150, Japan

United States Institute of Peace Press, 1550 M Street NW, Washington DC 20005, USA

Vietnam Veterans of America Foundation, 2001 S Street NW, Suite 740, Washington DC, USA

Washington Office on Latin America, 110 Maryland Avenue NE, Washington DC 20002, USA

Westview Press, 5500 Central Avenue, Boulder, Colorado 80301-2877, USA

The World Peace Foundation, 1 Eliot Square, Cambridge MA 02138-4952, USA

Zed Books, 9 Cynthia Street, London N1 9JF, UK

144

www.ingramcontent.com/pod-product-compliance
Lightning Source LLC
Chambersburg PA
CBHW080859030426
42334CB00021B/2606